Contemporary Political Cinema

Contemporary Political Cinema

Matthew Holtmeier

EDINBURGH
University Press

For Chelsea

Edinburgh University Press is one of the leading university presses in the UK. We publish academic books and journals in our selected subject areas across the humanities and social sciences, combining cutting-edge scholarship with high editorial and production values to produce academic works of lasting importance. For more information visit our website: edinburghuniversitypress.com

Edinburgh University Press Ltd
The Tun – Holyrood Road
12 (2f) Jackson's Entry
Edinburgh EH8 8PJ

Typeset in Monotype Ehrhardt by
Manila Typesetting Company, and
printed and bound by CPI Group (UK) Ltd, Croydon, CR0 4YY

A CIP record for this book is available from the British Library

ISBN 978 1 4744 2341 0 (hardback)
ISBN 978 1 4744 2342 7 (webready PDF)
ISBN 978 1 4744 2343 4 (epub)

Contents

Figures

Acknowledgements

Thank you to all of the colleagues, mentors, and interlocutors that inspired this project. I have been associated with a few remarkable institutions that afforded me the occasion to have conversations linked to this project. At Western Washington University, thank you to Kaveh Askari, Dawn Dietrich, Mark Lester, Doug Park, and Chris Wise. At the University of St Andrews, thank you to William Brown, Robert Burgoyne, Yun-Hua Chen, Cheung Tit Leung, Richard Dyer, Fredrik Gustafsson, Dina Iordanova, Saër Maty Bâ, David Martin-Jones, Serazer Pekerman, Diana Popa, Kathleen Scott, Leshu Torchin, John Trafton, Chelsea Wessels, Joshua Yumibe, as well as the opportunities provided by the Centre for Film Studies, including conversations with Mohsen Makhmalbaf and Jonathan Rosenbaum. At Ithaca College, Carlos Figueroa, Diane Gayeski, Nancy Menning, Sueyoung Park-Primiano, Wade Pickren, Tyrell Stewart-Harris, Andrew Utterson, and Patty Zimmermann. Thank you also to the larger academic community that has helped me think through aspects of this project, including Patricia Pisters, Richard Rushton, Steven Shaviro, David Sorfa, and many others I am certainly forgetting to name (if you have been forgotten, I expect a sharply worded e-mail).

A special thanks to Mark Lester for introducing me to philosophy. Endless gratitude to David Martin-Jones both for his provocations and his constant encouragement. I am always grateful to Kaveh Askari and Joshua Yumibe for their mentorship on a variety of levels. Many thanks to Patty Zimmermann for helping me to think in new ways and reinvigorate the old. And much appreciation to friends that provided unqualifiable support on this project: Gretchen Coulter, Jeff Coulter, and Eddy Troy.

This project received generous support from the Center for Faculty Excellence at Ithaca College in the form of the Summer Research Grant, as well as a small grant that was used to start a writing group. It also received support from the Office of the Provost at Ithaca College, which awarded it the Provost-Mini Grant. Finally, this project received the James B. Pendleton Grant for Research. Thank you to Jane Banks for her editorial work on this project. Thank you to Dean Gayeski in the Roy H.

Park School of Communications for helping to navigate potential sources of funding for this project.

Sections of this book were developed in earlier published journal articles, and I am grateful to the blind peer-reviewers and editors that looked at the earlier genesis of these ideas as a result. This includes "The Wanderings of Jia Zhangke: Pre-Hodological Space and Aimless Youths in *Xiao Wu* and *Unknown Pleasures*" published in the *Journal of Chinese Cinemas*, volume 8:2 (2014), pp. 148–159 (www.tandfonline.com), and "The Modern Political Cinema: From Third Cinema to Contemporary Networked Biopolitics" published in *Film-Philosophy*, volume 20:2–3 (2016), pp. 303–323. Thank you as well to the peer-reviewers at Edinburgh University Press for their helpful responses to this project. I apologize that I do not know the names of all of these peer-reviewers, but hopefully you receive this thanks some day!

Love and thanks to my partner Chelsea, not only for her intellectual insight, but for helping this project in every way possible.

And finally, I want to acknowledge the precariat around the world: refugees, immigrants, contract workers, adjuncts, victims of environmental degradation and climate change, and those generally uprooted. Living under uncertainty is a constant state of psychic, social, and economic violence. May your precarity be short.

Introduction

Filmmakers have long depicted the production of political subjectivity as a decisive shift that takes place within filmic characters, communicated through film form. In *Battleship Potemkin* (1925), the sailors revolt rather than endure intolerable conditions. After a sailor reads the words "give us this day our daily bread" on a plate he is washing, Sergei Eisenstein uses 15 shots in montage, moving between furrowed brows and the irony of the words before the sailor finally smashes the plate, acknowledging his newly politicized status. In *Battle of Algiers* (1966), Ali la Pointe witnesses the execution of fellow prisoners at the guillotine. The film cuts to three shots of the prison walls lined with cell windows, and then to a rapid zoom into Ali's eyes as the guillotine falls, suggesting not only the role that violent colonialism plays in Ali's politicization, but also its role in politically mobilizing an entire population. These classic examples of revolutionary cinema operate according to a grand dialectic: the people are oppressed, and their oppression leads to large scale political mobilization in which one population overthrows another. Since the 1980s, however, these classically grand gestures of political cinema have declined, though the depiction of political upheaval and turmoil have not. This book explores a set of films from across the world that examines the shift from earlier styles of political cinema to new ways that the politicization of characters is depicted in contemporary film.

The films in this book are diverse in their global sites of production and were produced from the 1990s to the 2010s, because a core argument of this project is that these shifts stem from increasing globalization and neoliberalization, which produced a new type of politics and a new cinematic subject. Accordingly, the films in this book have a conflicted relationship with commercial industries and forms of distribution, and most often circulate transnationally. This often takes the form of the "festival film" produced for an international audience with global flows of films, information, and economies already at the fore. Often the case studies are complicated, such as Bahman Ghobadi's *No One Knows about Persian Cats* (2009), which used online distribution and international distributors to circumvent its illicit status in Iran, and the filmmakers illustrate an acute awareness of the tension between the local and global both formally and in their modes of production. It is within this networked sphere that the aforementioned grand dialectic withers, and films become a symptom of the complicated effects global networks have on the production of subjectivity. The films are not only passive expressions though, but expressions of a new global logic, often at odds with the logics of nation states, at least as far as certain political theorists such as Samuel P. Huntington understand them.[1] This new logic suggests a reciprocal relationship between cinema and global politics, where cinematic expression shifts to document contemporary politics, and while in so doing the films themselves produce new forms of political thought.

Despite their conflicted relationship with commercial film industries, I used the term festival film above not to pigeon hole the films I discuss in this book, but to give a broad sense of the industrial articulation of these films globally. The term is familiar to most people, although it is imprecise. Similarly, I title this book with austerity, *Contemporary Political Cinema*, to suggest that there is a relatively popular network of distribution and exhibition for films with political content post-1990, a period that witnessed a sharp rise in festival exhibition and so-called independent film distribution. Accordingly, this approach does not intend to cover all potential expressions of political cinema, particularly because the global festival networks I have described shape the form of such films, as David Martin-Jones and María Soledad Montañez argue (Martin-Jones and Montañez 2013). The title of the book is also meant to distinguish my approach from the political modernism that D. N. Rodowick identified in the late 1980s. He explains that "political modernism is the expression of a desire to combine semiotic and ideological analysis with the development of an avant-garde aesthetic practice dedicated to the production of radical social effects" (Rodowick 1994: 1–2). Only six years after the original publication of *The Crisis of Political Modernism*, Rodowick wrote an updated preface to the second edition in which he questions the continued relevance of the discourse surrounding political modernism in cinema. He does not do so to invalidate his own work, but to historicize it. He writes:

> the impasse of political modernism has more to do with its particular organization of concepts and the kinds of rhetoric it deployed. For example, the rhetoric of the break, the apocalyptic desire to begin anew after the end of film history and theory, tended to line up with concepts in mutually exclusive categories of opposed terms. (Rodowick 1994: xxvi)

The main opposition or break he refers to here is that between a real-ist commercial cinema and a modernist critical cinema. Such clear breaks, he suggests, are increasingly unlikely post-1990, and the films in this book are testament to this argument though not lacking in formal experimentation.

What emerges is something like the hybridized second/third cinema Mike Wayne discusses in *Political Film: The Dialectics of Third Cinema*, where he argues "ideas, themes and strategies shuttle back and forth between these cinemas and change as they do so" (Wayne 2001: 23). Responding to Wayne's dialectical understanding of the legacy of Third Cinema, Patricia Pisters notes, "In varying dialectic dynamics these relations that started, amongst others, with colonialism, always crystal-lise differently in increasingly complex transnational networks" (Pisters 2006: 190). I echo Pisters's argument that "political cinema has arrived at another stage," though rather than the remix culture she focuses on, I look to the ways international art cinema has been exploited to illustrate the production of political subjectivity (Pisters 2016: 158). In other words, post-1990 political cinema is no longer identified with a break but an inter-mingling of political signification with the quasi-commercial industrial modes of independent production, festival exhibition, and transnational distribution.

I focus on the production of political subjectivity in this book as a measure for political statement. By subjectivity, I mean the perspectives, emotions, and ideologies of characters insofar as they are communicated through film form, which is not limited to the direct expression of charac-ters via dialogue or narrative. In other words, the films in this book commu-nicate the subjectivity of their characters through editing, sound design, mise-en-scène, and cinematography, and shifts in perspectives towards the political contexts of the films provide a metric for understanding their critical approach. I focus on the production of this political subjectivity to emphasize the processual politics of these films. The films depict acts of transformation rather than providing blueprints for a particular political future. I understand subjectivity through Gilbert Simondon's process of individuation, the ontogenesis of the subject as it goes through the process of becoming an individual. Simondon seeks "to understand the individual from the perspective of the process of individuation rather than the pro-cess of individuation by means of the individual" (Simondon 1992: 300). Simondon's approach provides a processual politics by emphasizing the shock to a system that starts the process of individuation, or the trans-formation of the subject. In the context of political cinemas, I emphasize that which is intolerable to a subject or community, which prompts the production of political subjectivity.

Simondon's perspective on individuation provides the means to analyze films that move beyond the classical, dialectical politics of *Battleship Potemkin* and *Battle of Algiers*. He describes his process-based philosophy as following a particular method:

> *to follow the being from the moment of its genesis, to see the genesis* of the thought through to its completion at the same time as the genesis of the object reaches its own completion . . . the above-mentioned course is obliged to play a role that the dialectic is unable to play, because the study of the process of individuation does not seem to correspond to the negation that follows as the second step, but rather to an immanence of the negative in the primary state (Simondon 1992: 314)

One of the foundational philosophers and critics of cybernetic theory, he argues that the conditions of systems are immanent to the subject and process of individuation. Later in this book, I discuss this further in relation to the films of Jia Zhangke, but I foreground it now to emphasize the shift from thinking of subjects as coherent individuals, towards a process of becoming political. Such a focus seeks not to understand how revolutions occurred, but the conditions in which political subjects are mobilized. The films in this project suggest that such mobilization is increasingly diverse in relation to global networks of protest.

Speaking of political film in *Cinema 2*, Gilles Deleuze hypothesizes, "There will no longer be conquest of power by a proletariat, or by a united or unified people" (Deleuze 1989: 219–220). Written in 1985, this seems to have been a prescient proclamation, but Deleuze's prediction has evolved alongside globalization. At present, we see not a depoliticization of film and activism, but a shift in political expression. The 1999 World Trade Organization (WTO) summit met with opposition in the streets of Seattle, Washington as swarms of protesters gathered in an attempt to prevent the meetings. At the time no one expected such fierce opposition at an event of such global importance nor the level of co-operation amongst the diverse individuals who arrived to protest. College students joined the ranks of environmental organizations, labor unions, and others without obvious affiliation. Those taking part in the protest had a common goal despite their diversity: to speak out against the exploitation of less powerful countries or entities and the wielding of global power in favor of a rich minority of countries. The individuals that converged in Seattle during the WTO summit were taking part in anti-globalization, anti-capitalist movements combating the spread of neoliberal economic policies, even though their basic claims may have been for a less clearly defined notion of global justice. Significantly, perhaps as a sign of the success of these protests, subsequent summits of the WTO, the International Monetary Fund (IMF), and the World Bank met with similar opposition across the world.

While momentous in 1999, the WTO protests have now been surpassed by much larger movements for social justice, such as Occupy Wall Street (OWS). OWS started with a very basic purpose, to protest in favor of the 99% against the 1%—stemming from a basic claim that 1% of the population in the United States holds a majority of the wealth, and Wall Street is a major center of the wealth for this 1%. While OWS was even more diverse and diffuse than the WTO protests, the size, breadth, and duration of OWS protests have greatly outstripped them to the point where major cities across the world, and even some relatively small cities, sustained their own Occupy movements. The arrival of this similar but far larger global protest movement just 12 years later suggests something important about the period from the late 1990s to the early 2010s. There are a multitude of issues influencing the arrival of these protests, and each protester undoubtedly has their own unique agenda, but they have been prompted by the increasing gaps between classes, growing socioeconomic uncertainty, greater channels for communication and the dissemination of information, and ultimately, the desire to come together in the face of something intolerable.

Responding to contemporary protests around the globe, political theorists have articulated various frameworks for understanding these events (see Hardt and Negri 2011, Chomsky 2012, Purcell 2013, Mitchell, Harcourt, and Taussig 2013, Mouffe 2013, Sassen 2014). Often these discussions revolve around what they consider to be the efficacy of particular protest movements, echoing, though not always affirming, Carl Schmitt's critique of liberalism in 1927 where he positions the friend/enemy distinction as the basis of politics (Schmitt 2007). Chantal Mouffe highlights a disparity, for example, between political strategies in terms of "withdrawal from" or "engagement with" political institutions (Mouffe 2013: 109). As this is a book about film, however, the chapters address the ways that cinema philosophizes this political moment and where it converges with these contemporary debates. The clearest convergence between this discourse and the cinematic project I identify relates to the production of subjectivity. Speaking of the role art plays within this political paradigm, Mouffe suggests:

> If artistic practices can play a decisive role in the construction of new forms of subjectivity, it is because, in using resources which induce emotional responses, they are able to reach human beings at the affective level. This is where art's great power lies – in its capacity to make us see things in a different way, to make us perceive new possibilities. (Mouffe 2013: 96–97)

Looking at films around the globe within their specific political contexts raises the following questions. What subjects are revealed in the films produced by and responding to the global flows that these contemporary protest movements respond to? How do these films organize affectively in order to produce extra-filmic subjects themselves? If not new possibilities, what political problematics are revealed by these films?

These questions take on increasing relevance with the rise of racial, ethnic, and religious nationalisms since the mid-2010s. Such movements are examples of the most repressive form of biopolitics: the control of who lives and how they live through policy or ideology. Elections with far-right candidates, whether successfully elected or not, sparked nationalisms, including Recep Tayyip Erdoğan in 2014 in Turkey, Theresa May in 2016 in the United Kingdom, Donald Trump in 2016 in the United States, Geert Wilders in 2017 in the Netherlands, and Marine Le Pen in 2017 in France. In the midst of these elections, ostensibly latent racist ideologies became public as seen in the white nationalist rally in Charlottesville, VA in August 2017 or the Rohingya crisis in Myanmar (Taub 2017). Outside of these relatively democratic elections, identity-politics have spread through militant and terrorist organizations such as the self-proclaimed Islamic State as it spreads through the Middle East, North and West Africa, and Southeast Asia. These are not national issues, however, but transnational issues as they are all sparked to some degree by migrations due to war, economic disparities, and environmental precarity. The degradation of the environment will only hasten this process. If the post-colonial moment of *Battle of Algiers* reflects on the resistance of indigenous populations against their colonizers, the contemporary political context of films in this book reflect on the attempted consolidation of nations under specific racial, religious, and ideological criteria against perceived outsiders, whether truly foreign or not. Deleuze's hypothesis takes on a particular valence in this context: not a lament of disempowered class struggle, but a return to his earlier anti-fascist stance in his works with Félix Guattari. The contemporary political cinemas in this book take their own anti-fascist stances by exploring how such repressive biopolitics become intolerable to the individual lives of their subjects.

As these intolerable experiences modulate aesthetic strategies – through episodic narratives, disjunctive editing, sound design, and other formal techniques that interrupt and fragment – contemporary political films provide affective nodes that promote the production of political subjectivity and create spaces for nascent political formations to emerge. This engenders a new form of political organization, distinct from the aforementioned revolutionary and dialectical politics. Within cinema, the sensory-motor schema, a linear time based on cause-and-effect relationships, has long supported majoritarian discourses that produce the intolerable. The role of sensory-motor connections is important to the political project of film, I argue, because contemporary political films rupture the teleology inherent in this oft-dialectical form of cinematic time that relies on resolving conflict by introducing a new norm. The films herein resist this causal relationship with a banal, seemingly disordered realism that focuses on existential narratives and the daily lives of their subjects, rather than grand objectives. To explain the importance of this formal aspect of contemporary political films, I will first turn to an explanation of how cinematic time has been structured historically. I will then give an overview of the contemporary context I address, discuss the political mode of these films in more depth, and finally explore their interaction with cinematic subjectivity.

Movement in Classical Politics, Time in Contemporary Politics

The historical shift in Deleuze's writing on film, from *Cinema 1: The Movement-Image* (1983) to *Cinema 2: The Time-Image* (1985), provides an important context for understanding the political significance of cinematic time in contemporary political films. Deleuze's transition between these texts charts a trajectory that moves from an insistence on causal, linear movement and action in films prior to World War II to an acknowledgment of new forms of time in film after World War II and the sensory-motor collapse that defines this shift. My contention is not that we remain in the post-War context that Deleuze defines, but as Patricia Pisters argues in *The Neuro-Image* (2012), that this first shift provides important background for other shifts that are now taking place, which were only in their most nascent form at the time Deleuze wrote *Cinema 1* and *Cinema 2*. Speaking to the mutation in post-War films, Deleuze points out that "Marxist critics have attacked these films and their characters for being too passive and negative," but also that this "is not the cinema that turns away from politics, it becomes completely political, but in another way" (Deleuze 1989: 19). Whereas Deleuze's passage from movement-image to time-image seems like a historical trajectory on the surface,[2] I am more interested in the rupture in majoritarian signifying systems akin to a minor use of cinematic time – the "completely political in another way." If history plays a role, it is only in that post-War technologies and forms of social organization have allowed this rupture to emerge more readily as a new political logic.

The sensory-motor collapse that defines this shift refers to the breaking down of causal relations in cinema. In other words, in traditional forms of narrative and editing an act leads to a changed situation, with most films culminating in a resolution of the driving complication. In *Cinema 2*, where he more directly addresses the deterioration of the sensory-motor schemata, Deleuze focuses on particular historical events which led to its demise in cinema. He cites the rise of Hitler and Stalin as examples (Deleuze 1989: 216). In each of these cases, he argues, beliefs regarding nations, democracy, and the rational acts of individuals were compromised by the horrors of World War II and the ways in which "the people" as a unified subject were co-opted in order to be exploited by individuals like Hitler and Stalin. As a result, the sensory-motor schemata with its rational coherence and clear causal relationships begins to make less sense for a war-torn world where the ability of individuals to believe in a cause and commit their entire being to a particular subject-position (in a unified people) has been compromised. While Deleuze attributes a great number of features to the time-image that arrives to address this dearth in belief – the co-presence of past-present-future, the mobilization of the powers of the false, and the emergence of a new type of political cinema – its arrival itself can be understood in terms of the inability of post-War subjects to believe in the sensory-motor schemata.

Theodor Adorno's critique of enlightenment rationalism provides a particularly useful way to understand this break in the notion of belief for Deleuze. Understanding this break is core to the philosophical importance of contemporary political films, because it is predicated upon, as D. N. Rodowick argues, "Belief [that] is no longer belief in a transcendent world, or in a transformed world, but a belief in *this* world and *its* powers of transformation" (Rodowick 1997: 192). In other words, belief in one's ability to take action in the world and to affect one's environment. While arguably part of the larger project of the Frankfurt School, Adorno directly critiques the concept of enlightenment rationalism in *The Dialectic of Enlightenment* (originally published 1944, during World War II). His argument tracks a trajectory beginning with the construction of enlightenment rationality and ending with the co-opting of this so called rationality to exploit and even eradicate entire peoples, often under the aegis of capitalism, even though this rationality is purported to create an enlightened age (Adorno 2002: 1; 30). If one considers Deleuze's move from the movement-image to the time-image in the context of Adorno's critique of the enlightenment, the time-image and its cinematic products, such as what he calls the "modern political cinema," become a form of counter-enlightenment, "another politics" that critiques what Adorno called "an outright deception of the masses" (Adorno 2002: 34). In contemporary political cinema, I argue, this other politics comes not in the classical form of unifying a people, but in disillusionment with forms of enlightenment rationality that have become cliché, and that this disillusionment is the prerequisite for a belief in the world.

Deleuze turns to this problem of cliché when he asks what happens when the methods of Alfred Hitchcock, Eisenstein, and Abel Gance are taken up by mediocre directors. He responds: "When grandeur is no longer that of the composition, but a pure and simple inflation of the represented, there is no cerebral stimulation or birth of thought. It is rather a generalized shortcoming in author and viewers" (Deleuze 1989: 164). Deleuze sees something problematic in the repetition of the same old cinematic clichés, going as far as to say that this "mass-art . . . has degenerated into state propaganda and manipulation, into a kind of fascism which brought together Hitler and Hollywood, Hollywood and Hitler" (Deleuze 1989: 164). Deleuze's argument mirrors Adorno's critique of enlightenment rationalism in drawing a connection between Hitler and Hollywood in how they control the construction of subjects. In this comparison, Deleuze makes a strikingly pro-filmic argument: it is not just about directors making boring films, but boring films making boring people, or subjects locked into a particular ideology. As Anna Backman Rogers puts it: "It is this exposure of meaninglessness at the heart of supposedly meaningful human activity that is 'intolerable and unbearable'" (Rogers 2011: 4).

The political concern for Deleuze becomes how to counter the repetition of clichés, and how to promote a "belief in the world." In response, Ronald Bogue argues that "The only viable response to the intolerable is to think differently, to disconnect the world's networks of certainties and pieties and formulate new problems that engender as yet unmapped relations and connections" (Bogue 2010: 122). Bogue's argument gives insight into what Deleuze really means when he says "belief in the world" – namely, that it would be opposed to a belief in cliché, oppressive ideology, or the stories of a dominant/majoritarian power. In other words, Deleuze's belief in the world is a belief in the immanent or existential possibilities inherent in one's immediate experience. Offering a potential method of meeting Deleuze's challenge, D. N. Rodowick argues that the answer is not through simply formulating new problems by revealing the clichés at work, however, but working through "an anticipatory time—of contingency, the purely conditional, the nondetermined or not yet" (Rodowick 2010: 109). When the action, story, plot, or teleology of a film break down, Rodowick explains, the character of the seer emerges in cinema, and "the seer . . . alienated both within herself and from the world . . . sees farther, better, and deeper than she can react or think" (Rodowick 2010: 110). As a result, the figure of the seer does not take the automatic or clichéd narrative path, but instead engages in thought, or the production of new connections between subjects and their environments. For Julian Reid, in his reading of Deleuze, the ultimate political potential of Deleuze's cinematic thought lies in the possibility of "our becoming seers" alongside these characters on screen, because the seer has the potential to witness what is intolerable and unbearable in life (Reid 2011: 231). In other words, there is something about certain films that have a pro-filmic effect on spectators, which allows them the power to see through cliché and construct a belief in the world in turn.

With the emergence of the time-image in the post-War period, Deleuze notes five features that can be attributed to the weakening of the sensory-motor schemata: "the dispersive situation, the deliberately weak links, the voyage form, the consciousness of clichés, the condemnation of the plot" (Deleuze 1986: 210). The dispersive situation acknowledges the dangers of the universalizing function of enlightenment rationality. The deliberately weak links between cause and effect illustrates how causation is not so clearly articulable. The voyage form espouses an aimlessness, which rejects the clear teleologies envisioned by those ascribing to rational cause and effect relationships, and admits the experimental nature of the progression of time. The consciousness of clichés acknowledges the false-base of clichés themselves. And finally, the condemnation of the plot critiques the didactic function of cinema as an instructive narrative form.

These aspects of the coming time-image that Deleuze lays out in *Cinema 1* are useful in transitioning to a discussion of contemporary political cinema. With the unstable belief in nationalisms, rational acts, and universal principles, political cinemas shift away from didactic functions and engage in a new mode of consciousness raising and subject-creation. While this project turns away from World War II as a turning point and the films that Deleuze himself discussed, it shares the break with a majoritarian regime of signification. As a further stage, this project focuses on the period of the 1990s to 2010s, because of political shifts engendered by the contemporary networked era, with the spread of networked societies and multifaceted subjectivities.

Networked Subjects and the New Era of Globalization

Noam Chomsky identifies the economic deregulation of the 1980s and 1990s as a new era of globalization, because of the rapidity at which transnational flows began to circulate at this time, even if globalization itself was nothing new (Chomsky 1999: 68). This period is characterized by global leaders taking a neoliberal stance (such as Ronald Reagan in the United States and Margaret Thatcher in the United Kingdom); the establishment of the WTO and its co-operation with the earlier established IMF and World Bank; and general economic strategies prescribed by the Washington Consensus.[3] Furthermore, the communications and information technology growth of the 1990s has contributed to the ubiquity of globalization as a cultural experience, increasingly mitigating the digital divide. The contemporary political films I highlight range from the mid-1990s to 2010, and are marked by Chomsky's new era of globalization through their narratives and their modes of production and circulation.

Chomsky's critique of globalization is shared by many contemporary writers such as Naomi Klein, David Harvey, Guy Standing, Zygmunt Bauman, Michael Hardt, and Antonio Negri. At the core of their critique is the criticism of a particular brand of capitalism: namely, the neoliberal, free-market Chicago school of capitalism popularized by Milton Friedman. These critics take issue with Friedman's argument that if capitalism were freed from all controls, state or otherwise, then it would naturally balance the economy and bring prosperity to all members of society. Its naturalization in the 1980s during the Reagan administration facilitated the export of these policies to non-Western countries, sometimes through forceful restructuring. Historically, what results from this deregulation is the widening of the gap between rich and poor. Klein argues that this is a process that has been operating since Central Intelligence Agency intervention in Iran in the 1950s (Klein 2007: 58), and Harvey adds that it also includes Mexico, Argentina, South Korea, Sweden, and China (Harvey 2007: 87-120). Often neoliberalism is forced upon countries through debt-restructuring plans. In other words, countries who are deeply indebted to the IMF are given a break if they restructure their country's economic regulations to comply with the neoliberal model. Ostensibly, this opens them up to international trade, but as Naomi Klein argues in *The Shock Doctrine* (2007), in practice it allows wealthy countries to buy up local industries and resources.

This history of economic globalization has also enabled increased communication, migration of peoples, and the export/import of cultural commodities that simultaneously results in a socio-cultural globalization. This is emphasized in David Held's description of globalization as a "process (or set of processes) which embodies a transformation in the spatial organisation of social relations and transactions – assessed in terms of their extensity, intensity, velocity and impact – generating transcontinental or interregional flows and networks of activity" (Held 1999: 16). Such networks result in the production of what I will refer to as networked subjects, with more complicated affiliations and desires than were assumed by classical political cinemas. Neither the Kurds nor French-Algerians, for example, are simply "national" subjects.

The larger argument of this project contends that filmmakers have used cinema to show how such networking complicates Samuel P. Huntington's claims in *The Clash of Civilizations and the Remaking of World Order* (1996). Demarcating "The World of Civilizations: Post-1990" Huntington argues, "In the post-Cold War world flags count and so do other symbols of cultural identity, including crosses, crescents, and even head coverings, because culture counts, and cultural identity is what is most meaningful to most people" (Huntington 1996: 26–27; 20). Huntington suggests that, post-1990, conflict proceeds according to the political philosophy of Schmitt with binaries of friend and enemy predicated upon civilizational identities, such as the West, Islam, and Asian civilizations, and "not . . . between social classes, rich and poor, or other economically defined groups" (Huntington 1996: 28). Crucially, Huntington refers to the growth of globalization as "forces of integration," which "generate counterforces of cultural assertion and civilizational consciousness" (Huntington 1996: 36). In other words, when subjects are impacted negatively by the forces of globalization, subjectivity forms in relation to these global flows, such as the anti-colonial radicalization in *The Battle of Algiers*. He rejects the possibility of understanding globalization as a force that both fragments and networks, because such an understanding is not useful for building an operable foreign policy. I argue, however, that this is the political mode of contemporary political cinema, which pays closer attention to the lived experiences of individuals and reveals the complexity that emerges in this dual movement of being fragmented and networked. Such a contention is important, because it entails a uniquely cinematic political philosophy based on the existential experiences of subjects in relation to globalization.

I do not mean to suggest that networked identities suggest some sort of global utopia. Speaking of the circulation of images and media in an increasingly networked world, Patricia Pisters argues, "The up-tempo world will make people more fluid and creative, even if that creativity can also be used to reinforce state power or can create all kinds of fundamentalisms to pose blocks of fixed identities (as "safe havens") in the sea of data, images, and possible ways of life" (Pisters 2012: 218). As will be discussed in subsequent chapters, these "blocks of fixed identities" are created through the organization of religious identity, censorship, and/or economic ideologies and provide grounds for majoritarian discourses to establish a norm, not unlike Huntington's vision. It is the political contestation of the filmmakers in this book which argues that underneath the normative subjects composed by majoritarian discourses exist multifaceted, networked subjects who cannot wholly conform to said discourses. As Shaviro points out in *Connected, or What it Means to Live in the Network Society*, being networked is not always a positive thing, subjects are increasingly compromised, distracted, and fragmented by networks that can pull an individual subject in a multitude of directions, "intensely involved, and maximally distracted, all at once" (Shaviro 2003: 26). Unsurprisingly, given the analysis of neoliberalism from the aforementioned authors, increasing inequality often plays a prominent role in contemporary political cinema, particularly in terms of potential mobility – a separation of the locals and the globals.

By way of trickle-down economics, neoliberal economic policies promise spreading prosperity. If the elite do well, or the corporations turn profits, this prosperity will inevitably trickle down to the less well off. The contemporary political films discussed in this book counter this concept by highlighting a feature of globalization that Zygmunt Bauman focuses on in *Globalization: The Human Consequences* (1998). Bauman points out that globalization does indeed "globalize" certain individuals. That is, they are liberated from a place-based experience: they are able to travel freely, consume products of other cultures, and generally benefit from the increased flow of capital across the world. As a result, these individuals are great examples of the ideological and economic freedom the free-market espouses – they are not subject to regulations, do as they please, and are allowed to fulfill their great potential.

At the same time, however, Bauman argues that others are localized by the very same processes. Due to increasing inequality, Bauman argues, there are even greater populations that are stripped of their freedom to move about the world and engage in global trade through this process of localization. These individuals become a servant-class that performs the manual labor for the globalized elite, such as the Indian or Filipino maid in Dubai. These peoples may be moved, but they do not have the freedom to move – they relocate based on where work is available, regardless of the (often dangerous) conditions. The mass-migration in the films of Jia Zhangke, addressed in Chapter Four of this book, provide a useful illustration, as characters move for work but then become trapped as a result of lack of finances or the more direct power exerted by those that traffic these individuals, such as the withholding of passports. Contemporary political films often document this dual process of globalization and localization, critiquing the promise of prosperity in particular. The films studied in this book highlight the production of subjectivity in relation to globalization, revealing localized populations to the spectator. The opposition inherent in this other(ed) class is generally both economic and cultural. By focusing on these aspects simultaneously, contemporary political cinemas reveal the identity-constructing nature of these global flows. People, characters and perhaps viewers, realize their own precarity in relation to these global flows of information, people, and commodities.

Focusing on the economic impetus of neoliberal-globalization helps to explain the increasing ubiquity of globalization as the context of these films. Because the modus operandi of neoliberalism is, as Harvey argues, to force open closed markets, this period of globalization is particularly pervasive and helps explain why certain filmmakers feel the need to respond to these forces in their films. This does not mean, however, that the concerns of these films are purely economic. I argue, instead, that these issues become immediately biopolitical. The idea that economic globalization engenders biopolitical issues stems from the arguments that economic globalization is intimately tied to cultural globalization as argued by writers such as Arjun Appadurai and Saskia Sassen – for example, Sassen's argument that "The multiple processes that constitute economic globalization inhabit and shape specific structurations of the economic, the political, the cultural, and the subjective" (Sassen 2001: 260) – but I further extend this into the realm of the biopolitical using Hardt and Negri's definition of class.

For Hardt and Negri, class is not purely a socio-economic term, but invokes discussion of race, sexuality, and identity more broadly, because for these authors, potential lines of resistance define class. They suggest that "There are, of course, an infinite number of ways that humans can be grouped into classes—hair color, blood type, and so forth—but the classes that matter are those defined by lines of collective struggle" (Hardt and Negri 2006: 104). There is an important point to make in that class need not be defined purely by level of income. If working from this definition, theorists like Michel Foucault would argue that class determines the way one operates in and understands the world. In other words, the global economic and cultural flows enacted by globalization, particularly forceful globalization, affect subjectivity on a biopolitical register – not just by mobilizing global products, but by mobilizing the very composition of peoples, constructing particular populations, and creating classes. On a macro-level, this is seen in Bauman's articulation of a globalized-people and a localized-people. On a micro-level, the contemporary political films in this book address the specific subjectivities of their characters in order to examine more closely where and how these global flows affect persons.

While Chomsky argues that we have entered a new era of globalization, the importance of technology in shaping this era and the formation of networks are fundamental to the construction of modern subjects. These networks reveal global desires that point to the immobility of certain classes. Starting in the mid-1990s, innovations such as networked computers and wireless technology have rapidly increased in power and decreased in cost. While even recently it has been popular to discuss what is referred to as the digital divide, that only the privileged have access to technology, recent trends have rapidly mitigated such claims of non-access to technologies.[4] As Manuel Castells argues in *The Rise of the Network Society* (2000), we are faced with "a common information system, and . . . process such information at increasing speed, with increasing power, at decreasing cost, in a potentially ubiquitous retrieval and distribution network" (Castells 2010: 32). I would revise his argument, already over a decade old, to say an increasingly ubiquitous retrieval and distribution network rather than a potential one. While there are undoubtedly still many without access to these communications technologies, the trend is changing. Many of the films I examine in this book, particularly those post-2005, explicitly address communications technologies such as cellphone and internet-based communication within the space of their narratives, even in spaces with complex geopolitics such as Kurdish-Iran. The case of Kurdish-Iran – where the state does not prioritize communications infrastructure, yet the Kurds use satellite connections, cellular technologies, and cultural networks to remain connected – is discussed in Chapter Three of this book.

Not just a question of more powerful/affordable technologies, Castells also notes the role these technologies play in promoting globalization:

> Because networks do not stop at the border of the nation-state, the network society constituted itself as a global system, ushering in the new form of globalization characteristic of our time. However, while everything and everybody on the planet felt the effects of this new social structure, global networks included some people and territories while excluding others, so inducing a geography of social, economic, and technological inequality. (Castells 2010: xviii)

What Castells says here is more nuanced than the general argument regarding the digital divide that only some people have access to technology. The films I address here show that the ubiquity of these technologies creates a consciousness of one's localized or globalized existence. This situation is reminiscent of the "cramped space" of Deleuze and Félix Guattari's *Kafka: Towards a Minor Literature* (1975), where an individual desire actually reflects a political reality. The globe and global movements become a more tangible desire when only certain individuals have access. Facing this reality, Castells asks the question: "Then the key issue becomes . . . in a world characterized by simultaneous globalization and fragmentation, 'how to combine new technologies and collective memory, universal science and communitarian cultures, passion and reason?'" (Castells 2010: 22). While this is a broad problem that no single solution will ameliorate, the contemporary political cinemas I address in this book offer one subtle solution in the mobilization of subjects.

In the context of inequality, I argue that contemporary political films have the potential to show the relationship between the daily experiences of individuals and seemingly intangible forces and flows of globalization. Unfortunately, this is not a particularly happy task in the films I examine here, which often end in an encounter with something intolerable to the individuals depicted. Returning to the sensory-motor break that Deleuze suggested political film is predicated on, he argues that: "The sensory-motor break makes man a seer who finds himself struck by something intolerable in the world . . . [and] the intolerable is no longer a serious injustice, but the permanent state of daily banality" (Deleuze 1989: 169–170). While expanding inequality is a common feature of the type of globalization I outline here, its naturalization through mainstream cinematic discourses prevents its critique, but that transition from man to seer describes the process by which characters and viewers come to articulate clearly what is intolerable. It is possible for contemporary political films, I argue, to illustrate cases at the limit of what is tolerable, and thereby highlight the conditions that mobilize subjects like the people involved in OWS. These films require the viewer to think about the connections between intolerable situations and the features of globalization they take as their setting, without the extreme break of political modernism.

In linking the intolerable to lived populations, contemporary political cinema establishes a site for political exchange and begins to form a base of common ground despite the massive deregulation, privatization, and dubious freedoms granted by the unrestricted globalization of 1990–2010. At the same time, while the majoritarian discourses I identify in this book seem to suggest something akin to Samuel P. Huntington's *Clash of Civilizations*, the films I address illustrate the falsity of such a future for the actual people these political discourses attempt to regulate. In other words, the nuanced, networked, and hybridized subjects that are produced by modern relationships with economic, technical, and cultural globalization often serve to mitigate the conflict Huntington refers to, because the emergence of these subjects does not support the classical politics his argument relies upon. Instead, the films reflect a diversity that comes from within otherwise restrictive and majoritarian discourses.

Becoming-film: From Minor Literature to Contemporary Political Cinema

> If the writer is in the margins or completely outside
> his or her fragile community, this situation allows the
> writer all the more the possibility to express another
> possible community and to forge the means for another
> consciousness and another sensibility
> *Gilles Deleuze and Félix Guattari*

My focus up to this point has been on historicizing the contemporary, first through thinking historically about film by looking at the fault lines between certain shifts between formal modes and themes in particular eras, and second by defining the contemporary in terms of technological advances and contemporary economic modes. I turn now to the film-philosophical production of subjectivity by way of Deleuze and Guattari's concept of the minor literature. The concept of minor languages ranges through Deleuze and Guattari's texts, with significant developments appearing in *Kafka: Towards a Minor Literature*, *A Thousand Plateaus* (1980), and *Cinema 2*. Briefly described, the minor is a textual product, voice, or enunciation – often simply called a "language" by Deleuze and Guattari – set within, but not against, a major language or discursive source of coding. As mentioned previously, the films in this book often have a conflicted relationship with commercial modes of production. They are commodities, and they have national sites of production, but as banned, transnational, or festival films, they elide majoritarian structures of production, distribution, and exhibition and, like Deleuze and Guattari's minor literature, begin to create expressive spaces for political subjects outside of these dominant structures – "from the margins" as Deleuze and Guattari suggest in the epigraph.

Kafka: Towards a Minor Literature is the second collaboration between Deleuze and Guattari, written three years after their collaborative debut *Anti-Oedipus* (1972). The book centers on the issue of Kafka writing in German as a Czech-born Jew, or the particular uses he makes of the German language coming from a different cultural and linguistic background.

As a result of this particular situation, Kafka's writing does not produce different meanings, but different writing-machines:

> We believe only in a Kafka *politics* that is neither imaginary nor symbolic. We believe only in one or more Kafka *machines* that are neither structure nor phantasm. We believe only in a Kafka *experimentation* that is without interpretation or significance and rests only on tests of experience. (Deleuze and Guattari 1986: 7)

As Réda Bensmaïa notes in the foreword, this approach to Kafka is radically different from previous interpretations, because it ultimately makes no recourse to a transcendental meaning or interpretation (Deleuze and Guattari 1986: 7). In reading Kafka, readers are faced with an experimental process, "a writing machine or mass of writing machines that are made of assemblages of nouns and effects, of heterogeneous orders of signs that cannot be reduced to a binary structure, to a dominant or transcendental signifier," which ultimately "lead[s] readers out of the impasse created by so many readings of exegesis" (Deleuze and Guattari 1986: xi, x). Where previous readers attempted to come to hermeneutical terms with Kafka's project, Deleuze and Guattari find unexpected, unthought experience. This theoretical understanding of Kafka's work, an experimental rather than hermetic understanding, lays the groundwork for minor enunciations. Deleuze and Guattari outline three principles of minor literatures – they operate in a deterritorialized and deterritorializing manner, they immediately connect the private sphere with public politics, and they always express a collective enunciation – which are then very nearly mirrored in *Cinema 2*.[5]

The oscillation between minor and major seems to suggest an opposition that would run counter to my overall claims in this book, but it is important to note that this is not a binary or oppositional relationship. Instead, the minor puts the major into variation: rather than coming from the outside of the major language, and opposing it, the minor comes from within the dominant discourse. Deleuze and Guattari briefly mention "what blacks in America today are able to do with the English language" (Deleuze and Guattari 1986: 17). African American Vernacular English provides a clear example, because it derives from American English, but allows for more means of expression than standardized American English – it deterritorializes the English language. By marking a rupture with the dominant discourse, the minor engenders a collective enunciation in that it immediately speaks for a multiplicity, "in it everything takes on a collective value" (Deleuze and Guattari 1986: 17). Individuals who find a voice or representation as a result of this rupture become part of a nascent community of "people to come" that may be diverse but are a collective in their shared investment in the minor language or text. Introducing the concept of the minor literature to the cinematic context I've provided helps me to argue that we should not be understanding the time-image as an image of modernity or the natural evolution of a cinematic language, but a rupture in a commercial signifying system that has become so codified and widespread that it has become majoritarian or cliché.

Ultimately, what is at stake for Deleuze in any discussion of the minor is the ability for a text "to forge the means for another consciousness and another sensibility" (Deleuze and Guattari 1986: 18). I will return to this argument in the next section, but considering film is an affective medium, it is important to note that Deleuze is referring to the production of subjectivity or even desire here. While some might consider this a form of identity politics, it is important to consider the notion of contingency in his argument, because this focus on the future departs from the grand dialectic, which depends upon an opposed identity that might assume the majoritarian position. For this reason, I choose to focus on subjectivity rather than national or racial identity (though these formations, as constellations of desire, do matter), because while the contemporary political cinemas I address here might mobilize political desires, they resist political imperatives. In other words, they might suggest something intolerable about the context they address in relation to new flows of globalization, but never depict a resolution. Such resolution, my argument suggests, does not belong in the fictive world, but in the spectator's extra-filmic reorganization of "another consciousness and another sensibility."

In order to resist the political imperative in the form of a majoritarian political subject, such as the *Battle of Algiers* epilogue that reveals a victorious and cohesive public, the minor literature or cinema is founded on the fragmentation of subjects. In *Cinema 2*, Deleuze links the minor literature to what he repeatedly calls a "modern political cinema," the filmic equivalent of his earlier work with Guattari, arguing: "Acknowledging the failure of fusions or unifications which did not re-create a tyrannical unity, and did not turn back against the people, modern political cinema has been created on this fragmentation, this break-up" (Deleuze 1989: 220). This fragmentation mirrors his discussion of "deterritorialization" from *Kafka*, albeit in cinematic terms, and scholars connecting his work in *Kafka* to *Cinema 2* have referred to films following these strategies as minor cinemas (Marks 2000, Marshall 2001, Yau 2001, Butler 2002, Martin-Jones 2004, Hjort 2005, White 2008, Szymanski 2011, Maimon 2012, Brown and Holtmeier 2013, Frangville 2016). Formally, this provides a strikingly different model than that of *Battleship Potemkin* or *Battle of Algiers*, because rather than a cohesive population it suggests a multiplicity of peoples, each subject being unique and not reducible to the whole. Speaking of "black American cinema" after the 1970s, much like he spoke of African American Vernacular English in *Kafka*, Deleuze explains this function by arguing that "instead of replacing a negative image of the black with a positive one, [black American cinema] multiplies types and 'characters', and each time creates or re-creates only a small part of the image which no longer corresponds to a linkage of actions, but shattered states of emotions or drives" (Deleuze 1989: 220). This fragmentation describes the process by which the minor as a philosophical and creative mode of textual production fragments majoritarian subjects and national identities and thereby resists the recreation of a "tyrannical unity" and works against cliché.

For political theorists and philosophers, this is contested ground – how can we have politics without a population that embodies political will? If the fragmentation of global networks and the filmic response to globalization precludes the return to a coherent cinematic subject, at least within the space global and transnational cinemas, how are political positions articulated?

The answer in this book, via an articulation of what is intolerable to a population, is that the fragmentation of a homogenous people does not preclude co-operation among a heterogeneous people, because within a film diverse subjects find a voice. By creating a rupture in the majoritarian discourse, modern political films allow room for a collective enunciation in speaking for potential subjects silenced by that discourse. As a result, the fragmentation of subjects creates the potential for new or previously othered subjects to find political representation and therefore "produce collective utterances as the prefiguration of the people who are missing," and creating a people to come by mobilizing subjects (Deleuze 1989: 224). These two points taken together, the fragmentation of the people and the production of collective utterances, provide an important foundation for the political efficacy of the films in this book, despite their resistance to political solutions and reflects the larger context in which the films are produced. Subjects are not only fragmented by global flows as they participate with extra-national flows, but are also networked by the increase in communications technologies. As mentioned previously, Huntington acknowledges this simultaneous fragmentation and networking of subjects that globalization prompts and then summarily dismisses it as not being an operable theory for international relations. In other words, it is too nuanced and complicated to develop public policy accordingly. Films, in contrast, effect a uniquely cinematic critique (a point to which I will return at the end of this Introduction) by providing access to diverse, fragmented subjects that nonetheless share their desire to articulate the intolerable political formations in the contemporary world.

The concept of the minor, as a philosophical strain in Deleuze's work, always points towards what he calls molecular identity, which is made up of diverse elements, whether a "people to come" or an identity based on the impossibility of cohesion. As a result of this function of contemporary political cinemas, I turn to the biopolitical production of cinematic subjectivity. In some respects, this approach is similar to the identity-based approach identified previously, but differs in that it focuses more explicitly on the fragmentation of subjectivity against social, political, cultural, and economic forces trying to contain it. As Adam Szymanski points out, "Though there is a political potentiality to identity politics, and any truly politicized cinema must be sensitive to gains made through these avenues of struggle, identity also has its limits and minor cinema must not be qualified solely as a cinema of minority identities" (Szymanski 93: 2011). Shifting the conversation regarding political cinema from representation to action, Vered Maimon argues for new forms of political subjectivity: "in order to bring into existence the claims of emancipatory politics, one must take leave of representation . . . [cinema] might also become the site where this idea is no longer presented but *enacted*" (Maimon 2012: 331). Here I use Foucault's notion of regulatory biopower as a way to explain how majoritarian subjectivities are produced, and Hardt and Negri's development of the production of subjectivity within this notion, and apply them to political cinema. Furthermore, subjectivity replaces identity to illustrate the way that subjects are products of the discourses that contain them, but may also exceed them. This way, subjectivity takes on an existential layer, important for the films in this book that discuss daily life, labor, and experience.

Biopolitical Production and Cinematic Subjectivity

At this point, I have situated the contemporary political cinema in this book as post-1990 films symptomatic of a decline in grand narratives, produced through global flows of information and economies, and containing characters both fragmented and networked by these global flows. In drawing upon the concept of minor literature from Deleuze and Guattari, I argue that these films are producers of nascent political communities by virtue of their peripheral relationship to commercial film production industries. In this section, I show how the films produce political arguments through the production of cinematic subjectivity, a form of cinematic biopolitics. I have two main concerns in this section: first, how we move from the negative concept of biopower, negative insofar as it is based on regulation, in Michel Foucault's work to a generative framework through the production of subjectivity; second, the role that intolerable political realities play in this production of subjectivity. These features together show how contemporary political cinema mobilizes subjectivity. As Pisters argues from a neurological perspective, "images *as images* . . . operate on the mind, can change our perception, and are therefore a 'political player'" (Pisters 2012: 220). In doing so, they do not just create new political communities or "people to come," but also offer new ways of seeing and being in the world.

In Foucault's original formulation, biopower was a term used to explain how nations and governments regulate populations in order to exploit their productive capacities or form ideal subjects. In his 1976 lectures at the College de France, Foucault distinguishes between two biological registers of power: that of disciplinarity and that of regulatory power (Foucault 2004: 242–243). Disciplinarity, he explains, is a product of "institutions" whereas regulation is a function of the state. The former treats the body as a source of capacities, which might be exploited for profit or must be contained because they are dangerous: "[disciplinarity] centers on the body, produces individualizing effects, and manipulates the body as a source of forces that have to be rendered both useful and docile" (Foucault 2004, 249). This concept of power is the same that was popularized by Foucault's *Discipline and Punish* (1975), and mirrors the process by which individuals are required to conform to an ideal subject in classical political cinemas. In the first chapter of this project, I use the examples of *Battle of Algiers* and *Outside the Law* (2010), where subjects are actively individuated to produce an effective revolution(ary) – by actively, I mean that the viewer witnesses individuation or politicization as the subject of the film.

Within the contemporary period, this individuation does not take place in Foucauldian institutions such as the prison, the clinic, or the asylum however, but within much more mobile assemblages. As Deleuze argues, "the disciplines underwent a crisis to the benefit of new forces that were gradually instituted and which accelerated after World War II: a disciplinary society was what we already no longer were, what we had ceased to be" (Deleuze 1992: 3). For Deleuze, the disciplinary powers of the institution have been freed, from the confines of the school, the prison, the hospital, etc. and they now operate as "ultrarapid forms of free-floating control that replaced the old disciplines operating in the time frame of a closed system" (Deleuze 1992: 4). This does not mean Focault's insight regarding the formation of subjectivity is unimportant, only that it has taken more rapid, complex forms post-World War II, and increasingly so in the post-1990 period. As Steven Shaviro notes in relation to this shift:

> Workers are still being exploited . . . regardless of how this process is described. But this does not mean that neoliberal dogma is simply mystification, or ideology. Rather, we should see the theoretical shifts dissected by Foucault as performative utterances. The expression of such theories is a particular sort of *action*, which is coordinated with other kinds of political, social, and economic actions. (Shaviro 2011: 78)

While Shaviro refers to operations within the political realm, such as economic policy, films can also become concrete sites where neoliberal policy becomes an expression of biopower. An example of this will be discussed in Chapter Five with the case of *The Pursuit of Happyness* (2006). In contemporary political cinema, however, the normalization of subjectivity provides a backdrop for the struggles of every character who faces a majoritarian regime attempting to harness these regulatory measures.

The second side of biopower concerns more the regulation of populations through state intervention and/or policies. Foucault argues, "we also have a second technology which is centered not upon the body but upon life: a technology which brings together the mass effects characteristic of a population, which tries to control the series of random events that can occur in a living mass" (Foucault 2004: 249). This second technology concerns statistics such as birth rates, mortality rates, spread of disease, life expectancy, and other health concerns. He calls this a technology of "security" – in other words, a method by which the state regulates and reassures its population. These are still concerns of the body and biological functions and, as a result, a biopolitical concern. While seemingly abstract compared to the narratives of films, the question of populations concerns contemporary political cinema where censorship and majoritarian signifying regimes are established, both within the narratives of films and the extra-filmic context of production. For example, *Bab El-Oued City*, examined in Chapter Two of this book, addresses the efforts of Islamic fundamentalists to regulate a city's population within the narrative of the film itself, whereas in Chapter Three of this book we see that the extra-filmic Ministry of Culture and Islamic Guidance in Iran controls what types of subjects are allowed in Iranian film. These regulatory measures are mirrored more subtly in Chapters Four and Five of this book, which focus more explicitly on the production of economic subjects. In these latter chapters, the mechanisms of control become more diffuse, resembling the culture industry described by Theodore Adorno. Adorno's argument that

the culture industry produces ideal subjects for its own perpetuation –
subjects that desire to see a certain type of cinema, spend their time a
certain way, and labor so that they may do so – provides an example of how
societies of control wield biopower in the realm of the arts to maintain a
generous market. Like Adorno's example of the young woman on a date,
who acts according to supposed societal norms, biopower operates on and
structures subjectivities in service of clichés (Adorno 2002: 136). These
naturalized structures are important to understanding the political importance of the intolerable in contemporary political cinema.

Foucault qualifies the separation between these two registers of biopower
by arguing that they actually exist simultaneously. He argues: "the two sets
of mechanisms . . . are not mutually exclusive and can be articulated with
each other" (Foucault 2004: 250). Furthermore, the macro and micro views
of biopower here share an important feature: the norm. The concept of nor-
mality lies at the heart of Foucault's political critique and is a core feature
of disciplinary and regulatory functions, as well as Deleuze's societies of
control. He explains: "The norm is something that can be applied to both
a body one wishes to discipline and a population one wishes to regularize"
(Foucault 2004: 253). The norm is important to Foucault's political critique because it illustrates how racism enters into questions of biopolitics.
This racism can be but is not confined to questions of race and skin color.
Racism, for Foucault, is a more basic question of "the break between what
must live and what must die," which is not always a question of murder,
but also "political death, expulsion, rejection" (Foucault 2004: 254; 256).
This most fully illustrates why biopower is a negative concept in Foucault's
articulation. For him, it is inherently racist and largely a concern of regulation and the creation of productive individuals in service of the state
(or institution), or the disavowal/reformation of non-productive subjects.
Deleuze mirrors this concern by explaining Guattari's imagined dystopia,
where the movement and access of individuals would be delimited by an
electronic key-card system in the societies of control, micro-managing the
"norm" for each individual (Deleuze 1992: 7). In contemporary political
cinema, characters continually run up against and come into conflict with
this negative biopower. In other words, while negative biopower may be
abstract, films make visible the conflict between existential experiences of
characters and attempts to regulate populations for political, religious, or
economic agendas. Such a capacity returns to the exceptional quality of
contemporary political cinema discussed earlier in relation to its response
to Huntington's larger political project: the making visible of power and
the production of political subjects offers a crucial contribution to larger
political conversations regarding ideologies, nations, and political actors.

The discourse surrounding biopower need not be thought of only in repressive terms, however. Deleuze and Guattari discuss an alternative in *A Thousand Plateaus*. They suggest that while the body or subject can be subordinated by biopower, it can also be disciplined in experimental and productive directions (Deleuze and Guattari 1998: 149–166). For them, the subject is allowed an element of agency, which is missing from Foucault's project. Hardt and Negri take up this shift from repressive to productive concepts of biopower. The progression between *Empire* (Hardt and Negri 2000), their first work together, and *Multitude* (2005), their second, provides a good example of this transition. In their first project, they outline a "global power" they call Empire, which largely promulgates the interests of the wealthy and large conglomerates independent of any nation, similar to Deleuze's societies of control. As part of the larger neoliberal project, one can connect Empire to the forced migrations of populations and other disciplinary functions of biopower. In their second project, however, they begin to illustrate a concept of the Multitude, a grassroots reclamation of "what is common" from Empire. Multitude's resistance to Empire comes through its fragmented yet co-operative nature, similar to OWS, and thus eludes regulatory measures. Hardt and Negri term this fragmentation of a population via the creation of new subjectivities biopolitical production.

Foucault notes fragmentation already at work within the wielding of biopower, which he identifies with the racism inherent in the normalization of populations. He argues: "That is the first function of racism: to fragment, to create caesuras within the biological continuum addressed by biopower" (Foucault 2004: 255). This fragmentation, however, is between political classes and works to purify a population, providing it security (Foucault 2004: 255). Returning to the larger framework for this project, I argue that this is the domain of classical politics, however: to fragment and to create discord among factions, or a caesura between two factions (French and Algerian in *Battle of Algiers*). These factions are comprised of cohesive populations, peoples with coherent histories, religions, and cultures that can come into conflict with one another. For writers such as Carl Schmitt, this is the basis for a concept of politics, a point which I emphasize in Chapter One of this book. There is another type of fragmentation that can exceed this control and categorization, which overflows the limits of conflict so that the friend/enemy distinction becomes compromised (not simply French or Algerian in *Outside the Law*). Contemporary political cinema illustrates this process, which is based upon the proliferation of identities, subjects, and ways of being in the world that are not immediately compatible with a particular faction or ideology, and which may be united by something they find intolerable.

Biopolitical production is an active process of producing something new rather than maintaining order, and as such, it opposes repressive biopower. In other words, it no longer draws upon the regulatory function Foucault identifies with biopower, but utilizes the disciplinary function to create new subjects. Hardt and Negri illustrate this process by highlighting a progression in guerilla warfare. They argue that pre-1968, guerillas were relegated to the countryside, and traditional military operations were their goal. Post-1968, guerillas moved to the city and took up a different political project. They explain: "It was not just a matter of 'winning hearts and minds,' in other words, but rather of creating new hearts and minds through the construction of new circuits of communication, new forms of social collaboration, and new modes of interaction" (Hardt and Negri 2006: 81). In other words, this new revolutionary action was the production of subjectivity, no longer based on antagonizing an opponent, but of creating a new way of life altogether. Biopolitical production is certainly not limited to guerilla warfare, and I argue that the creation of alternative subjectivities is also the political project of contemporary political cinema.

For Hardt and Negri, biopolitical production is important, because it has the potential to mobilize what they call the "Multitude" toward a form of co-operation. While a diffuse concept in Hardt and Negri's work, the Multitude can be described as the unmediated masses: not the unified people of a nation, but the individuals in all their diversity that make up the population. This framework is timely considering not only the increasing diversity of populations resulting from transnational migrations in the post-colonial context, but also the increasing diversity of intra-national subjectivities as communications technologies encourage the fragmentation of subjectivity through revealing alternative (to the nation) networks of affiliation. Despite the diversity of the Multitude, Hardt and Negri claim that it is possible to articulate something that the Multitude can hold in common – not a universal, but instead agreed-upon values proper to each singular-individual in the Multitude. The role of biopolitical production in creating this common is that it "constantly creates a new social being, a new human nature" appropriate to the well-being of all individuals in the Multitude rather than keeping the people in a form of homeostasis (Hardt and Negri 2006: 248). The question for contemporary political cinema is how this common ground or political problematic might be articulated, or what is intolerable to the diverse subjects collected within the space of the film.

The depiction of what circumstances or conditions are intolerable to a people is a feature common to the films in this project. The question of what is intolerable helps to elucidate how these films work politically, without the dialectical operation that Carl Schmitt would argue is requisite for politics. In *Cinema 2*, Deleuze argues that a film's ethical value is based on its ability to construct a belief in the world, and elsewhere I have illustrated how Deleuze distinguishes between films with characters that follow a morality or pre-determined/disciplined choice from films with characters that "choose to choose" or choose choice itself (Holtmeier 2010). Ronald Bogue describes this as producing in the individual "belief in the possibilities of the world," which affords the individual the ability to change the world by recognizing how it could possibly be different (Bogue 2010: 129). This belief resists the homeostasis Foucault identifies in the normalizing function of biopower, but something is required to mobilize the individual, or to make the individual believe (in the world, and one's power to change it). The intolerable nature of societies portrayed in such films prompts the individuals to attempt to change their environments for the better.

Deleuze suggests that political cinemas can be identified by their lack of a people – that is, their lack of a population conforming to a stable identity – but he also argues that they are marked by their creation of a people to come. With this in mind, I suggest that the recognition of the intolerable in films is a way of mobilizing biopolitical production in order to postulate a future-oriented politics based not on revolution, but the creation of a people, which suggests a non-determinate futurity (future-oriented, without being dialectical). More importantly, I want to suggest it engenders a pro-filmic[6] futurity as viewers see these films and are affected by seeing the intolerable alongside characters with whom they identify or about whom they care. If this is true, these films potentially draw their viewers into the biopolitical production being depicted on screen. It is not new to say that the viewer becomes "sutured" to the film in terms of its formal operation (Baudry 1985, Mulvey 1975, Oudart 1990, and Silverman 1983), but contemporary political cinema also has the potential to suture the identities of viewers with identities on screen in a mutual becoming-political. The pro-filmic effects of these films may generally be subtle, but it is worth mentioning their potential for larger political projects in concert with alternative methods of distribution and dissemination, such as the way Bahman Ghobadi released *No One Knows About Persian Cats* (2009) online in Iran to view for free. By releasing this film for free to the audience that the film depicts, his motivation can be only to show the possibility for this type of political mobilization, which was evident in the Green Movement following the 2009 elections in Iran.

The Contemporary Political Film in a Global Context

While the logics that structure this book will be outlined shortly, if there were one feature uniting these films it would be the production of dispossession in contemporary cinemas that circulate transnationally or are produced for the global market. Athena Athanasiou and Judith Butler define the dispossessed subject as precarious, stripped of land, community, autonomy, history, or impacted by a general process of biopolitical subjectivation. They argue: "being dispossessed refers to processes and ideologies by which persons are disowned and abjected by normative and normalizing powers that define cultural intelligibility and that regulate the distribution of vulnerability" (Butler and Athanasiou 2013: 2). These normative or normalizing powers are the same majoritarian structures within which subjects in the following films exist. Athanasiou and Butler discuss the process of "becoming-dispossessed" whereby subjectivity is shaped not by Foucauldian institutions, but injustices that mobilize the production of subjectivity. They argue:

> dispossession is a condition painfully imposed by the normative and normalizing violence that determines the terms of subjectivity, survival, and livability . . . dispossession involves the subject's relation to norms, its mode of becoming by means of assuming and resignifying injurious interpellations and impossible passions. (Butler and Athanasiou 2013: 2)

The sources of such dispossession in the following films are diverse, but they share a relation to shifts in ways of living as a response to global forces that upset local circumstances. As Bauman argues, "Globalization divides as much as it unites; it divides as it unites" (Bauman 1998: 2). This premise carries out in these films on a macro level as bodies are forcibly moved in response to economic flows, but also psychologically or subjectively as passions and ideologies are shaped by such dispossession. The contemporary political cinema charts these ruptures in supposed normative and normalizing powers in the becoming-political of its characters.

This book is divided into three overlapping sections organized around forces that structure the production of subjectivity: the first section – Chapters One, Two, and Three – focuses on the contexts of Algeria, Mali, and Iran and addresses ways in which Islamic identity is mobilized for revolutionary purposes; the second section – Chapters Four and Five – focuses on precarious labor in relation to global capitalism as it is introduced in China and enforced in the United States, as well as the shifting subject-positions that come with this economic program. To this end, I emphasize thinking through these contemporary films that focus on cinematic subjectivity, rather than applying an overarching theory to all films. Chapters Three and Four provide a third connection through their focus on censorship. Whereas I suggest contemporary political films promote plurality, censorship is used to restrict to proliferation of identities and desires. This dichotomy, between proliferation and restriction, is a core feature of the modern political film: in every case a diverse population overflows the coding of a majoritarian regime, but it comes up against the wielding of biopower by a dominant force (the state, a religious majority, an ideology, a community, etc.).

In Chapter One, I return to the classic example of political film, *Battle of Algiers*, because it is exemplary of the features I suggest are untenable in post-1990 political cinema: namely, the formation of clear class boundaries as lines of conflict. Aside from the film's popularity as an example of political cinema, the immediate post-World War II context of *Battle of Algiers* situates the film within the transitional period I discuss, whereas contemporary political cinema and its fragmentation of cinematic identities increasingly replaces dialectical or revolutionary cinema. While *Battle of Algiers* gives an analytic account of the events that led to revolution in Algeria, Rachid Bouchareb's *Outside the Law* serves as a modern rendition, even contestation, of the same events, albeit with a focus on the struggles inside France. This modern retelling of anti-colonial struggle critiques arguments regarding the coherent identities of revolutionary subjects taking part in the bid for an independent Algeria. Despite this critique of the older film's politics and its status as a post-1990 film, *Outside the Law* still focuses on a historical moment (in the past) rather than a contemporary political context.

While critics have looked to *Battle of Algiers* as the ideal example of third cinema (Stam and Spence 1985), Mike Wayne argues that its formal features elaborate more nuanced aesthetic and economic strategies that span the political modes of first, second, and third cinema, which Pisters argues has given the film a political afterlife as it contributes to later political struggle and military action (Wayne 2001 and Pisters 2012). These formal modes are relevant to the film's political status, but I focus more explicitly on the treatment of cinematic subjectivity within the film in order to examine the role of oppositional conflict in more traditional forms of political cinema. *Battle of Algiers* constructs this conflict formally and thematically in the film through the construction of screen space by depicting the mobilization of subjects, presenting a dialectical view of conflict that progresses according to the sensory-motor schemata. All of these features of the film work to separate and define two opposing peoples, the basis for politics according to Carl Schmitt (Schmitt 2007). Schmitt's argument is significant in this regard, because it explains why film that relies on traditional class struggles and dialectical conflict provides such an immediately political experience for the spectator. Films like *Battle of Algiers* suggest that it is only under these conditions that the revolutionary event is possible.

Rachid Bouchareb intervenes in the discussion of *Battle of Algiers* regarding cinematic subjectivity through his film *Outside the Law*. This later film argues that the identity-building assemblages of *Battle of Algiers* are not as effective or as clear cut as this earlier film suggests by fragmenting the idea of a pure revolutionary subject. *Outside the Law* begins to break down the notion of a homogenous people through the three brothers in the film. Each brother loosely corresponds to one of the cinematic modes of first, second, and third cinema. One brother mimics Ali's status as a revolutionary from *Battle of Algiers*, inhabiting the role of third cinema, another is wrought by personal conflict between his newborn child and political ideology, taking on the private register of second cinema, and the last brother cares mostly about training the next champion boxer, a narrative arc suiting a first cinema film. Though the formal dimensions of this film do not vary to this degree, this difference between the brothers illustrates the way that attitudes toward political projects have shifted since *Battle of Algiers*. Though the vastly different contexts of production complicate how one might understand the difference between these representations of the same conflict, I argue that the latter film revises understandings of the post-World War II context and reveals the networks taking part in the production of subjectivity.

In Chapter Two, I turn to a contemporary example within the Algerian context through Merzak Allouache's *Bab El-Oued City*. This film addresses Algeria's difficult movement towards democracy in the 1990s, including the rise of Islamic fundamentalism and political violence on part of the military dictatorship. Amongst these political struggles, the film highlights growing global networks among the population of the Bab El-Oued neighborhood, which influence desires and ways of living in 1990s Algeria. These networks erode the efficacy of both the fundamentalists and the dictatorship to mobilize citizens towards revolutionary action. For this reason, I pair *Bab El-Oued City* with *Timbuktu* (2014), which provides similar scrutiny of political extremism by exploring the humanity of subjects caught up in the rise of terrorist organizations.

Merzak Allouache's *Bab El-Oued City*, delves into the daily lives of individuals in the Bab El-Oued neighborhood of Algiers in the midst of conflict between rising Islamic fundamentalism and the violent repression of the military dictatorship. While dealing with explicitly political issues – the potential emergence of democracy in Algeria and socio-economic issues more generally – the film illustrates the impossibility for cohesive revolutionary action on the part of any constituent because of the formation of global networks among the population of Bab El-Oued. This film again addresses the attempt to discipline a population, but the attempts continually fail, and the conflict produces no dialectical movement. Instead, the stuttering narrative ends inconclusively with several characters leaving Algiers to go abroad. This ending constructs a sense of open ended futurity, opposed to the dialectical sensory-motor schemata of both *Battle of Algiers* and *Outside the Law*. This new time reflects the prevalence of global networks and impossibility of traditional revolution.

Like *Bab El-Oued City*, *Timbuktu* focuses on a group of Islamic militants inspired by the Ansar Dine, an actual militant group operating in West Africa, in their attempts to discipline a population. Despite this ostensible mission, the militants themselves are shown to be complicated subjects, forbidding music and sport to those they discipline while secretly discussing whether Zidane or Messi is the better player when alone. The film was criticized for humanizing terrorists, and was even banned at one point by a mayor in Paris, but the film neither glorifies nor asks for sympathy for the militants, it simply places them within the same world of global flows and access to information that fragments subjectivity in *Bab El-Oued City*. Both *Bab El-Oued City* and *Timbuktu* then suggest that the attempts to forcefully organize subjectivity are intolerable for civilians and militants alike.

In Chapter Three, the national film industry of Iran constitutes the subject-creating assemblage. Since the 1979 Revolution in Iran, an Islamic-Iranian identity has become the standard national subject in Iranian film, enforced through specific requirements placed on film, post-production censorship, and funding schemes controlled by a religious elite. While the New Iranian Cinema, with films emerging soon after the 1979 Revolution, has been lauded by critics for its poetic qualities – some critics, such as Hamid Naficy, illustrate how these qualities derive directly from the restrictions themselves. Post-1979 developments also bear directly on the construction of cinematic subjectivity. In some films, this results in a seeming depoliticization, because regulations and censorship diminish the potential representation of conflict among differing subjects. Over time, however, filmmakers including Jafar Panahi and Bahman Ghobadi, have emerged who challenge this homogeneity of subjects in their films. In Chapter Three, I focus on the Kurdish filmmaker Bahman Ghobadi who fragments the notion of a singular Iranian national subject by revealing networks of subjectivity outside of official representation despite the attempts of the Iranian state to discipline subjects.

I begin by looking at Ghobadi's *Half-Moon*, a film that follows a group of Kurdish musicians traveling to a freedom concert in Iraq after the death of Saddam Hussein. Through travel, musical celebrity, and Kurdish tradition, the film constructs a Kurdish bio-network that overflows and thus fragments notions of a particular Iranian national subject. *Half-Moon* is attentive to the restrictions placed on these ethnic subjects, however, and illustrates their inability to proclaim their status as sovereign subjects through sound situations, where audio takes precedence over visuals, that punctuate and fragment the film. The sound situations rupture linear time in short scenes in the film that glimpse into the future. These sound situations culminate in a freedom concert, which takes place after the death of the protagonist and cannot be depicted as a result of the intermingling of censorship and suggestion of a politicized population. From within the character's coffin, viewers hear the sounds of the concert, however, suggesting the continued operation of a Kurdish bio-network that cannot be completely delimited by the Iranian state.

While one might argue *Half-Moon* sets up an oppositional relationship between Iranian subjects and their ethnic Other, the inability to represent such an oppositional relationship, as a result of censorship and formally communicated through sound situations, mitigates the potential for the re-emergence of a friend/enemy distinction. Ghobadi moves further way from an oppositional politics in his next film, *No One Knows About Persian Cats*. Set in Tehran, this later film no longer focuses on Kurdish subjects exclusively, but instead acknowledges the fragmentation of an Iranian national subject within Tehran itself through similar formal strategies including music videos that fragment the narrative. I argue that Ghobadi advances his previous political project further in this later film by showing how bio-networks constructed by the Kurds also form within the musical communities of Tehran. As a result, despite charges that Ghobadi is a 'rural' filmmaker, he forwards a political strategy through several communities in Iran that resists a move to repeat the events of 1979 by the construction of Kurdish identity as other.

In Chapter Four, like their Iranian counterparts, Sixth Generation Chinese filmmakers have faced constraints on their filmmaking, including difficult circumstances in state-run studios and censorship. In the early 90s, young Chinese directors decided to make independent films in order to circumvent the studio system that privileged a set of older, established directors. In doing so, they brought new images and formal strategies to Chinese film with their focus on the quotidian experiences of Chinese citizens in urban settings. After avoiding the state-run system, however, their films were censored by the People's Republic of China (PRC). In this chapter I focus on the films of Jia Zhangke in particular, because of his interest in documenting the effects of economic reform in China. In his banned films, such as *Xiao Wu* (1997) and *Unknown Pleasures* (2002) he focuses on the discrepancy between official messages of economic progress and the lived examples of individual Chinese citizens. Through their use of post-socialist realist time, these films construct seer-like characters who bear witness to economic modernization in China and report these discrepancies to real world viewers. Through circulation in film clubs, bars, and university screenings, these films take part in the production of a critical network of cinephiles who discuss these films, not unlike the original film-events of third cinema. Despite the critical assemblage they construct, these films do not create a revolutionary environment as a result of the status of seers in these films and their use of post-socialist realist time. Rather than revolutionary action, these films promote a form of witnessing. While Jia was eventually invited back into the state-run studio system in China, I argue he continues these critiques in films such as *The World* (2004) and *24 City* (2008).

Jia's earlier films focus on the collateral effects of rapid economic modernization on urban youths. *Xiao Wu* creates a dichotomy between two subjects: one representative of pre-global economic activity, a local pickpocket, the other an idealized capitalist who exports cigarettes, but also runs a brothel. While either might be called a criminal, the pickpocket is criminalized as a leftover from pre-capitalist times whereas the capitalist is championed as the business man appropriate to China's increasing economic growth and the new economies emerging from market reform. Depicting relatively banal events, the use of post-socialist realist time in the film disconnects sensory-motor relations and serves to counter the dominant myths perpetrated by the PRC that idealize capitalist growth. Rather than establishing a dialectical movement where the proper subject replaces the other, this realist time illustrates how both subjects persist, as the pickpocket becomes a seer-like figure. The witnessing of the seer-figure is compounded in the end of the film, which turns non-actors passing by into a network of seers.

Unknown Pleasures focuses more explicitly on the impotence of urban youths in the face of rapid economic modernization. Without the ability to act upon their surroundings, the protagonists of this film also become seers as they wander changing (semi)urban environments. Eventually, unable to act, the young protagonists of the film try to construct a causal narrative for themselves by robbing a bank. This unsuccessful act illustrates the complete inability of these youths to take part in the economic reform rapidly reconstructing the city around them and which prefigures the local/global divide in Jia's later films.

Seeking a larger audience for his films, Jia eventually re-entered the state-run studio system in China. Despite his claims to the contrary, Jia's desire for a larger domestic audience suggests a political motivation, considering the already formidable global circulation of his films. His first film after being unblacklisted, *The World*, takes place in a theme park in Beijing that contains miniatures of various wonders from around the world. While not as deliberately paced as his previous films, *The World*'s depiction of the daily life and labor of the theme park's staff creates the same seemingly meandering (lack of) narrative. This approach reveals a divide between the better-off theme park staff and migratory workers who come to Beijing seeking lower-paid work. Though the migratory workers initiate a global, or at least regional, movement by coming to Beijing, this film examines the local/global divide critically by illustrating how they are abused by these global flows. In doing so, the film bears witness to the way economic globalization in China results in a negative form of biopower that separates and relegates populations to particular, and particularly dangerous, forms of labor.

Chapter Five turns to the United States and what I call Contemporary American Realist Cinema. While the United States is often associated with Hollywood, I argue another set of films has emerged in the late 2000s in response to the global economic crisis. This realist cinema counters the glossy, ideologically captivating nature of many Hollywood films, particularly in relation to depictions of the American Dream. I use *The Pursuit of Happyness* as an example of a film that propagates the American Dream as a feasible desire if one just works hard enough. While dreams of economic success have largely come to define what the American Dream represents for citizens and immigrants in the United States, I show that this is a contemporary post-Cold War phenomenon, and that the term was initially coined to define the co-operative network of individuals working in common. Hollywood films such as *The Pursuit of Happyness* promote particular ideologies through teleological narratives that imagine a cause and effect relationship between hard work and success. Contemporary American realist cinema, on the other hand, depicts the more arbitrary nature of reality through a less teleological understanding of time. Similar to Jia's films, they depict the daily, banal experiences of their protagonists and promote the emergence of seer-like figures within their narratives. In the films of Ramin Bahrani, an Iranian-American director exemplar of Contemporary American Realist Cinema, immanent-seers emerge when the American Dream is revealed to be a broken cliché.

After looking to *The Pursuit of Happyness* to provide an example of a film that endorses the American Dream, I turn to Ramin Bahrani's first commercial feature, *Man Push Cart*. *Man Push Cart* focuses on a network of Pakistani immigrants in New York City and working class laborers more generally. This film counters the contemporary myth of the American Dream by invoking a Sisyphean time rather than a teleological narrative of progress and success. The film follows a pushcart vendor in New York who is saving up money to purchase his own pushcart. After finally purchasing his own cart, however, he immediately loses it, stripping him of his dream and putting him back where he started in the beginning of the film. In this way, both the organization of time in the film and the role of labor itself become Sisyphean in nature. By stripping the protagonist of the ability to act, the film suggests that he becomes a seer. Bahrani's film expands upon those of Jia, however, by suggesting that the seer-status of these characters allows them to form an immanent relationship with their environments, rather than one overcoded by popular ideologies.

Bahrani's next film, *Chop Shop*, focuses on similar issues of ideology and labor, this time set in the Iron Triangle, an assemblage of autobody shops. The protagonist of *Chop Shop* is also pursuing the American Dream of financial security and success but similarly runs up against insurmountable issues along the way. These setbacks eventually deny linear progression towards the protagonist's goal of owning a food truck, and once more reveal the American Dream as a broken cliché. This revelation, however, produces a new subject in the protagonist unclouded by the American Dream. Without this overarching ideology, this character produces new relationships with the individuals around him. Ultimately, this suggests an ethical and political turn towards a belief in the world, not through the triumph of one ideology over another, but as the production of subjectivity itself.

These examples of contemporary political cinema present a turn away from previous forms of political rhetoric that construct coherent subjectivities, and focus instead on subject-positions outside of mainstream discourses. It might be more accurate to say that the ways of living perpetuated through the myriad of components that make up (mainstream) discourses cannot attend to the unique specificity of life, even as they attempt to constrain and direct it. In certain contexts, such as those addressed in this project, the difference between the actual lives of subjects and the control perpetrated by these discourses becomes intolerable. This leads characters to act: to depart, to die, to steal, and to fight. While none of these acts are solutions – they do not reconstitute a dialectical or sensory-motor moment where the action leads to a changed situation – they reveal the intolerable to viewers of these films, prompting the potential mobilization of politicized subjectivity.

The relationship between what is intolerable across a set of films worldwide in relation to spectator subjectivity reflects on how the festival circuit itself constructs a cohesive political argument, not unlike the shift in post-War/post-classical films after World War II. Discussing the potential of becoming-democratic in Deleuze's political philosophy, Paul Patton articulates the intolerable as the point in which political norms reach their limits, hypothesizing that in liberal discourse "if we accept that the contours of the intolerable will be historically determined by the mechanisms through which we are governed and by the ideals and opinions expressed in the prevailing political culture, then there is every reason to think that there is no definitive escape from the intolerable" (Patton 2008: 189). For this reason, he argues that there will be "as many ways of becoming-democratic as there are elements of the concept of democracy" (Patton 2008: 190). In arguing such, Patton returns to the larger discussion surrounding political efficacy for Huntington that I raised earlier in relation to understanding the existential circumstances of fragmented networks. While the films in this book do not all take place within the context of a democracy, nor with the goal of becoming-democratic, a similar problem might be raised with the question of what is or is not intolerable to a society in a global context. Surely it must differ, from region to region?

Of course the answer is yes, to an extent. In *Bab el-Oued City*, a character who is relegated to "women's work," finds it intolerable, whereas in *Timbuktu* certain gendered norms surrounding labor are followed without conflict. At the same time, both films share their positioning of Islamic extremism as intolerable. This suggests that across the set of films in this book, a certain baseline is established in determining what political intolerable prompts the production of political subjectivity to such a degree that characters must act. Of course we should not forget Martin-Jones and Montañez's argument that this is a select set of films, but we might thereby posit a much larger cinema-centered network of subjects that not only produce these films, but consume them as well, which are in broad agreement with regard to which acts constitute the production of political affect: that move us to feel or think politically. In all of these cases, that political affect stems from the precarious foundation of the dispossessed – that leads characters to depart, to die, to steal, and to fight – whether that stems from colonial histories, radical religious ideologies, racial normativity, economic transitions, migrations, etc. In other words, individuals being uprooted from land, society, or ideology. And though the individual cases in this uprooting vary, they all share an emphasis on the effects of globalization – not necessarily as the source of displacement, but certainly its catalyst.

I begin my introduction to this book by charting the larger political and aesthetic shift from pre-war cinema to post-War cinema as a means of setting up a structure that I see the films here extending with their approach to newly formed networks from the 1990s to the present. Constantin V. Boundas associates the intolerable with the disruptive event, which reveals the importance of Deleuze's great interest in and friendship with Foucault (Boundas 2006: 219). Foucault was able to see the intolerable, yet prevalent norms, and from that his psychological, sociological, and philosophical critiques were born, but for Deleuze it was precisely this power of seeing, being able to see, the intolerable through cliché that relegates Foucault to historical significance. "To see deeply is to see the intolerable, that is, to engage in a critique of the received truths and realities of the present," Boundas argues (Boundas 2006: 219). The films discussed in the following pages see deeply, evidenced by the production of political subjectivity as characters or film-form responds to the sources of dispossession. They in turn ask us as viewers to see deeply, to see cliché in order to see through cliché, and consider the precarity that pervades the contemporary world, which only increases with environmental degradation, growing economic disparities, and the global networks that connect us.

Notes

1. In *The Clash of Civilizations and the remaking of World Order* (1996), Huntington argues that nation states will increasingly align themselves with ideologies and other nations organized around particular civilizations such as the West, Islam, and Sinic civilizations.
2. Most critics of Deleuze's film philosophy dispel the notion that this is a historical trajectory. D. N. Rodowick, for example, argues that these two regimes are "images of thought", which are not "images[s] in the sense of cultural representation of the forms, means, and ends of thinking in a historically specific moment" (Rodowick 1997: 176). Angelo Restivo puts it more bluntly: "Of course, Deleuze is not 'doing history,' as he is the first to admit" (Restivo 2000: 171). For a more detailed discussion, see Martin-Jones 2011: 203–205.
3. Coined in 1989, the strategies in the Washington Consensus tied the IMF and World Bank to the development of global policy later via the WTO, which was signed into existence in 1994.
4. The Pew Research Center found that adults owning a cell phone in countries previously discussed in terms of the digital divide rose from 10% to 65%–83%. This level of saturation is not far from the so-called "centers" of global information. "Cell Phones in Africa: Communication Lifeline", *Pew Research Center*, April 15, 2015 (http://www.pewglobal.org/2015/04/15/cell-phones-in-africa-communication-lifeline/).

5. In *Cinema 2*, Deleuze's cinematic politics include four organizing principles: a people that is missing, or the lack of a coherent identity that unifies the subjects of the film (Deleuze 1989: 216); the collapse of boundaries that would separate private from public, political actions (Deleuze 1989: 218); the proliferation of identities and struggles, rather than one identity being replaced by another (Deleuze 1989: 220); and, collective utterances that do not speak for a people, but speak for co-operation among people (Deleuze 1989: 222).
6. The pro-filmic is that which the camera captures, rather than what is represented on screen.

CHAPTER 1

From *Battle of Algiers* to *Outside the Law*: Translating the Algerian Revolution for the Contemporary Era

Political cinema often relies on the formation and transformation of subjectivity. These films depict a becoming-political of their characters, like Ali LaPointe's transformation from bricklayer and boxer to revolutionary in *Battle of Algiers* (1966). As subjects are politicized, they reveal social, moral, existential, or ethical exigencies that drive the politics of the film. In classical political films, the exigencies are clear. Political concerns include the subordination of certain classes – as in *Battleship Potemkin* (1925), *Barren Lives* (1963), *Black God, White Devil* (1964), and *The Hour of the Furnaces* (1968); the expression of colonial/postcolonial relationships – as in *Battle of Algiers*, *Black Girl* (1966), and *Xala* (1975); or the experience of political turmoil – as in *Entranced Earth* (1967), *Lucía* (1968), or *Memories of Underdevelopment* (1968). Depicting the active construction or transformation of subjects provides cinema its uniquely existential perspective on biopolitics through the intersection of political power and ways of living in the world.

In this respect, most narrative-driven political cinema is biopolitical cinema in its address of who or how individuals exist in relation to regimes of power, although its expression shifts from film to film or from one period of time to another. In the Introduction, I discussed Gilles Deleuze's articulation of such a shift in his two works on cinema, *Cinema 1: The Movement-Image* and *Cinema 2: The Time-Image*. Specifically, he points to the breaking of the link between action and reaction that marks a shift from pre-World War II cinema to the post-War film-making environment. To update Deleuze's project on political cinema, this chapter provides an example of the qualitative shift in political cinema stemming from the emergence of neoliberal economic policies and the growth of networked information systems from the 1990s to the present. This shift renders earlier models of political cinema obsolete and results in a contemporary political cinema based on the fragmentation of political publics and the formation of new political exigencies.

An observation on the changing nature of political cinema in response to contemporary socio-economic formations is timely in response to the analyses of political theorists attempting to understand the evolution of politics in the twenty-first century. Samuel P. Huntington's *Clash of the Civilizations* (1993) provides a key site of this debate. He argues that the future of politics and violent conflict will be drawn along the lines of civilizations such as Western, Islamic, and Asian communities (Huntington 1993: 22). With the emergence of terrorist organizations formed along cultural lines, such as the self-proclaimed Islamic State, Huntington's argument seems increasingly prescient. Nonetheless, critics like Arjun Appadurai have noted significant failures of his model, pointing to its ahistoricity and its assumption that cultures themselves are not interlaced with global networks (Appadurai 2006: 115–116). While an important topic in contemporary political theory, little has been argued in the way of how cinema might contribute to this discussion, despite the appropriateness of the cinematic medium to enter into this discourse.

Specifically, cinema brings verisimilitude to politics by depicting the lived experiences of individuals caught in the midst of these cultural clashes. By providing this unique insight into the lived experiences of individuals in sites of conflict, cinema complicates Huntington's assumptions regarding the formation of subjects belonging to this or that civilization. Instead, along the lines of Appadurai's argument, certain films historicize these subjects and place them within the flows of socio-economic models and networks of globalization. This chapter explores two different examples that work as models for understanding this debate, while continuing the topic of the Algerian Revolution: *Battle of Algiers*, where subjects conform to a particular identity in order to further their political goals, and *Outside the Law* (2010), which depicts the difficulty of doing so for networked or globalized individuals.

While I make a distinction between the post-War period that Deleuze discusses in *Cinema 2* and the timeline that I address in this book, his conclusions about post-War political cinema are important here in relation to Huntington's claim that in the future political conflict will be between civilizations and cultures. Specifically Deleuze's contention that: "Art, and especially cinematographic art, must take part in this task: not that of addressing a people, which is presupposed already there, but of contributing to the invention of a people" (Deleuze 1989: 217). For Deleuze, the political role of cinema is like Chantal Mouffe's notion of the role of art in relation to political theory: an affective medium that through its means of representation might "make us see things in a different way, to make us perceive new possibilities" (Mouffe 2013: 96–97). This overarching concept of invention separates a political cinema that might resonate with Huntington's *Clash of Civilizations* from one that might critique it. Namely, Deleuze's separation of classic and modern cinemas. In classical cinema, the people are already formed as a people, however oppressed they may be, whereas in modern cinema, the people do not exist a priori, but must be constructed (Deleuze 1989: 216). If the subjects of political cinema are not preconceived, such as the Algerians of *Battle of Algiers* who resist the forces of colonialism or the migrant laborers of *Barren Lives* who scrape by on the parched earth, then the film must actively construct them out of the materials provided by history, culture, and the possibilities of cinematic representation. This act is necessarily political, because the film lays claim to a political reality in doing so, and if this reality strains majoritarian discourses, it effects a uniquely cinematic critique.

There are three important arguments to make in relation to this cine-politics: first, the construction of the subject is important to contemporary political thought, and global networks complicate the identification of a cohesive public; second, cinema takes pre-existing materials – history, culture, images – but works through them in novel ways via cinematic aesthetics; three, the existential emphasis of certain narrative films on the construction of the subject enters directly into the debate outlined in the *Clash of the Civilizations*. A film like *Outside the Law* illustrates the difficulty in assuming a model where pure cultures clash violently. That is not to say such violence does not exist, but that it exists within a world transected by global economies, desires, ideologies, and the lived experience of individuals.

The Classical Political Cinema: *Battle of Algiers* as Revolutionary Cinema

Battle of Algiers provides an example of a political project that presupposes an existing people through its presentation of successful revolutionary activity enabled by the existence of a homogeneous population. In addition to being regarded as a hallmark of political cinema and a classic example of political cinema from the 1960s, it also grounds the present discussion within the context of Algeria and helps determine how the changing geopolitical, cultural, and historical situation necessitated a shift in political modes, as we will see in *Outside the Law*. Moving from the historical context of the *Battle of Algiers* into the new era of globalization we see a fragmentation that helps to explain why "there will no longer be conquest of power by a proletariat, or by a united or unified people" (Deleuze 1989: 219-220). Specifically, three elements become problematic in this transition: a singular political vision, a unified people with a coherent subjectivity, and collective action against identifiable oppressors.

The present focus on cinematic subjectivity responds to Stam and Spence's call to action in their essay, "Colonialism, Racism and Representation." They argue that scholarship focusing on "The privileging of social portrayal, plot and character . . . has led to the slighting of the specifically cinematic dimensions of the films" and that the "insistence on 'positive images' . . . obscures the fact that 'nice' images might at times be as pernicious as overtly degrading ones" (Stam & Spence 1983: 3). Following suit, rather than looking to *Battle of Algiers* and *Outside the Law* for either positive or negative portrayals, this book understands the films as analytical frameworks which provide insight into particular political moments and strategies. The creation of a cohesive set of subjects, for example, is a particularly effective political strategy explored in *Battle of Algiers*.

Indeed, as Michael J. Shapiro notes in *Cinematic Geopolitics*, the US government used *Battle of Algiers* as a case study of insurgency in 2003. Acknowledging the difference produced by this viewing context, Shapiro suggests that "we can use the contrast between Pontecorvo's cinematic efforts and the Pentagon viewers' project to think about a politics that crosses geopolitical boundaries" (Shapiro 2009: 4). This extends the argument at the beginning of this chapter to the larger framework of this book: what might films tell us about the production of subjectivity, and in turn, how do films reflect the extra-cinematic production of political subjectivity? Stam and Spence rightly laud *Battle of Algiers* for its complicated positioning of the spectator, and its demystification of "The French colonial myth of 'assimilation,' the idea that select Algerians could be first-class French citizens," arguing that "Algerians can assimilate, it is suggested, but only at the price of shedding everything that is characteristically Algerian about them – their religion, their clothes, their language" (Stam & Spence 1983: 16). Rather than focus on only the negative aspect of assimilation, however, the following analysis suggests there is also a productive potential in the production of subjectivity explored in the film. Not just a vague nationalism, but a specific political program with the aim of creating effective, revolutionary Algerian subjects.

Battle of Algiers takes place in Algiers from roughly 1954 to 1962, the years of the Algerian Revolution. The film begins in media res, with the capture of iconic revolutionary Ali La Pointe. At the point of his probable capture, a dissolve takes the viewer back to the beginning of the revolution in 1954. After the dissolve, the European Quarter appears, but then the camera pans and zooms in on the Casbah. Through its cinematography, the film opens with an oppositional relationship between the Europeans and their Other in this movement of the camera, and emphasizes the separation of these two spaces/peoples. Voice-over narration strengthens this separation by reciting the Front de Libération Nationale or National Liberation Front (FLN) revolutionary mandate:

> National Liberation Front, Communiqué Number 1. People of Algeria, our combat is directed against colonialism. Our aim is independence and restoration of the Algerian state, in accordance with Islamic principles and the respect of basic liberties, regardless of race or religion. To avoid bloodshed, we propose that the French authorities negotiate with us our right to self-determination. Algerians, it is your duty to save your country and restore its liberty. Its victory will be yours. Onward, brothers! Unite! The FLN calls you to arms.

Composed of men, women, and children going about their daily business, this sequence stands apart from the main narrative of the film itself. Its expository nature mimics the instructional tone of the communiqué, and the subjects targeted by this communiqué are depicted inhabiting the Casbah. With this short sequence, the film surveys the larger political narrative: the construction of clearly separate subjects, Algerian or FLN resistance against European colonists, and the eventual capture of FLN leadership. History tells us that this is not how the story ends, but the ultimate point of *Battle of Algiers* is not a revelation of what happened during the Algerian War, but how revolution became possible. Namely, the unification of the Algerian people that allowed the rise of the proletariat, prompted by the opposition of classes, the reification of the subject, and the homogenization of the people.

The scene directly after the exposition of FLN directives illustrates how the film explains the struggle between two classes formally. After the scene at the Casbah, the film returns to Ali La Pointe's origins before joining the FLN, beginning with his time as a street hustler. While running a card game in an alley, a woman points out Ali to a police officer saying, "He's always there!" Ali, noticing, runs down the alley as the officer gives chase. It appears as if Ali is making a clean break until he passes a group of Europeans crowded on the sidewalk. One of the Europeans asks, "What's his big hurry?" and another yells, "Stop him." A young man in the crowd trips Ali as he runs by, and the camera cuts to a close-up on the young man's grinning face. The close-up allows the viewer to examine the young man's European features in detail: with his light complexion and straight blonde hair, he is clearly not Algerian. Ali stands up, furious, and although he sees the police officer closing in on him, he punches the young man in the face. The crowd of Europeans jumps Ali, and he is captured by the police officer. While the Europeans attack Ali, a brief montage of close-ups reveals faces similar to the young man's, fair-skinned and European. Here we see that the distinction between peoples is not only political, a question of independence, or religious, a matter of an Islamic state, but also racial, ideological, and biopolitical insofar as it concerns ways of living in the world: an us and a them. The manifest distinction between groups of people is a core facet of revolutionary or classical political cinema and is articulated insightfully by Carl Schmitt in an earlier treatise on political philosophy: "The distinction of friend and enemy denotes the utmost degree of intensity of a union or separation [the enemy is] the other, the stranger . . . in a specially intense way, existentially something different and alien, so that in the extreme case conflicts with him are possible" (Schmitt 2007: 26–27). In this scene, Schmitt's distinction is clear, the European friends can jump the Arabic enemy without incurring any existential anguish. Furthermore, this distinction between friend and enemy is possible because each subject is actively opposed to the other.

As Ali is carried off to jail, another voice-over details his personal history and previous criminal offences. The details, "Occupation laborer, bricklayer, boxer. Currently unemployed. Military status draft dodger . . . one year in reformatory for vandalism . . . two years for disorderly conduct," describe a working class subject, angered by colonial order, with a history of disobedience. Though disgruntled with authorities of any kind, Ali lacks a unified cause at this point in the film, which constitutes the second component of classical political cinema. Although the cause of the FLN has already been delivered to the spectator in the form of Communiqué

Figure 1.1 *Battle of Algiers* (1966).

Number 1, *Battle of Algiers* also highlights Ali's revolutionary awakening in prison, or the point where Ali develops an explicitly revolutionary subjectivity. The prison Ali is incarcerated in seems to be made up exclusively of Algerians, but beyond racial unity, the Algerians also express a solidarity in political sentiment. As a man is being taken to his execution by guillotine, he yells, "Allah is great!" and "Long live Algeria!" The guards try to silence him by covering his mouth, but the inmates begin cheering together and gesturing to Ali to join in. Ali does not share their fervor, but when he witnesses the execution itself, that changes. As the prisoner approaches the guillotine, the inmates grow quiet, and Ali jumps up to the barred window for a better view. The film cuts to an eyeline match that links the execution to a close-up on Ali's intent eyes, showing his transformation as he bears witness to an act that affects the way he understands the world. In other words, the act of witnessing radicalizes Ali's subjectivity and presents him with a clear, unified cause, developing a desire that leads him to join the FLN. Through editing, *Battle of Algiers* positions French colonial order as the political force that necessitates revolutionary action, and through voiceover the film adds a didactic dimension. With this combination of strategies, affect is harnessed for a particular political cause. *Battle of Algiers* cements this connection by transitioning directly to Ali's enrollment in the FLN after this act of witnessing.

These early scenes illustrate the way that the film constructs opposed identities and the unified cause of the FLN, revealing how the Algerian Revolution started and some of the necessary conditions for its emergence. The film then turns to the depiction of militarization and the political goals of the FLN. While not all classical political films contain the same focus on militarization as *Battle of Algiers*, this aspect shows the film's unique method of establishing the unequivocal focus required by a classical politics. In other words, the way that *Battle of Algiers* establishes a revolution seeks to construct a sensory-motor schema that describes a singular vision for the future of the Algerian state, or a causal relationship between the building of Islamic-Algerian subjects and revolutionary emancipation. Although Communiqué Number 1 mandates freedom of religion, *Battle of Algiers* suggests the creation of a very particular subject to inhabit post-Revolutionary War Algeria: Islamic-Algerian.

The FLN's revolutionary methods are depicted throughout the film and include identity-based austerity measures and collective action in addition to the terrorist activities for which the film is most memorable. Leader Ben M'Hidi relates FLN strategy to Ali before the two-week strike, "Acts of violence don't win wars. Neither wars nor revolutions. Terrorism is useful as a start. But then, the people themselves must act." This conversation gives an overview of the general direction of FLN efforts, starting with the attacks on police officers and bombings, as M'Hidi says, "useful as a start." Although it is a platitude to say that terrorism causes divisions among people, it is important that *Battle of Algiers* carries this division out programmatically. After assaults on police officers, a scene depicts French authorities responding by cordoning off the Arab Quarter known to pro-tect FLN militants, emphasizing the construction of a barbed-wire barrier that constricts the flow of bodies. Although viewers have already seen divi-sion among the Algerians and French in the editing and cinematography in the example of Ali being tripped by the French man, this second level separation makes the division public and more explicitly biopolitical. It allows French police officers to sequester and terrorize the Algerian pop-ulation through bombing. Similarly, the Algerian reprisal targets specifi-cally French locations/populations. The three targets the FLN bombers strike include two Western-style cafes and an airport. While bombing the airport may be a strategic acknowledgement of global colonial links, the cafes are sites of colonial/foreign ways of being in the world with their Western-styled music and dancing – images and sounds imported as part of the larger colonial project. As Ben M'Hidi suggests in the film, the FLN's strategic terrorism is only part of an identity-building assemblage with the overall project of mobilizing a particular population. Conversely, this assemblage also mobilizes French identity, such as when the popula-tion of the French Quarter falsely accuses a random Algerian on the street of being a terrorist. Regardless of whether the unification of a French identity was part of M'Hidi's plans, it enforces the overall thrust of the classical political cinema in polarizing identity and erecting oppositional relationships so that the ensuing violence seems inevitable.

Subjectivity-based austerity measures compose the second facet of this identity-building assemblage. A voice-over narrates FLN, Communiqué Number 24:

> People of Algeria, the Colonial Administration is responsible not only for impover-ishing our people, but also for corrupting and degrading our brothers and sisters, who have lost their sense of dignity. The FLN is leading a campaign to eradicate this scourge and requests the population's help and co-operation. This is the first step towards independence. As of today, the FLN assumes responsibility for the physical and moral well-being of the Algerian people and has therefore decided to ban the sale and use of all drugs and alcoholic beverages and to ban prostitution and procuring. Offenders will be punished. Repeat offenders will be sentenced to death.

While the voice-over narration relays this message, a drunk stumbles down the street as Algerians walking alongside scowl at him, and a veiled woman pushes him, saying, "You have lost your dignity." He is followed down a side street by a group of children who begin to harass him, tugging and pushing him, chanting "wino, wino." An older man whistles, calling a large group of children that drag the drunk to the ground and then down a flight of steps. In this concrete example of biopolitical power, the FLN goes so far as to police desire, ways of living, and identity. Later, Ali executes a drug dealer, enforcing this FLN ordinance, but the police action on the part of the children is more significant as it signals the reformation of a particular subjectivity, not just attacks against the Other or enemy subjects. As James D. Le Sueur argues, the extra-filmic FLN's program consisted of:

> violent theories of authenticity articulated most clearly by the adopted revolution-
> ary Frantz Fanon, culminat[ing] in the state's vision of the nation that pitted unity
> against individuality, authoritarianism against liberalism, national identity against
> ethnic and regional differences, and Arabic against other indigenous languages and
> French. (Le Sueur, 2010: 2)

In each of these dichotomies, there is a correct subject position to assume: unity, authoritarian, national, Arabic, and, in *Battle of Algiers*, Islamic. It should be noted that Le Sueur's historical analysis does not necessarily map directly on to the film *Battle of Algiers*, nor does my analysis follow Le Sueur's suggestion of dehumanization. As Stam and Spence illustrated, for example, part of the anti-colonial power of *Battle of Algiers* comes from the way it humanizes normally othered subjects, and places the spectator in the Casbah with these subjects. Nonetheless, Le Sueur points to a historical correlate in the political strategy of delineating political subjects. To energize this subject-creating machine, Communiqué Number 24 also calls for collective action, the last stage of Ben M'Hidi's revolutionary program.

Eventually, the FLN receives attention from the United Nations, who are set to debate the question of Algerian independence. Responding to this debate, the FLN organizes a two-week strike to show the extent of support for an independent Algeria. This collective action on the part of FLN members and supportive Algerians exemplifies the final important facet of classical political cinema: the unified action of a well-defined group of people. As M'Hidi points out, this means that "Every striker will be recognized as an enemy." The collective action of the strikers is tantamount to declaring allegiance and assuming a particular subject position. In the eyes of the FLN, and they hope the world, each Algerian striker becomes a member of the FLN at least for the time of the strike. Unfortunately, this also becomes judicial truth and allows French paratroopers to storm the Casbah and treat all strikers as terrorists. At this point in the film,

Figure 1.2 *Battle of Algiers* (1966).

the Algerian population becomes biopolitical in its most negative sense: because of racial and more generally class-based positions, individuals can be apprehended and treated as the political enemy. The two-week strike works to amplify and separate biopolitical entities between potential friends and clear enemies, the basic necessity Schmitt envisions for political violence.

After requisitioning the Algerian strikers and sending them to labor camps, the leader of the French paratroopers, Colonel Mathieu asks his soldiers, "Any of you ever suffer from tapeworm?" At this point in the film, the organism of the tapeworm becomes a metaphor for the organization or resiliency of the Algerian resistance. Mathieu continues, "It is a worm that can grow infinitely. You can destroy its thousands of segments but as long as the head remains, it rebuilds and proliferates. The FLN is similarly organized. The head is the Executive Bureau. Several persons. As long as they're not eliminated, we're back to zero." The metaphor of the tapeworm underscores an analysis of *Battle of Algiers* as a classical political cinema, because while the worm might be segmented and have the potential for infinite regrowth, it remains the same organism, the same tapeworm. Within the life cycle of a tapeworm, there is no possibility for evolutionary growth. This sameness of the tapeworm indicates the uniformity among those proclaiming Algerian independence, at least insofar as they are portrayed in the film *Battle of Algiers*.

Toward the end of the film, Mathieu succeeds in eliminating the FLN leadership, and proclaims: "The tapeworm's headless now." Reflecting on the success of their campaign, one of Mathieu's men comments, "But Algiers isn't all of Algeria," and Mathieu replies, "No, Algiers isn't all of Algeria." And accordingly, several sequences that take the form of an epilogue relate the resurgence of Algerian resistance two years later and the eventual independence of Algeria. The reintegration of the Algerian people into a French state falters before the ultimate alterity that the Algerian people have constructed. Speaking of the ululation of Algerian women, a voice-over narrator states towards the end of the film, "The Muslim quarter still echoes with those unintelligible and frightening rhythmic cries," completely missing the very much intelligible (to non-Europeans, the commentary suggests) cultural connotations of this practice in the narrator's strict othering of the Algerians. Perhaps the tapeworm was longer than Mathieu anticipated, but ending with this historic victory of the Algerian resistance emphasizes the singular focus and efficacy of the classical political cinema: a political project carried out by a unified people involving collective action and the construction of a coherent subjectivity opposed to that of the oppressors.

Outside the Law: Three Brothers, Three Politics

The appropriateness of classical political cinema, while useful for articulating singular political struggles, becomes complicated with the advance of global capitalism and the proliferation of desires, identities, and collective affiliations. Though in many ways a very similar film, *Outside the Law* illustrates how the classical political cinema begins to break down once identity begins to fragment and global networks begin to form in a less idealistic reimagining of past political struggles.

Outside the Law retraces the steps of *Battle of Algiers*, offering a different perspective on the Algerian Revolution and the history of Algeria from 1925 to 1962. Where *Battle of Algiers* suggests that the struggle against colonialism took place within Algeria's borders, *Outside the Law* argues that this conflict was a global phenomenon because of the forced relocation of Algerian peoples, increased protest in Europe, Asia, and the Americas, and the rising importance of global public opinion. To illustrate the global nature of the Algerian people's struggle, *Outside the Law* focuses on the struggle of the FLN inside France. Whereas *Battle of Algiers* erects solid geopolitical boundaries through reinforcing the friend/enemy distinction and the almost complete non-presence of an exterior, *Outside the Law* begins to establish a network of connections linking Algeria to not only its French colonizer, but also to globalized identities, conflicts in French Indochina, peace talks in Geneva, and music in the United States. While these examples suggest globalization in a nascent state, they highlight an important lack in *Battle of Algiers*, and the inability of this earlier film to illustrate these global flows suggests a reason why classical politics are no longer possible for Deleuze. If the classical political cinema is predicated upon its ability to construct oppositional identities and clear lines of conflict or struggle, this political project begins to break down in *Outside the Law*, despite its ties to *Battle of Algiers* and its focus on the same historical and political context. In other words, *Outside the Law* reveals how the interrelation of global political activity begins to alter the political project at hand. This difference is shown in the conflict between the three brothers Messaoud, Abdelkader, and Said and their various responses to the effects of globalization.

When discussing the introduction of global flows and subsequently fragmented and/or networked subjectivities, the two films' production history becomes important. Whereas *Battle of Algiers* was commissioned by former FLN members that entered into the post-revolution Algerian government, *Outside the Law* was written and directed by the French-Algerian Rachid Bouchareb, received funding from both France and Algeria (as well as Tunisia and Belgium), and circulated primarily as an international art house film. It premiered at the Cannes Film Festival, and was a nominee for Best Foreign Language Film at the 83rd Academy Awards (submitted by Algeria). As such, the production and reception of the film are completely bound up in the global socio-economic flows that this book suggests have impacted the way *Outside the Law* operates as a political film. Its economic hybridity, no doubt inspired by the director's hybrid identity, extends to the generic elements it takes on, borrowing from both the gangster film and the western, as well as the fact that it is primarily an economic and prestige piece for the auteur Bouchareb and his funding bodies. The industrial narrative of both *Outside the Law* and *Battle of Algiers* provide insight into the two different portrayals of Algerian anti-colonial struggle, as well as the shifting strategies for addressing the production of political subjects post-1990.

Outside the Law's most noticeable difference from *Battle of Algiers* can be discerned by the way in which it dramatizes its story through focusing specifically on a single family rather than on class struggle more generally. The story begins on the family's farm in 1925, with the gendarmes – officials representing French colonial rule, whether European or indigenous Algerians – arriving to seize land to hand over to French farmers. Despite the family's protest that the land has been passed down from generation to generation, the gendarmes cite the family's lack of documents showing ownership as reason enough to take their land. The patriarch exclaims indignantly: "we have no deeds." In this instance, the family's private trouble with the gendarme Khaid portrayed in this scene stands in for the much larger colonial project of uprooting and displacing Algerian farmers in order to exploit the natural resources of Algeria. As was the case with many families historically, the protagonist-family of *Outside the Law* is forced to move to Algiers in order to seek another source of income. The film transitions to 1945 by way of newsreel style footage, which first shows French citizens celebrating in France on May 8, 1945, the day Germany surrendered to the Allied forces in World War II. The film then cuts to Setif on the same day, and the newsreel aesthetic fades, leaving the viewer amid a very different and less well-known event taking place on May 8, 1945 in Algeria: the Setif Massacre in which violence broke out between French police and anti-colonial protesters with Algerian flags, no doubt inspired by the defeat of Germany's imperialist ambitions.

A rich semiotic-strategy, the fading in and out of the newsreel footage is a movement between historical events in the classical sense, where a clearly identifiable group of people is showing their support for a cause or historical outcome, and the more modern representational strategy of collapsing public sentiment with private narratives. As the Setif Massacre erupts over the struggle between a French police officer and an Algerian youth who will not relinquish an Algerian flag, the camera hones in, among the ensuing carnage, on two brothers introduced in the beginning of the film as part of the family whose land was confiscated. First, in action-packed sequences, the camera shows how the brothers avoid getting killed during the massacre, but then the pace slows to reveal the murder of the brothers' sisters and father. This extreme personal trauma, sets up the premise of the narrative: the bond between brothers caught up in colonial conflict. This struggle, however, is more specific than the struggle between the Algerians and the French as depicted in *Battle of Algiers*. Instead, the focus on a particular set of actors portrays the struggle of *Outside the Law* as a personal conflict, between the brothers and the enemy that perpetrated the tragedy beginning with uprooting them from their ancestral home to murdering their father and sisters. In this way, the film dramatizes historical events for the sake of entertainment and also collapses the distinction between private stories and political struggles. In other words, the personal tragedy of the protagonist-family underscores larger political concerns over how we understand historical events tied to France's colonial past.

In addition to the way the film begins to dismantle the project of the classical political cinema by introducing a private narrative into the tale of class struggle, this sequence is poignant in terms of the connection between *Outside the Law* and *Battle of Algiers*. While the latter largely avoids the Setif Massacre as the specific event that fostered the revolutionary desires of the Algerian population, preferring to focus on general racism and identity-division instead, the sequence in *Outside the Law* nevertheless borrows certain images directly from *Battle of Algiers*. Patricia Pisters has documented the way that *The Battle of Algiers* has operated as an "open archive," providing materials for later films, social movements, and even military action (Pisters 2012). *Outside the Law* validates her argument, with many details and their formal representation borrowed directly from *Battle of Algiers*. In *Outside the Law*, for example, during the massacre the French are separated from the Algerians by virtue of their positions on the balconies in the city. This positioning illustrates a socio-economic difference on one level while simultaneously revealing the French occupiers' fear of the indigenous population on another. These images of the French watching the action on the street below from their balconies mirrors several similar instances from *Battle of Algiers*, such as when the Algerian man who appears to be living on the street is (wrongly) accused of taking part in crimes and the French call down accusations from their balconies. In *Outside the Law*, however, the French rain down bullets rather than insults. Despite the narrative's insistence on following the brothers specifically, these moments pay homage to *Battle of Algiers* and directly acknowledge the political project of the earlier film – even intensifying it with violence, which is not there merely to entertain. By acknowledging this earlier political mode, *Outside the Law* establishes an environment where two political projects, classical and modern, may be placed side by side. This juxtaposition plays out poignantly in the development or individuation of Abdelkader and Said's separate subjectivities.

Figure 1.3 *Outside the Law* (2010).

Abdelkader, characterized as being the brainy brother, is the most overtly revolutionary member of the family. In the beginning of the film, he marches for Algerian independence and urges his brother Said to do so as well. Said, preoccupied with a boxing match, seems to care little for the independence of Algeria or its continued occupation as a French colony. After violence breaks out during the Setif Massacre, Abdelkader is rounded up by French forces along with other Algerians that are lined up as instigators. Later, the viewer learns that he has been imprisoned in France. Abdelkader's imprisonment is an homage to Ali's imprisonment from *Battle of Algiers* through both its editing and cinematography. The prison scenes from each film show the prison as a meeting ground for like-minded revolutionaries, chanting slogans and showing an acceptance of their fate as revolutionaries when they are sent to the guillotine. Ali's act of witnessing in *Battle of Algiers*, described in detail previously, reoccurs here with Abdelkader in *Outside the Law*. A fellow prisoner is called to the guillotine and Abdelkader uses a chair to climb up to a tall set of iron bars to witness the execution. Although the cinematography is not as aggressive in *Outside the Law*, lacking the extreme close-ups and eyeline matches, the powerful effect that the execution has on Abdelkader clearly mimics Ali's revolutionary mobilization. *Outside the Law* offers slightly more explication in this scene, however, with a revolutionary leader speaking to Abdelkader directly afterwards in his prison cell, ordering him to begin gathering FLN recruits. Despite the contrast between Abdelkader's intellectualism and Ali's illiteracy, these two characters are made out to be revolutionary counterparts. In fact, in *Outside the Law*, Abdelkader's dramatic dynamic is that he is "married" to the revolution and has cast aside any notion of a personal life, even rejecting the romantic advances of another revolutionary later in the film. The other two brothers are quite different in this regard, illustrating the development of a less revolutionary, networked subjectivity. Like the identity-based austerity measures enacted in *Battle of Algiers*, which enforced a Muslim-Algerian identity within Algerian society, FLN directives in *Outside the Law* forbid Algerians to drink, smoke, or otherwise take part in French culture and industry. While Abdelkader easily follows this directive, showing less regret than either of his brothers and often reminding Messaoud that he shouldn't expect to have a family, Said has a difficult time shaping his identity and conforming to the revolutionary ideal required by the FLN.

Said's networked identity is established in the beginning scenes of the film, when Abdelkader asks him to take part in the march for independence. As mentioned previously, he declines because he is more interested in his boxing match. However, the boxing match is swept up in the chaos of the Setif Massacre, and Said is forced to run. He returns home to discover his father and sisters murdered – the only brother to have witnessed their deaths. It would be a mistake to say that the colonial struggle does not play a role in the construction of Said's subjectivity, because after the death of his family and witnessing an Algerian murder a police officer with a hidden pistol before running off (another homage to *Battle of Algiers*), he locates the gendarme, Khaid, who originally pushed his family off its land and kills him with a knife. This act is personal: Said seeks out an actor involved in his family's narrative and stabs him repeatedly, rather than employing the hit-and-run tactics of the other revolutionaries in the film. He calls the gendarme a traitor, because he is an Algerian who took a privileged position within the French hierarchy. By labeling Khaid a traitor, Said symbolically establishes a new Algeria and invokes the political bid for Algerian independence.

Later, once the story has moved to France, Said aids the FLN action there by contributing funds that he earns through his nightclub, The Casbah, to the revolutionary cause. Though the murder of his family gives Said good reason to take part in the revolution, he is completely unwilling to conform to the FLN austerity measures and sometimes appears fully integrated into French culture. In fact, in *Battle of Algiers* the character he most clearly corresponds with is the drug dealer Ali kills when the FLN first enforces its austerity measures. In *Outside the Law*, despite the fact that Said funds the revolution and is the brother of several leaders of the revolution within France, he is also in danger from the FLN. Abdelkader warns Said that the FLN will kill him and his prized boxer if they continue to participate in the French boxing circuit where the winner (in Said's case, an Algerian national) becomes the champion of France. Here, the film's treatment of Said most clearly departs from the strategies of the classical political cinema operating in *Outside the Law*. Whereas *Battle of Algiers* is almost impersonal, despite the fact that it largely follows Ali, *Outside the Law* introduces difference between potential political modes in the form of the three brothers. This is particularly the case for Said, who espouses a hybrid or fragmentary French-Algerian identity and Abdelkader, who denies his own desires for anything outside the revolution, such as the French revolutionary who shows romantic interest in him.

While Abdelkader and Said provide a useful distinction, the introduction of a third model, via the other brother Messaoud, illustrates how the political model of *Outside the Law* moves beyond dichotomies to a new representational model altogether. In other words, if Abdelkader represents the political potential of creating a homogenous or identifiable people, and Said represents the impossibility of doing so, Messaoud reveals that it is not a question of either/or, but of the impossibility of committing to such a singular political struggle. While Messaoud actively contributes to the FLN activity in France, working as a sort of enforcer presumably using the skills he learned in the military, he regrets his participation even while acknowledging the importance of Algerian independence – a lesson he learns during his capture in the Indochina War. There, the prisoners are subjected to a loudspeaker's invective: "You, from African colonies, take for example the successful fight of the Vietnamese people. Your brothers, your wives, your children deserve justice and freedom! Fighters, don't be slaves sacrificed by the colonizers anymore. See our victory and break your chain." Later, Messaoud invokes the successful Vietnamese resistance as an argument for resisting French colonialism. However, if Abdelkader is the revolutionary and Said the entrepreneur, Messaoud is the family man that would rather recede from political life altogether. Over the course of the film, he marries and has a child, and the fact that he does not see them due to his FLN activity weighs on him heavily. Later in the film, when Abdelkader threatens to kill Said, Messaoud yells at Abdelkader, "You shall not kill my brother. Nobody shall! Or, shoot my brother, shoot," as he points a pistol to his own skull. This moment reveals that Messaoud's commitment to family outstrips his commitment to Algerian independence – apparently not the case for Abdelkader.

Despite the way *Outside the Law* perfectly mirrors *Battle of Algiers* on occasion, it does not fully commit to the film's representational strategies as a classical political cinema. As Pisters points out, "Presenting a humanized past, this type of historical cinema . . . revisits the past but adjusts it according to the insights and changed needs of the present, giving the present a different past" (Pisters 2012: 226). The difference between *Battle of Algier*'s national insularity and *Outside the Law*'s insistence on a global context is important to note and may provide some insight into why *Outside the Law* cannot commit to a more nationalist political project. Though the United Nations makes an important appearance in *Battle of Algiers*, giving the FLN reason to embark upon their strike, it remains an abstract concept in the film, and ultimately does not impact the FLN's project. *Outside the Law*, on the other hand, shows the global nature of the FLN struggle. It does not remain in Algeria, but spans to France, Indochina, Switzerland, and Germany as well. It is set amongst other, similar conflicts, such as the First Indochina War. FLN leadership is shown meeting with international bodies in Geneva, representing public opinion more concretely than in *Battle of Algiers*. Abdelkader and Messaoud also encounter American music while meeting a weapons supplier in Germany. Predictably, Abdelkader rejects the music asking, "How can you dance to this?" while Messaoud admits that there might be some merit in it. This more recent film's open acknowledgement of the emerging globalization of the time reflects our contemporary globalization. It would be disingenuous to ignore these aspects of the conflict when they so clearly played an important role in how this period in Algeria's history is represented, but, more importantly for us, in acknowledging these contextual influences, the film must also begin to shift representational strategies.

Towards a Contemporary Political Cinema

Because they addressed the same historical moment, *Battle of Algiers* and *Outside the Law* are especially useful in illustrating the differences between two different cine-politics. Both center on conflict and political struggle, but they reimagine historical moments and political desires through separate formal strategies. Taken together, the two films help to isolate a turning point in political representations that is similar to the shift Deleuze attaches to World War II. *Battle of Algiers* depicts anti-colonial struggle, with the primary goal being emancipation from the colonial state of France. With this specific goal in mind, the film creates a polarized account centering on conflict and the constitution of a new national subject. *Outside the Law*, on the other hand, shows that seemingly national subjects are cut through with heterogeneous elements that gesture towards a more complicated, networked subjectivity, which is not surprising considering the director's own French-Algerian identity. This political approach matches the film's industrial narrative, with its multi-national funding from France, Algeria, Tunisia, and Belgium and its complex mixing of genres that mark it out as being a political drama, gangster film, and international art film all at once. As a result, the industrial form of the film itself reveals its integration with a global world of politics and entertainment, rather than a product of or homage to a singular political struggle, as was *Battle of Algiers*, which was commissioned by the FLN after Algeria's independence.

While *Battle of Algiers* will long be remembered in the history of cinema, contemporary Algerian cinema is relatively understudied and underrepresented because of a combination of recent political turmoil and diminished state funding for film projects. For example, *Bab El-Oued City* (1994), addressed in Chapter Two, was made by director Merzak Allouache clandestinely, often filming from car windows because of political violence stemming from the military coup and the cancelling of democratic elections in 1992. And although the Algerian Ministry of Culture provided the second largest source of funding for the film (21% of the film's approximately €20 million budget), historian Todd Shepard reports that this maxed out state funding for film production for that year, suggesting a relative lack of support for state-funded film projects (Shepard 2011). Given the costs and infrastructure required for film production, it is no surprise that increasing reliance on global economic flows and policies are essential to the production of Algerian films. The reliance on global interconnections, however, suggests that if the new era of globalization gives rise to a shift in political cinema toward acknowledging the fragmented and networked nature of contemporary subjectivity, it will continue in the same direction for Algerian cinema, as was the case with *Outside the Law*.

While the classical political film and contemporary political film differ in their representational strategies, they are not connected through linear passage of time despite what their names, and my somewhat historical analysis, suggest. Formal strategies distinguish the two, because it is entirely possible to return to a classical mode in a recent film, as *Outside the Law* suggests through the character of Abdelkader and the recreation of the famous prison scene from *Battle of Algiers*. There is still reason to conceive of contemporary political cinema as a unique cinematic project, however: through its production of difference, it lays the ground for a cinematic Multitude to emerge, to use the concept of Michael Hardt and Antonio Negri (Hardt and Negri 2006) – that is, a set of differing identities that may nevertheless come together for a shared political transformation. Hardt and Negri's articulation of the Multitude differs from the vision produced by *Battle of Algiers* in that their Multitude consists of diverse subjects with a shared political desire, but who nonetheless remain unique, whereas in *Battle of Algiers* like subjects are produced to strengthen political efficacy and desire. The notion of Multitude challenges Huntington's model from *Clash of the Civilizations* through the form of contemporary film, which is increasingly transnational, networked, and hybridized. The question of whether transnational co-production and financing necessitates a movement towards this networked model is one that must be examined through the analysis of individual films, but I hypothesize that the Multitude (of talent, of producers, of subjects) is the future of political film, and the answer to Deleuze's own hypothesis that "there will no longer be conquest of power by a proletariat, or by a united or unified people" (Deleuze 1989 219–220).

Deleuze sees this process as a product of crisis, which spurs the fragmentation of a people, but I have substituted the term "networked." He argues that "The death-knell for becoming conscious was precisely the consciousness that there were no people, but always several peoples, an infinity of peoples, who remained to be united, or should not be united, in order for the problem to change" and that "modern political cinema has been created on this fragmentation, this break-up" (Deleuze 1989: 220). The proliferation of voices and identities for Deleuze precludes the possibility for unity, but where does this proliferation come from? For Deleuze, it may simply be a natural part of the post-War environment, but I contend that the environment has shifted post-1990, so that we need to think not just of proliferation of peoples, but a networking of peoples within the process of individuation that produces not only diverse political subjects, but bonds between them. I do not conceive of this as either a fragmented or a networked model, but rather I believe that fragmentation is a politico-aesthetic process later taken up by networks, so that Deleuze's analysis of the impossibility of singular political struggles remains prescient, remembering that we need to think the production of political subjectivity a step further than the "people to come" (Deleuze 1989: 223).

While *Outside the Law* provides a useful case study for approaching the difference between the two models I have outlined because of its focus on the same historical moment as *Battle of Algiers*, films looking at the post-1990 political environment provide more developed models of a contemporary political cinema. Films like *Bab El-Oued City* and *Timbuktu* (2014), for example, are far more episodic and fragmentary than *Outside the Law*. Both address rising Islamic extremism: first in the context of 1990s Algeria when the Islamic Salvation Front began winning legislative elections and the national military responded violently prompting a civil war, and second in response to the occupation of Timbuktu by Ansar Dine, a militant Islamist group. These films share *Battle of Algiers* and *Outside the Law*'s focus on a group of individuals that attempt to homogenize a population, but rather than suggesting it as a viable political strategy, they reflect primarily on the impossibility of doing so. As films that approach the new era of globalization, this difference is a significant response to Huntington's proclamation that a fundamentalist Islamic civilization should be growing in strength, rather than fragmenting via the complicated networking of identities. As a result, this discussion of *Battle of Algiers* and *Outside the Law* should be read not as delineating a contemporary political cinema par excellence, but as juxtaposing two models of the production of political subjectivity to highlight the ramifications of globalization and a networked logic on post-1990 political films.

CHAPTER 2

Networks of Extremity:
Militancy in *Bab El-Oued City*
and *Timbuktu*

The first chapter discussed the production of politicized subjects with the aim of transforming social, cultural, and religious environments and encouraging a shift in centers of power. The films – *Battleship Potemkin*, *Battle of Algiers*, and *Outside the Law* – involved historical recollection. And while *Battle of Algiers* was filmed a mere decade after the events that inspired it, the film does not interrogate the current state of affairs in Algeria, but instead asks the questions: how did the Algerian Revolution come to pass, and why was it successful? *Battle of Algiers* and *Outside the Law* suggest that the success of the revolution was due to the creation of an appropriate Islamic-Algerian subject and the politicization of the public, though this is a political project complicated by nascent global networks of ideas, economies, and people in *Outside the Law*. Rather than a look towards history, my second chapter turns to films that capture contemporaneous events. These films are no less interested in what the production political subjectivity looks like and how such production exists in tension with transnational networks of information and economies. At the same time, they provide an exploration of this politicization in the present of the films' respective periods of production.

Bab El-Oued City (1994) follows a set of characters living in the eponymous neighborhood in Algiers amid conflict between military and Islamic groups vying for power as Algeria institutes democratic elections. With similar eponymy, *Timbuktu* (2014) follows a cast of characters in Mali as the Ansar Dine, a militant Islamicist group, arrive to enforce Sharia. Set just north and south of the Saharan desert, the films share a focus on the rise of religious extremism and militancy in the Maghreb: what William F. S. Miles refers to as political Islam (Miles 2007: 1–18). Despite the proximity of these two films with those of Chapter One of this book and the similar thematic interest in political Islam, they represent two widely different approaches to Islamic identity. Both *Battle of Algiers* and *Outside the Law* are revolutionary films, insofar as they depict the activity that makes up political revolutions as their narratives move towards a turning point in which political power changes hands. *Bab El-Oued City* and *Timbuktu*, on the other hand, depict daily life in the mode of poetic realism – despite its interruption by the rise of extremism and militancy. While speaking of *Timbuktu*'s director Abderrahmane Sissako, Michelle Stewart reflects on this aesthetic mode in relation to transnational cinemas in a way that encompasses *Bab El-Oued City* director Merzak Allouache's films as well: "His poetic style points to the necessarily hybrid forms of contemporary experience, subtly mapping out the way individuals traverse and produce subnational, national, and transnational networks, thus making Sissako a contributor to dialogues on globalization and culture" (Stewart 2007: 205). As such, these two films provide a drastically different perspective on the production of political subjectivity: rather than the key to revolution, it is presented as a facet of contemporary experience that conflicts with the everyday life of heterogeneous publics. As part of the larger project of this book, I will examine how individuals in these films are depicted as diverse in their ideologies and desires largely as a result of their participation with global flows of people, information, and economies.

While these films reflect on moments contemporaneous with their production, and thereby avoid recalling a historical moment, that is not to say that they completely dehistoricize their respective political environments. Instead, they reflect on their political environments obliquely, so as to provide minor stories in relation to these events. In each film, these stories are multiple and give a holistic rather than hermetic impression of their respective political contexts. *Bab El-Oued City* takes places at a crucial time in Algerian history as democratic elections are held after a long period of military rule. After 1965, there were several failed elections within an atmosphere of political unrest until the successful election of Abdelaziz Bouteflika in 1999. The failed elections were brought about by the success of popular Islamic groups and the subsequent retaliation of a military regime. Filmed in 1993–1994, *Bab El-Oued City* not only depicts its neighborhood of Algiers in the midst of this political turmoil, but was in fact filmed within this tumultuous moment. *Timbuktu* focuses on the Ansar Dine, which endeavored to spread Sharia throughout Mali. In particular, the film responds to an *Al Jazeera* article from July 30, 2012, which reported on the stoning of an unmarried couple in Aguelhok in northern Mali, the same year the group occupied Timbuktu. The film depicts this event briefly but unflinchingly in a sequence somewhat disconnected from the primary narrative of the film. As with *Bab El-Oued City*, the positioning of the events in the film suggests contemporaneity while ceding them to larger social currents within which they occurred.

As stimulus for political action, these films isolate the point at which the spread of extremism becomes intolerable to a population. As discussed in the introduction, the revelation that something in the world is intolerable provides a philosophical fulcrum through which subjects come to identify the limits of cliché in the world, providing the impetus to believe and/or act in the world. The combination of the style of these films (sharing a poetic realist focus on quotidian life) and their encounter with Islamic extremism provide what I call an oblique ethics. Oblique, because these films do not outline a morality, nor even an example of an ethical response – their fragmented subjects/narratives preclude this. Instead, they provide a framework for an ethical cinema in that they model the possibility of coexistence and co-operation for spectators brought together by the film's framing of intolerable violence. This cinematic ethics has the potential to engender subjective change in spectators, by revealing the intolerability of conflict and forced conformity, whether this conformity is biological, cultural, political, religious, or existential. And through their representation of a multifaceted people in the face of conflict from a military state and Islamic extremism, *Bab El-Oued City* and the more recent *Timbuktu* operate not just as political films, but biopolitically in revealing conflict between dominant discourses and diverse ways of being in the world.

Fragmentation and Multitude

I began Chapter One with a short taxonomy of conditions from the history of third cinema, which results in the politicization of cinematic subjects: the subordination of classes, the expression of colonial/post-colonial relationships, and the experience of political turmoil. The contemporary political films discussed in this chapter extend this taxonomy by stressing a non-oppositional politics in the discourse surrounding third cinema. Rather than suggesting a division of existing peoples, contemporary political cinemas contribute to the creation of a new people altogether, who affirm their belief in the extra-cinematic world and their ability to change it. A politics based on the co-operation of diverse individuals emerges, though in order to avoid a return to identity politics, the films themselves resist making such a politics programmatic.

The focus on creation, or the production of new subjects, is not to say that the subjects themselves did not pre-exist as living entities, but that these films allow the possibility for subjects to articulate positions that were previously either overburdened with meaning or suppressed by a majoritarian discourse. This ethical/political project of belief in the ability

to change the world, countering the role normative discourses play in mitigating this potential, already takes place in third cinema manifestos. In
Espinosa's *For an Imperfect Cinema*, for example, he observes that films
show us "'lucid' people . . . the ones who think and feel and exist in a world
which they can change. In spite of all the problems and difficulties, they
are convinced that they can transform it in a revolutionary way" (Espinosa
1979: 25–26). Philosophically, Espinosa describes a turn away from transcendental orders and the pursuit of perfection, where "truth is purged by
suffering," in order to turn toward the world itself and the redoubled effort
to improve existing lives. The similarity between Espinosa and Deleuze
in this instance hints at Deleuze's understanding of third cinema, which
included the work of directors Ousmane Sembène and Glauber Rocha.[1]
The important element that links third cinema thinkers and Deleuze is
that the resistance to dominant discourses – Hollywood models of production, distribution, and exhibition – multiplies the ways in which we might
understand the world. If there is one way that Hollywood moves forward
commercially, there are many other methods that might suit indigenous
stories and needs of media production. Michael Hardt and Antonio
Negri's concept of Multitude carries this philosophical resonance forward
by providing a more recent dialogue that addresses contemporary shifts in
the production of subjectivity.

In *Multitude*, Hardt and Negri note a significant change post-1968 in
forms of organization, labor, and revolutionary activity:

> After 1968, the year in which a long cycle of struggles culminated in both the
> dominant and subordinated parts of the world, the form of resistance and libera-
> tion movements began to change radically—a change that corresponded with the
> changes in the labor force and the forms of social production . . . The techniques
> of guerrilla warfare began to be adapted to the new conditions of post-Fordist pro-
> duction, in line with information systems and network structures. (Hardt and Negri
> 2006: 80–81)

Within the new era of globalization, Hardt and Negri argue that political
activity shifts from attacking a ruling regime, as in *Battle of Algiers*, to the
transformation of a place and its public. Accordingly, revolutionary tactics change from terrorism to cultivating cultures of disobedience, resistance, desertion, sabotage, and counter-power. This relationship between
models of economic and social production mirrors the post-Fordist move
away from traditional, factory models of labor to decentralized and mobile
units of production in globalized labor. In this equation, Fordist modes
of production compare to the organization of subjectivity and struggle in

classical political cinemas, whereby political subjects are mass-produced, such as with the communiqués of both *Battle of Algiers* and *Outside the Law*. If contemporary political films fit the post-Fordist model, on the other hand, in these films it is no longer "just a matter of 'winning hearts and minds,' . . . but rather of creating new hearts and minds through the construction of new circuits of communication, new forms of social collaboration, and new modes of interaction" (Hardt and Negri 2006: 81). These new modes of interaction more closely resemble a networked society.

Hardt and Negri equate this new political activity with a more lateral form of organization. Whereas hierarchical models of revolutionary organization require a particular subject, their lateralization allows for the proliferation of subjects. I argued earlier that the political project of *Battle of Algiers* focuses on the production of subjectivity as a key component in the Algerian resistance, but that this subjectivity is strictly limited. Communiqué Number 24 defines parameters within which this population can exist with draconian consequences if they are violated: no drinking or use of drugs, at risk of execution if they cannot conform. The strategic bombing of French cultural sites prevents any Algerian-French cultural experimentation or fusion. This political strategy requires this differentiation of friend and enemy, as well as subjects conforming to these clear roles.

Bab El-Oued City and *Timbuktu* contain conflict, but reject the oppositional project laid out in *Battle of Algiers*, not least because they center on a different historical moment. Also set in Algeria, *Bab El-Oued City* illustrates how the context of increasing globalization and proliferation of identities complicates such strategies. Similarly, *Timbuktu* suggests that the Ansar Dine's replication of these strategies in the sub-Saharan context highlights the fragmentation of subjectivity even among Islamic militants. Espinosa and Deleuze might suggest that such subjects are sick with desire, but this desire calls into question the truth of Islamic militancy. For Espinosa, Deleuze, Hardt, and Negri, the critique of dominant discourses and lateral political organization, and the creation of new modes of social interaction seems to suggest a concrete political strategy. A tension emerges between this notion of political organization and the response of the films themselves. Both films end not in emancipatory examples of these new forms of social organization, but instead in departures and deaths. The question becomes: How might films represent a politics based on fragmentation and multitude, when such concepts resist representation? Endings featuring death, desertion, and the like in the narrative, however, need not preclude the oblique ethics I mentioned at the beginning of this chapter. Rather, I argue that these endings combined with the formal construction of fragmented characters and narratives avoid retelling a history, and instead provide the intolerable event that brings together extra-cinematic audiences.

Bab El-Oued City: What is a Citizen?

Writing of *Bab El-Oued City*, David Prochaska suggests,

> At first, *Bab el-Oued City* presents itself as a disquisition on daily life, la vie quotidienne, a "this is the way it is" essay on making one's way in Algeria today that makes for a simultaneously kaleidoscopic and claustrophobic view of the working class Bab el-Oued neighborhood of Algiers. As a series of character sketches, it has people not politics (let alone revolutionary politics) occupy center stage. (Prochaska 2003: 138)

His initial assessment of the film accurately describes its generic nature as tending toward the neorealist in depicting daily life, but as I will argue, his separation of the private lives of characters and public realm of politics is more complicated than his initial assessment would suggest. Prochaska points out a number of real political events the film does not depict nor seem to take into consideration. He does not blame Allouache, however, but "The opacity of political power, for one thing; what can (and cannot) be said, for another" (Prochaska 2003: 142). Not only are political events often shrouded in mystery (Prochaska points to the suited men in BMWs that appear infrequently in *Bab El-Oued City*), but the facts are often contested by different political forces vying for support. I would also note the dangerous environment Allouache worked in during the filming of *Bab El-Oued City*. Despite the fact that Allouache is an Algerian, he is also secular and resides in France, which puts him and his production at risk at a time where Islamic fundamentalism was on the rise. In fact, Allouache's friend, Tajar Djaout, was murdered during the filming of *Bab El-Oued City* for being a popular secularist writer, critical of both Islam and the Algerian military state, indicating a real threat to Allouache's own life. While all of these extra-cinematic factors should be taken into account, it is also possible that Allouache chose not to focus on overtly political events in order to concentrate on the more existential registers of the film. By examining the quotidian experiences of individuals living in Algiers, Allouache reorients the film from a classical – overt and public – politics, to a more subtle contemporary politics centered on the formation and fragmentation of subjectivity.

Although *Bab El-Oued City* follows a whole cast of characters and explores the neighborhood in detail, Boualem the baker takes the place of the protagonist as he incurs the wrath of a young fundamentalist named Said. In the Bab el-Oued neighborhood, a loudspeaker broadcasts Islamic sermons during the day. One of these loudspeakers is situated across from Boualem's bedroom. But as a baker, Boualem works through the night and sleeps during the day. Despite attempts to block out the noise with pillows, the speaker keeps Boualem awake. Eventually, he grows frustrated and, in a fit, tears the speaker down. Explaining to a friend later, Boualem complains, "the noise was eating away at my brain." Though his actions are not necessarily religious in nature, he incurs the wrath of a group of young men in the Islamic community led by Said. Said and his band are mobilized by Boualem's act to "clean up the neighborhood" and find the culprit who has taken the speaker. Although Said is presented in the film as extremely religious, his violent brand of fundamentalism is not embraced by the local Imam. As a result, what transpires has little do with Islam, instead focusing on the creation and intensification of an extremist subjectivity against the rest of the inhabitants of the Bab el-Oued neighborhood. Rather than affirming Said's progress in cleaning up the town, *Bab El-Oued City* works as contemporary political cinema in three principal ways: first, through refusing to capitulate to a majoritarian impulse that would treat the subjects of Bab El-Oued as homogenous; second, by revealing a fundamentalism intolerable to the diverse citizens of Bab El-Oued; third, by refusing narrative closure, which might indicate a different majoritarian formation. In these three aspects, the film operates quite differently from *Battle of Algiers* while still focusing on the regulation and production of subjectivity (through enforcing Islamic values and fragmenting notions of the singular subject respectively) and raising political questions regarding the future of Algeria.

To illustrate the diversity of Algiers, the film introduces a number of characters with different desires, motivations, and goals, thereby fragmenting any notion of an Algerian national subject. It is significant, however, that an intense civil war contextualizes the story of *Bab El-Oued City*. Beginning in 1991, several years before Allouache began shooting his film, this civil war involved conflict between multiple pro-Islamist groups who eventually took up arms against a secular military state that shut down democratic elections when it appeared the Islamic Salvation Front was going to win a majority. Despite the fact that there seems to be clearly opposed sides in this historical conflict, there is no longer a national subject being fought for. Accordingly, there exists no Islamic-Algerian union of subjects in *Bab El-Oued City* as we see in *Battle of Algiers*, considering Said's militancy distances him from the Imam. *Bab El-Oued City* emerged at a time when democracy was becoming a possibility for the first time in Algerian history, despite fierce opposition from the military. The military's censorship of democracy, however, did little to repress the desire for democracy – indeed, Le Sueur points out that several terrorist groups promoted the re-institution of democratic elections. With the background of an emerging, yet repressed democracy, Allouache takes a different representational approach by eliding the big questions of this political confrontation altogether in what Prochaska noted as a seemingly apolitical approach. By doing so, he fragments clear understandings of Algerians, who, particularly to a global audience, might be identified as Islamic, violent, or non-democratic, because of the context of the civil war. Unlike *Battle of Algiers*, by relegating this violent movement to a fragment of the population, the film reconsiders ideas of what it means to be an Islamic militant in Algeria, and removes the idea that this is a national subjectivity. Messaoud, one of Said's cronies, is a useful case study in this regard.

Early in the film, Mabrouk, Boualem's friend and fellow baker, gives insight into Messaoud's position by greeting him, "Hi immigrant . . . Your beard is growing well," which seems strange considering he has only been identified as belonging to Said's fundamentalist crowd until this point. What Mabrouk knows, and which is not revealed to the viewer until later, is that Messaoud is not from Algeria, not Islamic, and certainly not a fundamentalist. Eventually, Messaoud reveals his situation angrily when Mabrouk jests about his prayer robes, "I was stuck in Algiers, with no papers or anything, kicked out of France like an asshole." It turns out that Messaoud is actually a French citizen, deported to a country he knows little about. Identified by his skin and dark complexion as Algerian, his deportation puts him in an alien environment. But, he continues, "It wasn't you [Mabrouk and company] who fed me! I slept three days, three weeks even, on cardboard behind the main post office. You know who took me in? The Imam. I'll never forget it." In the end, Messaoud finally receives his replacement passport and leaves on a boat for France, giving Mabrouk these parting words, "I leave you Bab el-Oued, the sun, and the beach."

Just as Messaoud's hybrid identity reveals the fallacy of Said's attempt to homogenize the population of the city, the sequence that follows this exchange indicates a general desire among the citizens of Algiers for a new political reality. As Messaoud boards the boat, an upbeat yet mournful song begins to play with the accompanying lyrics: "I want to get out! I want to split . . . my country is a rose. They've destroyed it, wilted it. I cry over its sad fate." As the song plays, the camera pans slowly to the right to reveal a group of characters from the film looking on from a nearby terrace. The close up on their wishful gazes and accompanying lyrics illustrate a desire to leave on the same boat. The camera then cuts back to the

Figure 2.1 *Bab El-Oued City* (1994).

boat, showing Boualem leaning on the railing of the ferry, a point I will return to shortly. After showing Boualem, the film cuts to another close-up of more citizens of Bab el-Oued intently looking off screen, and pans to the left to show the boat as the object of their gaze while it raises its gates, preparing for departure. This repeated connection between the desiring gazes of Bab el-Oued's inhabitants and the departure reveals the neighborhood's characters to be more complicated, here globally networked through hybridized identities and desires, even in characters initially marked out as Islamic fundamentalists.

Whereas the revolution of *Battle of Algiers* is supremely national, with increasing globalization comes the fragmentation of previously national subjects. In *Bab El-Oued City* characters overwhelmingly express this longing for a wider connection to the world, illustrating underlying networks of desire. Messaoud and the scene of departure, while a useful case study, is not the only instance in the film. Other global desires include Mabrouk's importing of goods unavailable in Algiers, characters invoking other global locations ("I'm off to Canada"/"Still dreaming of Marseilles?"), the expressed desire for foreign commodities such as BMWs and Mercedes, characters wearing foreign icons such as Mabrouk's Public Enemy hat, imported books, women who speak of marrying foreign husbands so that they can leave Algiers, and French tourists returning to Algiers with nostalgia. Whereas the other is targeted for attack in *Battle of Algiers* in the bombing of French cafes and airports in order to cement an Algerian identity in control of the Algerian nation, in *Bab El-Oued City* desire for this otherness returns in order to inhabit and fragment the national subject, even among Said's attempts to clean up the neighborhood and reassert the dominance of an Islamic subjectivity.

Rather than taking political events as the primary focus of the film, as one might imagine a political film would do, *Bab El-Oued City* follows the quotidian, seemingly apolitical experiences of its characters. This strategy operates on a narrative level as it dwells on daily routines and formally as the camera lingers on everyday labors. This is not to say that nothing happens, but that the causal narrative structure that uses action to replace one situation with a changed situation does not occur, as discussed in the Introduction of this book. These ordinary moments, however, reveal the interconnectivity between social, psychological, and economic factors that collapse private and political narratives. Boualem's inability to sleep and subsequent altercations with Said, for example, reverberates with this interconnectivity. As mentioned earlier, Boualem tears down the loudspeaker, because he cannot sleep while it broadcasts. Boualem must sleep while it broadcasts, however, because he sleeps during the day because of his job at a bakery. As a result, this act is immediately connected to the economic sphere and political realm of the greater economy of Algeria. Despite the fact that Boualem must work at night, he is lucky, the viewer learns, to have the job. Other families cannot even afford housing for everyone in the family. One family rotates family members into a car to sleep at night. Mabrouk drops off hot croissants in the morning to Fatah, who sleeps in the car, later saying, "They're lucky to have that car." Boualem asks, "There are 16 of them in 2 rooms?" "Eighteen," Mabrouk replies. This vast overcrowding illustrates the economic situation of Algiers, but also directly links to Boualem's tearing down of the speaker in that his economic situation is the basic condition for the event in the first place. Le Sueur even suggests that this is not purely an economic situation, but a historical and political one as well, as the "anticolonial inheritance left to the youth could no longer mask years of corruption and stagnation represented by staggering unemployment and a deadening lack of opportunities" (Le Sueur 2010: 3). In addition to delineating various classes in the film, Boualem's ability to work also reveals social concerns.

Yamina, Said's sister, expresses a desire to work in the film. As part of Said's family, however, her role as a woman is strictly confined, mostly by Said and his constant regulation under the banner of religion. Her strict position is defined early on in a conversation with her mother. As her mother fits her for clothing, she says, "I didn't realize. You're a woman now," and Yamina replies, "Woman or girl, it's the same. Nothing has changed. We're still locked up." The conversation continues with the mother suggesting that Yamina can go out like the other girls, which really means she can go to the mosque and to the baths, rather than wherever she wishes. Finally Yamina says, "You don't understand. I want to work. It would help us anyway," to which the mother replies, "What will help us, is that you marry well." Yamina's desire to work expresses a desire that overflows the narrow coding enforced by her family and in particular her brother. One might also understand this coding as majoritarian, insofar as Said's attempt to force an Islamic subjectivity on the community is an attempt to construct a majoritarian discourse – even if the film simultaneously suggests that this is an impossibility. Yamina's private desire is also immediately political, as it invokes the state of the economy in Algeria at the time of the film and illustrates a social level of Boualem's work. Boualem tears down the loudspeaker, because he sleeps during the day, because he is a man, which affords him the right to work. In *Bab El-Oued City*, the seemingly simple act of tearing down the loudspeaker, while perhaps criminal, speaks on a variety of registers including the psychological, economic, and social: psychological, because "the words eating at his brain" illustrates a basic difference to the Islamic subjectivities in the Bab el-Oued neighborhood; economic, because his actions illustrate a more systematic problem of unemployment in Algiers; and social, because his ability to work is defined in relation to the collective view of his gender. These public psychological, economic, and social factors precipitate the private stories not being told regarding basic experiences of people in Algeria.

As a result of these networks of reciprocity between single actions and systemic structures, *Bab El-Oued City* begins to issue collective utterances about the Bab el-Oued neighborhood. In the "struggle with informatics," Deleuze aligns "speech-acts" with the act of storytelling, an act that has the potential to overturn majoritarian formations by contributing something new to a stagnant discourse (Deleuze 1989: 270). The fragmentation of the people embodied in the characters with varying motivations construct speech-acts, which assume authorial agency in their ability to define an aspect of Bab el-Oued. Although Deleuze uses this term liberally, these speech-acts are acts, in terms of J. L. Austin's *How to Do Things with Words*, because they are not only communicative, but do something as well when they assume narrative agency (Austin 1975). Characters become intercessors as their statements can no longer be relegated to a character in a narrative, but take on an extra-cinematic existence in the act of story-telling. Yamina's statement of desire to work, in this regard, is a real statement that challenges already formed notions of what a woman can or cannot do. And because this statement addresses systemic concerns, not just private desires, it takes the form of a collective utterance. This is not just a state-ment of desire by one woman, but a statement of desire by many – other women in the filmic reality of *Bab El-Oued City* and real women living in Algiers. These speech-acts become collective not only in that the one can be substituted for the many, but also in that they pave the way for a more co-operative environment by allowing other statements to co-exist. Whereas *Battle of Algiers* settles on Schmitt's friend/enemy dichotomy, *Bab El-Oued City* paves the way for a more lateral social organization by constructing a multiplicity of desires and identities in the cinematic space.

The speech-acts of *Bab El-Oued City* indicate the filmic and pro-filmic production of subjectivity through the creation of new subjects beyond majoritarian notions about the neighborhood and about Algiers. Whereas Said in the film, and the various fundamentalist groups in 1990s Algeria outside of the film, posit a particular subject as proper to the future of Algeria, the film's speech-acts produce new subjects altogether. This pro-duction can be said to be biopolitical, because it directly addresses ways of living and being in Algeria (not to mention issues of race and nationality, as Mabrouk illustrates). When Deleuze writes "if there were a modern political cinema, it would be on this basis: the people no longer exist, or not yet . . . *the people are missing*," he speaks first of this fragmentation of the people (Deleuze 1989: 216). The notion of "people" that is missing is the unified subject of the classical political cinema. In *Cinema 2*, he sug-gests that the story-telling speech-acts of characters will invent a people in order to fill this void, "an act of story-telling which would not be a return to myth but production of collective utterances . . . the invention of a people . . . Not the myth of a past people, but the story-telling of the people to come" (Deleuze 1989: 222–223). In the case of *Bab El-Oued*, the people to come is less a people, however, and more the production of diverse sub-jectivities that characterize the new era of globalization. In other words, films like *Bab El-Oued* that focus on the invention of a people depict the production of subjectivity on screen without attempting to harness that subjectivity toward a particular end, as is done in *Battle of Algiers*. This intimates a new political mode, which cannot claim a particular solution as its goal. Instead, the fragmentation of the people, the attention to the politicized aspects of individual lives, their collective utterances brought into the forum of the film, and the prefiguration of a people to come all lay the grounds for questioning who a people is and what political direc-tion should be taken. Given the extra-filmic context of *Bab El-Oued City*, filmed in the midst of a violent upheaval after the promise of democracy has been challenged, the possibility for the formation of new subjects is directly relevant to the film.

Bab El-Oued City does not end on an optimistic note in this regard. While the possibility for democracy remains the concern of the film, its conclusion does not reveal the means to achieve it. After a violent conflict between Said and Boualem, Ouardya, an acquaintance of Boualem's, suggests they leave the country and that she has the money to do so. As the initiator of conflict in this film, Boualem's departure is significant, and marks his realization that the situation that has emerged in Algiers is intolerable. Rather than attempting to settle matters democratically between the constituents of the Bab el-Oued neighborhood, Boualem evacuates, signaling an end to any sort of democratic process that may have been possible. Boualem's departure is mirrored by the Imam's as well, who broadcasts over a newly-installed loudspeaker:

> Everything is clear now. Some people, among us, don't want peace in this neighborhood. Some people among us, and our children, want discord. Violence breeds violence. There will be no more peace in Bab el-Oued. Is this what we teach our children? . . . I've decided to leave this place of hatred . . . I want to warn you: You are responsible for what will happen in the future.

The Imam's closing note warns that the well-being of Bab el-Oued is a question for the people to come, of whether or not an existence where differences can be acknowledged without violence can be established in the future. Before leaving, Boualem promises Yamina, a romantic interest at this point, that he will return one day, telling her, "I'll come back for you." During Yamina's voice-over conclusion to the film, however, it is clear that Boualem has not returned. She narrates:

> Boualem, if you could see how Bab el-Oued has changed, like all the neighborhoods. Death prowls among us. Fear is constant. We observe a curfew. My brother Said is dead. He was gone for months. They found him in the morgue. Often I asked your brother what country you went to. He never answered me. Neither did your sister, Hanifa. Maybe they don't know. So I write and hide these letters. I'll give them to you when you come back.

While Yamina's non-diegetic narration proceeds, the viewer watches her brother Said making his way down a cliff towards a secluded beach. After looking around, to make sure he is alone, he pulls a pistol out of his jacket, a symbol, but also material effect, of the increasing violence in Bab el-Oued. He cocks the pistol, aims out at the water, and shoots. At the moment of the shot, the film cuts to a more direct angle on Said, and zooms in to a close up on his determined face. He shoots again and the film cuts to a close-up of the gun, while another round from the gun brings an extreme close-up on Said's face. As he finishes firing off the round, one of the suited men who gave Said the firearm earlier in the film looks out over the cliff at Said. If Prochaska is correct, and these suited men in BMWs are agents of the state, the film suggests that this fundamentalism is not only linked, but somehow encouraged by the military regime controlling Algeria in the 1990s. While Yamina states that Said has died, this death is never explained nor shown, emphasizing the lack of narrative closure. While this scene serves to formally intensify the escalating violence that the viewer must now assume is the future of Bab el-Oued, it also suggests that, despite the presence of an epilogue, which would seem to suggest a changed situation as in *Battle of Algiers*, nothing has changed at all. Fundamentalism and military dictatorship still typify the dominant regimes in Algeria.

Yamina's voice-over during this epilogue suggests Boualem's potential return, concluding the film by opening up a form of time characterized by Yamina's endless waiting. This refusal of narrative closure rejects the causal, finite time of films that operate according to a sensory-motor schemata. *Battle of Algiers*, in contrast, provides narrative closure through an epilogue that relates the final (successful) results of the revolutionary action depicted throughout the film. While the open-ended nature of the film gestures toward a people to come, the context of *Bab El-Oued City* and the civil war occurring in Algeria at the time suggests that contemporary political cinema does not rely on positive narrative conclusion. Instead, the film focuses its political critique around the intolerable violence in Algiers, thereby not suggesting a particular future or a new majoritarian formation, but rather creating a viewing environment ripe for political discussion and desires to emerge. Yamina's conclusion is an elegy for democracy, and reflects the escalating violence in Algeria at the time – what Le Sueur calls the "phase of absolute terror," which lasted from 1992–1998 (Le Sueur 2003: 5). Yamina's waiting, while personal in its relation to Boualem's potential return, also manifests the larger political desire for democracy that characterized this point in Algeria's history, as shown through the diverse subjects the film depicts. At the time of *Bab El-Oued City*'s filming and release, 1993–1994, however, there was little room for optimism. Even so, *Bab El-Oued City*'s political strength lies in its construction of a network of desires bubbling about the surface of the city.

Zidane or Messi? Jihad and Desire in *Timbuktu*

Like *Bab El-Oued City*, Abderrahmane Sissako's *Timbuktu* is a fragmented depiction of daily life under the stresses of a contemporary political moment. Rather than state politics informed by religious movements and military resistance, however, the influence of the militant Islamist group

Ansar Dine drives the events in *Timbuktu*. As discussed in the introduction to this chapter, *Timbuktu* loosely centers on a particular historical event, the stoning of an unmarried couple by members of Ansar Dine in 2012. The film does not simply tell the story of this event, but instead reveals the social and political context of this moment in time. When *Timbuktu* was released just two years after this stoning, the Ansar Dine were still active, merging in 2017 with the much larger militant Islamist group Al-Qaeda. Consequently, *Timbuktu* follows a similar cinematic strategy as *Bab El-Oued* in referring obliquely to a moment contemporary to the production of the film in order to explore Ansar Dine's effects on the individual inhabitants of Timbuktu. Sissako has said "What interests me is people in their present state, what happens when I am face to face with them," and *Timbuktu* follows suit by offering discrete encounters with the inhabitants of *Timbuktu* (Armes 2006: 193). To highlight the relationship between individuals in Timbuktu and this political moment, the film operates by fragmenting both narrative and individual subjectivities, collapsing public and private spheres, relying on the proliferation of identities, and simultaneously developing a collective resistance to the repressive mandates of the Ansar Dine. Like many sub-Saharan African films, *Timbuktu* is a co-production, with French companies as major partners, but director Sissako is also marked by his own global experiences, having trained at the Gerasimov Institute of Cinematography and now residing largely in France. As a film that is both a product and a depiction of global flows of ideas and individuals, *Timbuktu* complicates the viewer's understanding of the source of political violence without abdicating its intolerable presence in the lives of those who live there.

The narrative seemingly begins by showing the Ansar Dine leading a white hostage down into a canyon, to whom they give medication. A brief conversation occurs among the militants that quickly disrupts audience expectations of militant groups. It takes the form of a banal conversation about administering the medication to the hostage: "His medicine. Two tablets in the morning, two in the evening . . ." "They changed that one." "Yes, I know. A generic drug." While referencing the role the Ansar Dine has played in kidnapping journalists and foreign aid workers in Mali, this sequence immediately connects the militant group to a global world of pharmaceuticals, name-brand price gouging, and generics as an alternative. This brief moment of humor destabilizes preconceived images of religious militants in Africa, but the white hostage will not appear in the film again. Not returning to the kidnapping reiterates the point that this film is not about international intrigue or even terrorism, but a more subdued approach to the effects of Islamic law on the particular community of Timbuktu. It also breaks down the expectation that this film will have an overarching plot. Like Sissako's other films, the film focuses more on premise than careful plotting. These qualities are foreshadowed here, and the humorous mood of this scene tinted with seriousness, by two brief montages that bookend the title card. After production and distribution credits role, a group of men on jeeps chase an African gazelle, shouting "Tire it! Don't kill it!" in a moment that will be mirrored in the end of the film. After the title credit fades in and out, the film cuts to a sequence of African artifacts – carved wooden visages and mannequins, clay pottery in the pattern of a face crying out – being used as target practice. The artifacts are shown in detailed close-ups as the wood is splintered by bullets, markers of African tradition and identity decimated systematically through the careful choice of what is being destroyed, though carelessly by virtue of the wanton nature of target practice.

The film proceeds in mosaic fashion, weaving individual characters into a larger tapestry that becomes Timbuktu. As William Brown puts it in aptly describing *Timbuktu*'s political and ethical aesthetic, "Sissako's 'listening' and 'looking' camera . . . does not seek to impose an 'understanding' on these people (unlike the IMF and World Bank, which repeatedly tell Africa what it needs)" (Brown Forthcoming). Within the variety of individual characters and snippets of stories Sissako observes, the film returns a Tuareg family with more consistency, which provides a central thread. Many of the characters in the film are never named, but the viewer learns the history, hopes, and desires of Kidane, Satima, and Toya in greater detail, intensifying the tragic ending of the film in order to reflect on the intolerable nature of the Ansar Dine's militancy. Kidane is a rancher with a herd of cows, which a local boy helps him manage. A conversation among

Figure 2.2 *Timbuktu* (2014).

Figure 2.3 *Timbuktu* (2014).

the family illustrates the centrality of the herd to the Tuareg life. Kidane asks his family, "Guess what I'm thinking about?" After a pause, his wife says, "Your cows." And his daughter excitedly exclaims, "About GPS! His favorite!"

As the local boy shepherds the herd, however, the favorite cow GPS breaks away and runs into a fisherman's net. The fisherman responds by killing the cow with a spear in retaliation for destroying his nets, sparking a chain of events that allows the film to detail the Islamic legal process that the Ansar Dine has brought to Timbuktu. Upon learning of the death of his favorite cow, Kidane retrieves a gun and confronts the fisherman. It is clear that Kidane is angry, but that he does not necessarily have murderous intent. Nonetheless, a fight breaks out between the two and the gun accidentally discharges, killing the fisherman. After the gun goes off, the film cuts to an extreme long shot that depicts the entire width of the river, emphasized by the film's wide aspect ratio. Kidane trudges back across the river in a single, long take that builds upon the gravity of the moment and the fatalism of the rancher. As anticipated by this shot, the Ansar Dine arrive to apprehend Kidane, put him in a cell, and eventually put him on trial in a jihadist court that they have introduced to Timbuktu to legitimate their political and religious reform of the city.

As a historical crossroads of many cultures, language and translation provide a salient reflection on the role the Ansar Dine play as outsiders to the local population. As they enter town in the beginning of the film, the Ansar Dine announce "Important information!" as they outline new Islamic regulations in Arabic, "Smoking is forbidden. Music is forbidden. Women must wear socks and gloves." Resonant with the communiqués of *Battle of Algiers* and *Outside the Law*, and communicated via loudspeaker as in *Bab El-Oued City*, these commands are repeated in several languages – a key difference from the aforementioned films. The announcements are then repeated in Bambara, the national language of Mali, which sets the stage for the diversity of inhabitants and languages that will be spoken: Arabic and Bambara, but also Tamasheq, French, and English. Throughout the film, language acts as a biopolitical marker as it demarcates an external power that controls who lives and who dies, and mandates appropriate ways of living. The jihadist court forces marriages and assigns corporal punishment to young men playing football and to female singers, a theme that I will return to with Bahman Ghobadi's films in Chapter Three. As an example, the leader of the Ansar Dine, Abdelkarim, admonishes his driver after the driver expresses a belief that the people of Timbuktu are believers even if they don't follow strict Sharia, saying, "Omar, how badly you speak Arabic!" – to which he replies, "Yes, but I also speak English and Tamasheq." The tension between the two resonates with the interplay of power, the history of colonialism, and transnational movement in *Timbuktu*.

The jihadist that administers Kidane's trial does so through a translator, because Kidane speaks Tamasheq and the jihadists primarily Arabic. Through translation, Kidane is informed that his trial will be swift and that they will follow Sharia. He is told that the judge is a good man, and then the conversation goes to reparations, to which the jihadist tells him "We'll decide on blood money." After telling the jihadist and translator that he has seven cows left, since GPS was killed, the jihadist tells him, "You have to give 40 cows." Since Kidane cannot possibly pay 40 cows, he is sentenced to death. Upon realizing his fate, he asks the jihadist if he has children, and the jihadist tells him that he has two. Kidane proceeds to tell him that his daughter Toya is his entire life, and that while fate cannot be avoided, he fears not being able to see her before he dies. The sequence ends with the jihadist telling the translator, "Knowing that his daughter will soon be an orphan really hurts me. But don't translate that." While the film's setup of Kidane's crime is complicated by his anger and the accidental nature of the murder, the results of the trial are clearly articulated in that they will destroy not just the father, but the entire family. This central thread reveals both the extremity and strict application of Islamic law, contrasting the gaiety other moments in the film sometimes provide.

Numerous stories intercut Kidane's story in order to show both the diversity of tensions that arise from the arrival of the Ansar Dine, which are often communicated through comic absurdism. In Sissako's earlier film *Heremakono* (2002), Roy Armes suggests that it has a "narrative . . . from which all the normal signposts have been removed, and where the boundaries between actuality and pure fiction are not immediately apparent"

(Armes 2006: 197). While scripted, *Timbuktu*'s depiction of historical events and its fragmentary nature, via the removal of signposts that might point to a central story other than some consistency in characters, creates a similar effect in its approach to the historical world of Mali. In the first of these moments, an older man is told to roll up his long, flowing pants. He tries to roll them up to no avail, saying "all my pants are like this." Eventually he decides to just take them off and he walks away in his shorts. A female fishmonger is told that she must wear gloves, and she becomes irate because it impedes her work. She exclaims, "We're fed up. First they made us wear the veil. Now the gloves! How are we supposed to work?" In the film's most iconic moment, after a young man is assigned 20 lashes for playing football, a balletic sequence unfolds of a group of boys dashing through a field between two goalposts, kicking into the air imagining a time prior to the arrival of the Ansar Dine. With no diegetic sound and no football, their performance provides an imagined experience of how they would live without the presence of the Ansar Dine. Other individual stories lack either the poetry or the absurdism of these scenes, however, as a woman is forcibly married to a Jihadist of whom neither the local imam nor the parents approve. Another group of young men and women are caught playing music together, and a young woman receives lashes as her punishment. She begins to sing through the corporal punishment as a form of protest. As mentioned earlier in this chapter, the stoning of an unwed couple that inspired the film is shown, brief but brutal in its close up of a bloodied face, buried in the sand, being pelted with a rock. This last example not only reminds viewers of the real event that inspired the film, but through its formal depiction argues that while the film might humanize the jihadists, there is nothing humane about their actions.

The reception in the popular press highlighted the way the film appeared to humanize jihadists, though within the context of this larger project, I argue that they are not humanized so much as their militant subjectivities are compromised and complicated. In the *New Yorker*, Alexis Okeowo titles her review of the film "A Movie That Dares to Humanize Jihadists" (Okeowo 2015). She cites the attempted banning of the film by a Parisian mayor who deemed the film apologist, and that the Festival Panafricain du Cinéma et de la télévision de Ouagadougou (FESPACO), Africa's most prominent film festival, pulled the film. However, the mayor who tried to ban the film conflated the effort to humanize the jihadists with sympathy for them. As my previous examples have shown, the film provides little sympathy for the jihadists, except for the rare circumstances where a jihadist appears to be forced to perform – such as when a young boy is being told how to appropriately renounce his desire for rap music and proclaim his Islamic faith on camera. Often, this so-called humanization comes not from the films sympathizing with the jihadists, but a revelation that they are complicated, globally networked subjects rather than one-dimensional archetypes.

Unlike Ali in *Battle of Algiers* and Abdelkader in *Outside the Law*, no jihadist in *Timbuktu* expresses an uncomplicated Islamic revolutionary subjectivity. As they reveal desires informed by global networks, they conflict with the politics they impose on the community. The earliest example of this in the film shows a group of the jihadists arguing. At first the details of the argument are unclear, as they name dates, "He joined us in 1990. We beat them in 2001, 2003, and 2005." It almost seems they could be discussing jihad until one of them says, "I respect Zidane, he's a great player. But he hasn't Messi's track record. Messi scores 3 or 4 goals in a game." They continue to discuss football with a level of detail – "Don't compare Barcelona with Real" – that illustrates their intimate knowledge of global culture. Despite their own interest in it, they still administer lashings to local residents for playing football; the exposure of this hypocrisy clearly does not humanize the jihadists. Like its poetic rendition of a football match without a football, the film's complication of the jihadists culminates in another poetic scene, cut to directly after the stoning of the unwed couple, where Abdelkarim dances in front of the local woman Zabou. His performance is equally balletic, and similarly references a time before the Ansar Dine as he appears to be a trained performer. His performance is no longer on a public stage, but hidden from view on a terrace in Timbuktu. This private act complicates the larger political imperative of the Ansar Dine, not just through the transition from stoning to ballet-like artistic expression, but also by revealing suppressed desires that the film suggests all of the jihadists contain to some degree.

The themes of biopolitically imposed alienation from personal desire and transnational movement speak to Sissako's training at the Gerasimov Institute of Cinematography in Moscow (VGIK). In an article that positions Sissako as a key example of transnational filmmaking, Michelle Stewart argues that "Sissako promotes the role of filmmaker as a kind of mobilized exile, who can, with the aid of a technology that might itself be deterritorializing, explore shared experiences of diaspora and migration as conditions of African experience, at the same time pointing to the legacy of different phases of globalization on African peoples" (Stewart 2007: 201–202). In this regard, *Timbuktu* presents an evolution of Sissako's reflections on transnational life and experience. Born in Mauritania to a Mauritanian mother and Malian father, Sissako moved to Mali both for primary and for secondary education. Sissako then briefly spent time in

Mauritania again, before heading to Moscow for film school. Sissako's training at the VGIK is not without precedent. Josephine Woll explores the tradition of African filmmakers training in the Union of Soviet Socialist Russia (USSR) before returning to Africa, including luminaries such as Ousmane Sembène and Souleymane Cissé. Woll explains the general paradigm of support of African industrial development and aid as a way for the USSR to disrupt economic and political ties with the West. Even though the USSR no longer existed by the time Sissako finished his studies in Russia, a number of aesthetic and social, if not political, influences can be seen in his films, including "the intertwining of human relationships . . . and the social realities in which they exist" as well as the soviet preference for non-actors (Woll 2004: 231-232). The movement from Mauritania to Moscow was perhaps not such a difficult transition due to Sissako's earlier displacement. As Woll notes: "Sissako attributes the power that visual images hold for him to his childhood emigration from Mali to Mauritania, where Bambara, his mother-tongue, no longer served him as a medium of communication" (Woll 2004: 236). This personal experience of earlier transnational movements takes on a menacing tone in *Timbuktu*, where certain languages become power-laden and the pre-Ansar Dine cosmopolitanism brought to the fore by the insistence on particular languages in juridical settings.

The film ends with a reflection on the intolerable nature of the Ansar Dine's brand of Sharia as it is carried out in Timbuktu. A motorcyclist couriers Satima to Kidane's execution, and she runs at the executioner fist raised – presumably with weapon in hand. Foreshadowed by Kidane's trial, where the jurist expresses sadness that Toya will soon be an orphan, the injustice of the legal proceeding preempts death from the very beginning of its proceeding. She and Kidane are shot by the assembled jihadists, and the motorcyclist flees. Crosscutting then connects four figures as they run through the desert: the gazelle from the film's beginning, Toya, the young shepherd who witnessed the killing of GPS, and the motorcyclist that took Satima to Kidane's execution. There is a thematic rather than a spatio-temporal or narrative connection between these intersecting segments. Armes argued of Sissako's earlier film: "Though clearly a fiction, *Heremakono* is an intensely personal and lyrical piece, held together by the strength of Sissako's emotions rather than by any sort of purely narrative logic" (Armes 2006: 199). The same might be said of *Timbuktu*, but rather than Sissako's emotions, we have a response to the intolerable biopower of Islamic extremism as it suppresses the desires of those who inhabit Timbuktu, which includes the suppression of the jihadist's globally inspired desires as well. Both *Bab El-Oued City* and *Timbuktu* include the character of a local imam who tries to mitigate the extremism of militant enforcers of Islam, but both films end in death and departure. A multitude of political desires are reflected in these films, ranging from the non-religious to the extreme fundamentalist, but each film ends on a representation of that which becomes intolerable, with no solution other than death or departure. We are left with the conclusion that another political reality must be sought.

The Intolerability of Violence

Battle of Algiers, *Outside the Law*, *Bab El-Oued City*, and *Timbuktu* hinge on a relation between two very different politico-cinematic projects. All four center on conflict and political struggle, but their difference illustrates an attention to particular historical moments and political desires. *Battle of Algiers* depicts an anti-colonial struggle, with the primary goal being emancipation from the colonial state of France. With this in mind, the film creates a polarized account centering on conflict and the constitution of a new, unitary national subject. *Bab El-Oued City*, on the other hand, was filmed when the potential for democracy was emerging in Algeria. This democracy is represented in the film by the proliferation of identities, some co-operating and some coming into conflict. While the film's representational strategies allow for the possibility of democracy, the film ultimately argues that democracy is only on the horizon for the people of Algeria. *Outside the Law* has elements of both these films, with some characters displaying revolutionary fervor, and others preferring the capitalist, inter-national fragmentation of identity. *Timbuktu* complicates these politics even further, by suggesting even the militancy represented in the aforementioned films is more complicated than one might think.

While earlier I developed some resonance between the philosophical project of Deleuze and the political project of third cinema, the focus on the production of individual subjectivities in relation to larger political moments can be described cinematically as a hybridization of the categories of second and third cinemas. In suggesting Sissako's own hybridity between second and third cinema, Rachel Gabara defines these categories by arguing that "Third Cinema, to the contrary [of art cinema], was interested in the People, in popular history and living conditions, and not at all in individual psychology" (Gabara 2010: 321). The hybridity of filmmakers such as Allouache and Sissako places these individual psychologies in the context of popular history and living conditions, without the suggestion of "the People." This hybridity constitutes a larger political and cinematic project responsive to globalization's complicated effects on political cinemas.

Through the production of difference, second cinemas interpellation of third cinema lays the ground for a cinematic Multitude to emerge – a set of differing identities that may, nevertheless, come together with shared political desire. Earlier I referred to this as an oblique ethics. Oblique, because it does not directly analyze political problems nor offer political solutions. Ethical, because it explores the limits of political realities, what communities consider intolerable – the limits of a bearable life, and the possibility of coexistence and co-operation. This oblique ethics allows the individual viewer freedom to be and become other without directing the viewer who or how to become, while simultaneously admitting a biopolitical limit identified by the deaths and desertions of characters in these films. This cinematic ethics has the potential to engender subjective change in its spectators, by revealing the intolerability of conflict and forced conformity to a political logic that differs on a biological, cultural, political, religious, and existential, that is to say, a biopolitical scale.

Note

1. Deleuze uses the term third world cinema, but my argument suggests that his cinematic politics is congruent with many of the third cinema manifestos, so I opt for the more generally accepted third cinema here.

CHAPTER 3

Kurds on Screen and Bahman Ghobadi's Networks of Resistance

Chapters One and Two have argued that contemporary political cinemas address multi-faceted struggles in response to globalization, rather than the formation of a particular (national or religious) subject. Like scholars of transnational cinemas, this chapter posits the difficulty of considering the nation a center at all, although with a slightly different approach (Higson 2000, Andrew 2010, Ďurovičová and Newman 2010). While addressing particular geopolitical concerns – independence from France or religious extremism in North Africa – and although nations can be involved firsthand in certain instances – the censorship in Iran and China – these struggles often take place within different discursive communities that cannot be described as national. Instead, a minor subject position emerges from a dominant discourse, thereby fragmenting and critiquing majoritarian ideas by exposing another story the discourse does not account for. As an example, this chapter turns to Kurds in Iran and the ways in which Bahman Ghobadi organizes his films in order to address the Kurdish experience, culminating in his film *Half-Moon* (2006). Ghobadi extends this strategy to the musical communities in Tehran in his last film made inside Iran, *No One Knows about Persian Cats* (2009).

As I argued in Chapter Two, films that operate this way continue along the lines of third cinema, but extend such politics to elucidate the position of more fluid subjects – those without nation-states or institutionalized political representation to speak for them. This perspective underscores Deleuze's argument for the creative power of political cinema: "The moment the master, or the colonizer, proclaims 'There have never been people here', the missing people are a becoming, they invent themselves, in shanty towns and camps, or in ghettos, in new conditions of struggle to which a necessarily political art must contribute" (Deleuze 1989: 217). This does not mean instituting a new discourse, but the fragmentation of a dominant discourse to the point where new, minor stories might be told. Following this strategy of political cinema, Bahman Ghobadi introduces a hyphen to the Iranian subject as formulated by the state. Through sonic strategies, Ghobadi invents a Kurdish-Iranian subject missing from the mainstream cinematic discourse in Iran. He takes this strategy even further in *No One Knows about Persian Cats* through musical diversity in Tehran, despite laws at the time that restricted what the state perceives as western desires (Staff and agencies 2005).

Since the 1979 revolution in Iran, Islamic ideology has been established as a national and legal ethos. That is not to say that Islamic ideology is a simple thing. As Saeed Zeydabadi-Nejad notes, its complexity is revealed by discrepancies in issuing exhibition permits, for example, or the impact personnel changes have had on policy (Zeydabadi-Nejad 2010). Nonetheless, many laws in post-revolution Iran make recourse to Islamic ideology as grounds for their validity – for example, Sharia, or Islamic law, being enforced in films. Similar to the political strategies depicted in *Battle of Algiers*, the state uses film regulation to promote a particular, Islamic subject. As a result, these regulations operate as a form of biopower, structuring the creation of subjects and ways of living in contemporary Iran.

The repressive biopolitics of the Iranian state came to a head with the production of *Half-Moon*. Ghobadi was asked by the Ministry of Culture and Islamic Guidance to stop making films in the Kurdish language, because of its potential to promote separatism. In a discussion of dispossessed languages, Athena Athanasiou argues that "The erasure of singularity, or de-personalization, is a crucial aspect of biopolitics, much as individuation – in the form of individuated life (*bios*) and the capability to individuate and privatize – is a crucial aspect of biopolitical (self-)management" (Butler and Athanasiou 2013: 133–134). In this case, efforts by the state to restrict self-management in the realms of language and cultural production led to depression for Ghobadi, because he was restricted from working on films, but it also inspired the production of *No One Knows about Persian Cats*. As a result, these two films in particular, in revolving around Ghobadi's conflict with the Iranian state, are closely tied in with the precariousness of the Kurdish population and biopolitical concerns surrounding the production of diverse subjectivities.

To disrupt repressive biopolitics, Ghobadi develops formal strategies that interrupt otherwise linear narratives using music and sound-situations. These aural operations evoke an alternative form of time that reaches beyond the causal connections of narrative and editing. In *Half-Moon*, these breaks in causality are part of psychological sound-situations that afflict the protagonist of the film, heralding his imminent/immanent death – though imminent in terms of chronology, here I also mean immanent as part of the journey itself, suffused throughout the rest of the film through sound design. In depicting the final events of the film before its actual conclusion, these moments allow a glimpse into the future-time of the film and repeatedly interrupt the progression of the narrative. In *No One Knows about Persian Cats*, intermittent music videos detail the daily lives of individuals in Tehran, depicting a multitude of subjects, despite state biopolitics. The music itself, however, also attests to this diversity as it stands alongside, and equal to, traditional Iranian music in Tehran.

While these aural ruptures fragment the linearity of Ghobadi's narratives, they also engage in a form of biopolitical production by fragmenting notions of a particular national subject and revealing a diversity of individuals in Iran. Despite the banning of these films, or perhaps even enhanced by the ban, Ghobadi also prompts biopolitical production for viewers of these films as they encourage the formation of extra-national communities inside Iran. Ghobadi's release of *No One Knows about Persian Cats* online for free to the citizens of Iran suggests his political motivation. As two of his more pessimistic films, however, *Half-Moon* and *No One Knows about Persian Cats* also both end with deaths, juxtaposing his argument for biopolitical production with something intolerable about contemporary Iranian society. In light of the focus of these films on subjectivity, I argue that what these films find intolerable is the attempt of the state to wield a regulatory biopower in the formation of proper Islamic-Iranian subjects. These films, in turn, suggest the inability of the state to control the desires of populations through the wielding of biopower and censorship in contemporary Iran.

The 1979 Revolution, Censorship, and Cinema

> Because the direct gaze of desire was
> prohibited after the 1979 revolution, the averted,
> unfocused look has been predominant in film ever since.
> *Hamid Naficy* (1994)

In 1979, Ayatollah Khomeini overthrew the Pahlavi monarchy that had held power in Iran for 54 years, presenting an almost entirely antithetical political platform. Whereas the Shah promoted westernization and rapid modernization, Khomeini preached religious foundations for society. As a result of deteriorating socio-economic conditions in Iran, the Ayatollah overthrew the Shah with popular support. Once in power, the Ayatollah established an Islamic doctrine for the country and began to construct a dominant ideology aligned with Islam. The effects of this political shift on Iranian cinema appeared immediately, beginning with actions such as the institution of Sharia – for example, laws that govern the public appearance of women. However, the enforcement of Sharia on Iranian films was only a small part of how this new ideological force changed cinema in Iran. The attempt to create a norm for the Iranian population notwithstanding, this majoritarian discourse contains minoritarian elements that expose its suppressed stories.

Describing the most immediate effects of the 1979 Revolution on the production of film in Iran, Hamid Dabashi argues: "The development of Iranian cinema came to a standstill immediately after the revolution. The organs of the Islamic Republic actively used the medium for their own propaganda purposes. The state poured millions of dollars into films that supported and consolidated the revolution" (Dabashi 2001: 32). In addition to financial support, Khomeini set the stage for the role of cinema after the revolution with a series of proclamations about the medium of film itself. Although film had already held a tenuous position amongst religious groups in Iran before the revolution, Khomeini made these beliefs a public position. Ayatollah Khomeini proclaimed that "cinema and other manifestations of westernization (theatre, dancing and mixed-sex swimming) 'rape the youth of our country and stifle in them the spirit of virtue and bravery'" (Naficy 2001: 27). Cinema presents a danger for Khomeini, because of its power to transport the western world directly into Iran where it would threaten Islamic values. More significantly, Naficy argues that Khomeini was a "proponent of the hypodermic theory of ideology," which suggests that ideology has direct influence on people through cultural products such as foreign cinema (Naficy 2001: 28). Informed by this hypodermic theory of ideology, Islamic law banned Western products, but it is important to note that Khomeini did not oppose cinema technology itself: "The cinema is a modern invention that ought to be used for the sake of educating the people, but as you know, it was used instead to corrupt our youth. It is the misuse of cinema that we are opposed to" (Naficy 2001: 29). Instead of importing foreign entertainment, Khomeini advocated the spread of Islam through film technology to solidify a particular Islamic subject. In order to align film technology with Islamic principles, the Ministry of Culture and Islamic Guidance was established and charged with regulating film production, importation, and exhibition in Iran.

To enforce these regulations, the Ministry of Culture and Islamic Guidance required directors interested in producing a film inside of Iran to first submit a script and receive an exhibition permit for their film. The Ministry verifies that films work in accordance with Islamic law by ensuring it adheres to a set of regulations. For example, authorities will forbid an exhibition permit include films that:

> weaken the principle of monotheism and other Islamic principles or insult them
> in any manner;
> insult, directly or indirectly, the Prophets, Imams, the guardianship of the
> Supreme Jurisprudent (*velayat faqih*), the ruling Council or the
> jurisprudents (*mojtaheds*);
> blaspheme against the values and personalities held sacred by Islam and other
> religions mentioned in the Constitution (Naficy 2001: 37)[1]

Naficy contends that while "Clearly these regulations codify . . . Islamic values," the "regulations themselves contain many ambiguities" (Naficy 2001: 37). Zeydabadi-Nejad agrees, suggesting that filmmakers are not rejected out of hand by the Ministry of Culture and Islamic Guidance, but rather they must negotiate with Ministry authorities in order to earn exhibition for their films (Zeydabadi-Nejad 2010). While the filmmaker attempting to obtain an exhibition permit may know the regulations quite well, how to navigate them has remained a challenge. Additionally, the meaning a member of the Ministry of Culture and Islamic Guidance takes from a particular scene may be far different from what the director intended, making it a doubly difficult task. As a result, particular styles of filmmaking have emerged that work around the regulations in order to make it easier to attain exhibition permits. An example of particular strategies that emerged in Iranian film after the revolution include what Naficy has called a "unique system of looking" (Naficy 1994: 143).

Naficy traces the reason for this back to the constitution of Islamic law, which in turn affects the production of subjectivity (Naficy 1994: 136). Naficy argues that for Iranians, the individual is split between an outer, malleable self and an inner, pure self. This binary "necessitates a boundary zone— however amorphous and porous—which can be thought of as a veil or a screen" enabling "strategies [which] are used in Iran to hide what is most pure and valued—the inner self. Veiling thus is operative within the self and is pervasive within the culture" (Naficy 1994: 136). Contrary to Laura Mulvey's original argument in "Visual Pleasure in Narrative Cinema," the gaze does not arrest and objectify women in this context (Mulvey 1975). Not only does the veil literally block the gaze directed at Iranian women, Iranian women also,

> have a great deal of latitude in how they present themselves to the gaze of the male
> onlookers, involving body language, eye contact, types of veil worn, clothing worn
> underneath the veil, and the manner in which the veil itself is fanned open or closed
> at strategic moments to lure or to mask, to reveal or to conceal the face, the body, or
> the clothing underneath. (Naficy 1994: 137)

And while this describes Iranian culture outside of cinema as well, this particular system of looking has also replaced dominant forms of the cinematic gaze that previously may have been imported from foreign (Hollywood) films.

Although this unique system of looking that has supplanted the cinematic language of Hollywood seems to be an ideal strategy to present a rupture in a majoritarian cinematic practice, I want to be careful about what constitutes a majoritarian discourse when working in a global context. If we were to look at all of cinema, perhaps this unique system of looking does represent a rupture, but to argue this relies on a relation to Hollywood that posits Hollywood as the center of the cinematic universe.

Such an approach glosses over the particularities of the Iranian context, and I argue instead that this unique system of looking actually exists as an aspect of the majoritarian mode of Iranian cinema, because it emerges from the Islamic doctrine that has shaped current cinema in Iran through the Islamic Republic's rules and regulations. In other words, this aesthetic operates in relation to the dominant ideology of post-revolution Iran. As such, Naficy's point that the regulations codify Islamic values takes on more significance than just the formal style presented in the film; it also concerns the construction of a more total Islamic-Iranian subject with this system of looking as one component amongst others, such as the use of didactic narratives, reluctance to fund or accept films from rural filmmakers (a label often applied to Kurds), and the censorship of perceived Western and non-Islamic values. As Negar Mottahedeh argues of the tactile gaze of Iranian cinema, "the act of looking transforms the viewer's identity . . . the act of looking collapses the distance between the subject who sees and the subject looked at" (Mottahedeh 2008: 9). If, in the Iranian context, film has the power to transform individuals and individual subjectivities, then the question here is how Ghobadi's films articulate spaces outside of the standard Islamic-Iranian subject position favored by film regulations in Iran.

Iranian cinema provides a useful context for examining the role of majoritarian discourses and the ways in which contemporary political cinema fragments the normalizing function of such a discourse. Such an examination reveals that cinematic ideologies do not necessarily stem from a global center despite Hollywood's global pervasiveness historically, as Miriam Hansen illustrated with regard to her concept of vernacular modernism.[2] In the context of Iran, this ideological coding is both religious, like the construction of an Islamic-Algerian subject described in the previous chapters, and part of the operation of the Iranian state, as will be the case in the PRC discussed in Chapter Four. I now turn to the Bahman

Ghobadi, whose films similarly reveal several sources of political critique. These sources of critique are the Kurdish population in his so-called rural films and the musical communities of Tehran. Ghobadi's cinematic politics thus stem from the way his films construct emergent communities through landscape, music, and a play with time that merges cinematic form and subjectivity.

Interrupted Journeys: Bahman Ghobadi's Musical Travels

> I always insist that I am a normal, cultural
> Kurd fighting for the rights of the oppressed Kurdish children and
> their parents . . . The ones that are always seen in extreme longshots.
> *Bahman Ghobadi*

The start of Ghobadi's career is popularly considered to be his work on Abbas Kiarostami's *The Wind Will Carry Us* (1999). Although Ghobadi had started his filmmaking before – even referring to his early experiences with a camera as a child in an interview with Peter Scarlet (Scarlet 2007) – Kiarostami's celebrity as the great Iranian director seems to have a gravitational pull when discussing Iranian cinema. Regardless, Kiarostami and Ghobadi's friendship is a poignant way to define Ghobadi as a director because of their public disagreement in 2009. After Kiarostami admonished Ghobadi for criticizing the Iranian state, Ghobadi released an open letter to the press, attacking Kiarostami for not being political enough. Yet, despite Ghobadi's extra-filmic activity, his films are not overtly political. Rather than, for example, constructing the Kurds as an oppositional class, he sets seemingly personal stories within Kurdish territories. As a Kurdish-Iranian filmmaker, Ghobadi's films operate according to what Naficy refers to as the "politics of the hyphen" (Naficy 2001: 15). His films are Kurdish in their geopolitical boundaries, the topics and stories depicted, and the individuals who create them, but are Iranian in their funding, production, and the regulations to which they must adhere. Through this hyphen, Ghobadi develops the concept of an underlying network in his earlier films about Kurds, illustrated here via analysis of *Half-Moon*, and extends it to the political struggles of the Iranian people more broadly in relation to the regulation of subjectivity in *No One Knows about Persian Cats*. A spiraling locomotion of characters in Ghobadi's films defines this political aesthetic and reveals networks of connected individuals, but it also leads to something intolerable (here, death), which interrupts any articulation of a people independent from the Iranian state.

Speaking of media outlets such as the British Broadcasting Corporation (BBC) and the Cable News Network (CNN), and world leaders such as George Bush and Tony Blair, Ghobadi defines his cinema as being about the people that go unnoticed rather than events covered by the media and addressed by leaders of nations. Ghobadi takes part in the well-established tradition of using non-professional actors in his films to create a realism and focus on the everyday lives of ordinary people, but he also takes this particular brand of aesthetic realism further: "I believe the scripts of my films are not totally mine. Fifty percent is mine and fifty percent comes from the actors" (Ghobadi 2002). He not only casts non-professional actors, but allows them to act as agents in the telling of their own stories – defying subsumption by the script. While this is certainly an aesthetic choice, Ghobadi also shows that it is part of a larger political strategy by claiming that "Kurdistan has not been realized yet" (Ghobadi 2002). Pragmatically speaking, this is not only true of their status as a nationless people, but also indicates an emergent population – a people to come. While the Kurds have concrete traditions and culture, they have not established themselves as a political entity, nor have they branded their cultural products the way Iran has done with its own cinema. Ghobadi sees an emerging trend, however, highlighting the recent successes of Kurdish-Iranian short films in regional film festivals. Indeed, this statement proved to be prophetic as a number of Kurdish film festivals emerged in major cities around the world between 2004 and 2007, including London, Montreal, Hamburg, Paris, and Melbourne.

Unsurprisingly, the Iran-Iraq war and political tensions between Iran and Iraq are common issues in Ghobadi's films, and all of his feature films prior to *No One Knows About Persian Cats* (2009) take place along the Iran-Iraq border: *A Time for Drunken Horses* (2000), *Marooned in Iraq* (2002), *Turtles Can Fly* (2004), and *Half-Moon*. As a result, Ghobadi's films deal with a particular political geography reflected in a real landscape along national borders. Often, these films deal with displacement and movement resulting from the conflict between Iran and Iraq – landmines and smuggling in *A Time for Drunken Horses*, restricted travel across borders in *Marooned in Iraq*, orphaned and war-injured children in *Turtles Can Fly*, and more border-crossing issues in *Half-Moon*. *Turtles Can Fly* most explicitly addresses the Iran-Iraq conflict, but in all of Ghobadi's films the war exists as a backdrop that the characters traverse without much attention being drawn to its purpose or origin (border disputes between Iran and Iraq and religious unrest).

Instead, for the Kurds, smuggling and sneaking across borders is an everyday difficulty as they travel Kurdistan, a land cut through with borders enforced by nations that simultaneously claim and disavow the Kurdish populations. As a result, Kurds in Ghobadi's films often lead a nomadic lifestyle while crossing the smooth space of Kurdistan, whether it be to go to work, come to the aid of a family member, or hold a concert in a Kurdish cultural center on the other side of the Iran-Iraq border. I am not saying that Ghobadi attempts to downplay the effects of these disputes on the Kurdish people, but rather that he shows how integral they are to modern Kurdish life with a blunt realism. For Ghobadi, "The two defining features of Kurdish life are suffering and hardship," but Kurds have adapted to their harsh realities (Ghobadi 2002).

These border crossings lend the films a particular aesthetic centered on movement and traversing endless roads, interrupted only by borders or Kurdish settlements, in a stylized locomotion that connects Kurdish peoples in the form of "rhizomatic group affiliations" (Naficy 2001: 6–7). Rather than focusing on cultural centers, like the Kurdish capital city Sanandaj, Ghobadi films the landscapes, outposts, and crossroads of Kurdistan. While his later film, *No One Knows about Persian Cats*, is set in Tehran for the entirety of the film, it too focuses on movement among various locations in the city, from the outskirts, to skyscrapers under development, to the neighborhoods and the heart of the city itself. In each case, this movement shows a population intimately connected in some way: the Kurds through shared culture and the citizens of Tehran through a shared desire for musical expression.

In addition to the actual movement of the Kurds in Ghobadi's films, musical celebrity also points toward the Kurdish people's rhizomatic group affiliations. In Ghobadi's films, the Kurdish communities seem to be intimately connected, rather than shut off from one another despite physical distance and borders erected by the surrounding nations. This is often exemplified through shared cultural knowledge and musical celebrities – Mirza in *Marooned in Iraq* and Mamo in *Half-Moon* – whose reach crosses these borders. Each film shares scenes where the protagonists enter tea-houses in remote locations and are greeted either by name, or by patrons of the tea-house spreading the news: "look, it is Mirza!" or "this is Mamo, put on his tape!" These displays of recognition are significant considering the films were created and take place prior to the establishment of specifically Kurdish satellite television stations in 2007 (Semati 2008: 106). Additionally, in each case, the arrival of the musical star does not evoke sensational outbursts from the tea-house patrons, but a general approval from the crowd and a sense that Mirza or Mamo's arrival was inevitable. For the nomadic Kurds of these films, the musical stars are not beyond the Kurdish people as would be the super-celebrities of Hollywood, but are an immanent part of their culture connecting Iranian-Kurds and Iraqi-Kurds to Kurdistan through a biopolitical network.

While the characters' journeys in Ghobadi's films construct the notion of a Kurdistan that crosses borders, it is important to note that their journeys never come to a clear conclusion. At some point, they are interrupted either before reaching their goal – as in *Half-Moon* and *No One Knows about Persian Cats* – or when a goal is reached, but it is not the intended goal – as in *Marooned in Iraq*. In a study on cinematic journeys, Dimitris Eleftheriotis defines "two broad interconnected and often combined types of mobile vision that offer evocative comparisons with specific instances of cinematic movement . . . A steady, smooth and continuous movement of more-or-less linear direction [and] a circular type of movement around specific objects of interest" (Eleftheriotis 2010: 31). Further defining these two types of movements, Eleftheriotis explains, "In the first case a sense of destination, purpose and direction underpins the movement. In the second type a sense of completion informs the comprehensive observation of an object or event" (Eleftheriotis 2010: 32). These broad characterizations of cinematic movement are useful descriptors for Ghobadi's films as cinematic journeys, especially Eleftheriotis's argument that these movements are often combined.

Ghobadi's films – particularly *Half-Moon* and *No One Knows about Persian Cats* – are set up with the pretense that they will be linear journeys with purpose and direction, but as the films progress, the audience realizes that they are not about the destination, but the journey itself. Ghobadi himself has said that the plot is "just an excuse to take the audience around and show them different corners of Kurdistan" (Ghobadi 2002). In other words, what seems like purposeful direction ends up being the spiraling observation of Kurds and Kurdistan. Ghobadi uniquely plays with this movement in his films, however: though specifics are different in each film, the goals of individual characters is always thwarted. I will address two of these examples in this chapter: Mamo never arrives at his concert in *Half-Moon*, and Negar and Ashkan never escape to London to play their music in *No One Knows about Persian Cats*. The interruption of the characters' journeys in these films points at something Ghobadi finds intolerable in contemporary Iranian society: that Kurdistan may be explored and postulated, but never officially proclaimed as autonomous – or following this logic in *No One Knows About Persian Cats*, that other musical genres can be explored, but these genres may not be integrated into one's identity and freely expressed.

The seemingly meandering path of the protagonists in *Half-Moon* and *No One Knows About Persian Cats*, however, is not the same as the bourgeois protagonist's Sunday drive through an industrial site in Kiarostami's *Taste of Cherry* (1997). On the other hand, neither do they promote a distinct Kurdish film aesthetic, another discourse that might claim representation for all Kurds or present another myth about the Kurdish people. Instead, Ghobadi elaborates a cinematic experience on multiple levels that describes the daily conditions of Iranian-Kurds and their relationship with Kurdistan. First, he establishes a landscape that is not divided into strictly delineated areas, but a smooth yet textured space where boundaries are felt though still crossable. Second, he invokes Kurdish movement and musical celebrity that constructs rhizomatic and biopolitical networks across the spaces of his films. Finally, he presents a particular form of cinematic time based on the wandering of his characters that is marked by aural ruptures. Addressing these three facets of Ghobadi's films, I examine two of his later works, *Half-Moon* and *No One Knows about Persian Cats*. These two films focus on different people in Iranian society that the current regime restricts through laws that codify the subjectivities that are allowed in post-revolution Iran. *Half-Moon* shows the importance of Kurdistan despite its status as a non-nation, and locates a cross-border network of Kurdish subjects despite the contentious relationship the surrounding nations have with Kurdistan. *No One Knows About Persian Cats* looks to musicians in Tehran to show the importance of individual subjectivity in contemporary Iranian society as illustrated through the desire to play, and shape one's identity around, global music traditions. By revealing the multitude of different subjects within Iran, Ghobadi's films fragment concepts of a singular, hegemonic Iranian subject.

Kurdish Meta-narrative and Sound Situations in *Half-Moon*

> To me, border is a nonsensical, grim, and
> disgusting word . . . it's something imposed on us.
> It is thanks to these borders that the four Kurdish
> regions have always lived in deprivation.
> *Bahman Ghobadi*

Half-Moon, Ghobadi's second film about musicians on a journey, follows Mamo as he gathers his sons for a concert in Iraqi-Kurdistan. Along the way, Mamo also picks up a female singer named Hesho, an act that defies Iran's ban on female singers. The entourage faces many diversions and setbacks along the way, but they eventually make contact with Niwemang (*Half-Moon*), who, like some sort of metaphysical being, appears on the top of their moving tour bus to lead them to their concert. Two formal features of this film explicate the Kurdish experience while communicating the minor position of the Kurds within Iran: first, the exploratory nature of movement across the Kurdish countryside, compounded by Mamo's musical celebrity, which elaborates a (bio)network composed of Kurdish subjects; second, the sound situations that punctuate and interrupt the narrative, which indicate a non-linear form of time.

Each of these points constitutes significant political acts. The movement of Mamo – uncle in Kurdish – and his sons as they cross borders to hold a Kurdish concert, combined with Mamo's musical celebrity, reveals a rhizomatic network linking the Kurdish countryside spanning Iranian- and Iraqi-Kurdistan, as he visits various tea-houses, villages, and checkpoints. This biopolitical network indicates a Kurdish identity within Iran that is molecular in nature, as recourse to Kurdish nationalism in the past has led to severe reprisal from Iran and the surrounding states. The movement of Mamo and his sons amongst the Kurdish countryside resists the regulatory biopower implicated in Iranian law and censorship, a reading promoted by ruptures in the linear and causal narrative of the film. These ruptures take the form of sound situations, where the aural register of the film becomes intensified and the narrative slips from present to future, suggesting Mamo's imminent death. Embodied within Mamo, these sound situations explain the impossibility of a Kurdish revolution, the inability to realize independence, but also the vitality and persistence of Kurdish peoples more broadly.

The film begins with bus driver and trip enabler Kako quoting Kierkegaard at a cock fight, "I am not afraid of death because when I am here he is not . . . And when he is here I am not. No gain or loss is more important than death," and his audience echoes: "No gain or loss is more

Figure 3.1 *Half-Moon* (2006).

important than death." The use of Kierkegaard anticipates the poetic trajectory of the film as a narrative about Mamo's journey toward his own
death, a narrative reinforced by the first shot of Mamo, which shows him
lying still in an open grave staring upwards blankly, and by a scene near
the end of the film when Mamo climbs into a coffin that rests mysteriously
against a featureless, snow-covered hill along the Iran-Iraq border, where
one of his sons and the mystical Niwemang find that he has passed away.
The film constantly suggests throughout the narrative that Mamo understands he is dying, but knows he must move towards death rather than flee.
His determination is significant, and because he is the only clear bearer
of Kurdish national identity within the film, his death takes on symbolic
value. In the final scene of the film, as we hear Mamo's sons begin to play
at the concert they have been traveling toward all along, Mamo's body is
shown against the dark background of the coffin, opening his eyes, as if
moved by the music. One reading would be that it is through music that
Kurdish culture can thrive, but *Half-Moon* also shows a different, more
subtle logic at work, which articulates a non-oppositional and minor position that the Kurds might inhabit in relation to the majoritarian discourses
that exclude Kurdish identities.

I have used the term network above, because *Half-Moon*, despite its
rural setting, treats the Kurdish people as a biopolitical information system where Kurds in villages remote from one another share news, friend-
ships, and knowledge of particularly Kurdish phenomena like Mamo's
musical celebrity. It is worth noting, however, that both internet and
television satellite technology play a role in Ghobadi's films, suggesting a natural uptake of technologies endemic to the population. I call
the network biopolitical, however, because Kurds present an embodied
politics – that is, regardless of individual political leanings, the various
nation-states to which Kurdistan belongs all treat the Kurds as a significant political force, even through disavowal such as the neglect of public
infrastructure in Kurdish regions (Natali 2005: 39; Chaliand 1993: 244).
As a result of their biopolitical status (being considered political for who
they are and how they live, or because of their existential difference), there
can be no separation of public and private spheres as far as the Iranian
state is concerned, because the private sphere breeds the grounds for a
secessionist movement that must eventually be dealt with by the state. As
Fardin Alikhah points out, even satellite television stations that promote
Kurdish ethnic identity "might be exploited as [producing] ethnic divisions by political forces" (Alikhah 2008: 106). Even more significantly, a
particular fear of the Iranian state is that human rights defenders such as
the United Nations will take more interest in the Kurds, requiring fair

economic treatment of Kurdish populations and areas. As a result of that concern, "rights activists already under extreme pressure from the state seek to distance themselves from the Kurds, an issue that they know will inflame the authorities" (Yildiz and Taysi 2007: 33). Given the state pressure leveraged against Kurds, the political networks in Ghobadi's films become revelatory in relation to how they allow Kurds to respond to the effects of globalization, or in the case of *Half-Moon* international military conflict, on their own terms.

In *Half-Moon*, Mamo's musical celebrity drives the narrative as he organizes his sons' travel to Iraqi-Kurdistan in order to hold a freedom concert after the fall of Saddam Hussein. Evidence of Mamo's celebrity is reified by interactions with various Kurds throughout Kurdistan. The first instance is the driver Kako's insistence on borrowing a bus in the beginning of the film, bargaining for it by telling the owner that he'll be famous when the world knows it was his bus that transported Mamo from Iran to Iraq – as Kako says, "all the networks will be there, BBC, CNN!" From the beginning, Mamo's celebrity crosses borders – from Iran to Iraq (Syria and Turkey are implicated here as well), to the United Kingdom and the United States. Despite the Iranian state's attempt to quell Kurdish nationalism, this scene suggests that there is a global audience for displays of Kurdish music and culture. At the same time, however, Kako is presented as an idealistic and rather reckless character. For example, he learns towards the end of the film that the video recorder that he's been using during the trip to create a documentary about their travels has no tape. As a result, the extent to which Kako's ideas about the popularity of the concert are true is questionable. The tapeless recorder suggests the impossibility of expression for this Kurdish entourage, despite the fact that the audience is viewing a film about the very trip Kako cannot film. This is a point I will return to later, with the film's ending, which has its own way of positing the inability to present a strong Kurdish cultural presence or nationalism.

Despite the seeming inability to communicate this cultural moment through technology, there are three distinct scenes in the film where various groups of Kurds recognize Mamo as a Kurdish musical celebrity which indicate the success of networks sharing Kurdish culture. These scenes reveal the subjective and locational diversity of the Kurds who recognize Mamo's celebrity. Mamo's first scene of recognition is at the outdoor schoolhouse his daughter has constructed for refugee children. Towards the end of this scene, a group of children run up to Mamo for autographs. Though this scene appears incidental, it is one of the most significant scenes that announces Mamo's celebrity – despite the fact that

Mamo is an older, dying musician, the scene demonstrates his popularity with Kurdistan's youth, the demographic that will embody the next wave of Kurdish culture. Additionally, his music is traditional Kurdish music, rather than foreign inspired music that youth – as shown in Ghobadi's next feature, *No One Knows about Persian Cats* – might otherwise prefer.

The second scene in which Mamo is recognized for his celebrity is when he and his group arrive at the Iran-Iraq border after they are stopped by border guards. One of these guards turns out to be Kurdish, and proclaims his own Kurdishness: "Mamo . . . it is okay, I am Kurdish too . . . leave everything to me." In proclaiming his Kurdishness, the border guard exposes his minor position as a Kurdish agent of the Iranian state. The Iranian captain, after stopping their group the second time, refuses them passage across the Iran-Iraq border and takes Hesho, the female musician they had been illegally traveling with. Not only does the Kurdish border guard subvert his status as a border guard by finding a way for their group to secretly cross the border, he also manages to return Hesho to Mamo's group. The Kurdish border guard acts as a surreptitious counter-agent to the Iranian state, reversing its official decision to refuse passage to the freedom concert and detain the female singer. Whereas music may seem harmless, this scene reveals its political status in relation to policies of the Iranian state.

Finally, Mamo is recognized by the patrons of a tea-house in rural Iraqi-Kurdistan directly after Hesho leaves the group. This demographic often serves as the stereotype of the rural Kurd, but in this instance, it is also an example of the Kurdish population that lives without infrastructural support from the state – a legacy inherited from pre-revolutionary times, which is another sign of the relationship between the potential political force of Kurdish populations to nation-states (Yildiz and Taysi 2007: 35–36). Although seemingly apolitical compared to the previous two examples, the Kurds in this scene most clearly exemplify what I've referred to above as a biopolitical network. As Mamo and his sons enter, the owner of the establishment immediately greets him and calls for "a round of applause for Mamo." Though these Kurds have only an old tape recorder to play Mamo's tapes on, they are well aware of his celebrity. Though presumably lacking access to satellite television stations, through word of mouth and travel, Mamo's celebrity has reached even Kurds on the periphery living in mountainous regions on the Iran-Iraq border.[3] The vastness of Mamo's celebrity is indicative of the biopolitical status of Kurds as a networked community.

Mamo's musical presence operates differently from Western musical celebrity; whereas Western celebrity transcends its place in reality, Mamo in *Half-Moon* is immanently involved with the tea-houses and among his fans. Mamo's celebrity is embodied within the experience of the Kurds themselves. While perhaps not much of a philosophical commentary on Western musical celebrity, there is a clear difference between the internalization of Mamo's status in Kurdish culture, and the exteriorization of celebrity in Western cultures through media machines. The only media that communicate Mamo's music in the film are the scratchy cassette player in the tea-house and the sheets of music that are taken from Mamo's jacket at the end of the film. Both media are suggestive of something passed along among friends, rather than disseminated through mass media outlets such as satellite television (TV) stations. As mentioned previously, Kako's camera, having never had any film to begin with, also suggests an inability to take such representation outside of Kurdistan, despite the paradox that Ghobadi's film has found global success through the festival circuit.

The fact that a range of demographics recognize Mamo's celebrity is a poignant political point, because it indicates the collapse of the public and private sphere on a wide scale in the Kurdish community. In other words, the characters' consumption of Mamo's celebrity in *Half-Moon* marks them as resolutely Kurdish, and thus in a contentious position with the identity-building assemblage of the Iranian state. And despite Ghobadi's claims of being an apolitical filmmaker, the Iranian state is hyper-aware of displays of Kurdish identity, as argued previously by Alikhah, Yildiz, and Taysi. By displaying this interiorization of Kurdish culture through Mamo's celebrity, Ghobadi seems acutely aware of this situation for Iranian-Kurds – a concept he addresses directly when Mamo and his sons are refused entry into Iraq in order to hold a concert, which the captain pejoratively refers to as a "party." The idea that the Kurds in the film are internalizing Mamo's celebrity in particular must be reconciled with the overall trajectory of the film and its final conclusion: that Mamo is heading towards his death, and finally passes away on a featureless snowy hillside in Kurdistan. While one might take this to be the death of an oppositional Kurdish cultural identity, this internalization and collapse of public and private spheres suggests a new politics under a different heading. Namely, a politics embodied in a Kurdish, molecular identity shown most accurately in Mamo's sons, who are the bearers of the Kurdish music but reticent about marching into Iraq to hold a freedom rally. The sons as a group, often disagreeing but still brothers, present a fragmented version of Mamo's nationalism. This is further compounded by the fact that the spectator never bears witness to the concert in Iraq, which I will return to in discussing the ending of *Half-Moon*.

Earlier, I referred to the formal operation of sound situations in *Half-Moon*, which operate meta-cinematically. These situations are notable for their disconnection from the sensory-motor linkages in the rest of the film and, as a result, introduce a non-linear form of time in the film. Contrasting neo-realism and traditional realism, Deleuze argued that a "sound situation becomes established in what we might call 'any-space-whatever,' whether disconnected, or emptied" (Deleuze 1989: 5). Like Amy Herzog's concept of the musical moment, these scenes in the film deterritorialize the superficial narrative – that Mamo and his sons are traveling to Iraq to hold a freedom concert – poetically expanding the diverse ways the film makes meaning. Herzog defines musical moments "not as texts to be 'decoded' but as dynamic events, distinct temporal occurrences that are always open to the outside" (Herzog 2009: 16). And while Herzog acknowledges that musical moments rely on repetition, she also suggests that these "dreams of difference" are inherent in the event or musical moment.

Herzog makes a clear distinction between the repetition of cliché and "the most basic operations of perception and cognition . . . Habit here is not the mere repetition of a code but the introduction of difference, of something new, within the mind that is impacted by the perception and anticipation of a pattern" (Herzog 2009: 17). The sound situation in *Half-Moon* is in no danger of becoming cliché, because it repeats throughout the film with differences each time. As a result, the play between repetition and difference is key to understanding its purpose in the film. At face value, the repetition of these sound situations paint a psychological portrait for the viewer. On the other hand, they push the narrative towards its poetic and mystical conclusion, opening the film to the outside allowing a meta-cinematic understanding of it.

The first sound situation accompanies Mamo's introduction immediately after we see him lying in an open grave. From the start, the sound situations are directly connected to the anticipation of Mamo's death in the film by presenting a form of future-time. In revealing what appear to be Mamo's hallucinatory thoughts, however, these sound situations expand on their general progression throughout the film. Each time one occurs, Mamo enters a state of acute sound-perception – as opposed to a musical number as we might find in Herzog's musical moment. For the duration of these sound situations, it is as if Mamo, and the viewer with him, hear minute sounds amplified to such a degree that one experiences the aural texture of the surrounding materials: the crunch of dirt or snow under a boot, the roll of a die, the clinking of beads, or the hallow thumps of an empty coffin. This last item accompanies each sound situation in the form of a vision, appearing unexpectedly while Mamo is in the throes of acute sound-perception. In these scenes, the film cuts between close-ups on

Mamo's distracted face, his surroundings marked by the hollow detachment of environmental sounds, and a coffin being dragged by a woman toward the edge of a mostly static frame. Both the hollow detachment from the sounds of Mamo's immediate environment, and the seeming introduction of another time-space in the image of the woman dragging the coffin create the trance-like feeling of these scenes.

While these scenes do not operate as they might in a musical or music video, they do share the moment of being open to the outside through their rejection of immediate narrative causality. Mamo experiences these acute sound-situations four times throughout the film: when he is introduced; while visiting a wise man after one of his sons urges him to delay the trip; at the tea-house after Hesho leaves the group; and finally, at the time of his death, when he finds the coffin from his dreams before him. Each scene shares the image of a coffin being dragged and sounds associated with its dragging – the hollow thump of the coffin and the clinking of the beads worn by the person dragging it – forming a framing narrative that exists outside of the narrative arc provided by Kako's planned journey. Providing a hint to the nature of this framing narrative, when the woman who is gradually revealed through Mamo's visions shows up in narrative reality, he gives no indication of recognizing her. As a result, these dreams seem to be non-diegetic, at least within Mamo's film-world. Each vision, in breaking with narrative causality, points towards an outside – here in the case of the characters' experience – but they also point to another outside, a meta-cinematic reading of the film that comments specifically on the place of Kurdish identity within the film.

These sound situations reveal that *Half-Moon* is not just about Mamo's death, or even the death of Kurdish nationalism, but rather that the difficulty of representing Kurdish nationalism or culture on film in Iran is intolerable. The poetic, non-causal sound situations in *Half-Moon* also reveal the outside to be the real world conditions and difficulties in the production of cultural artifacts, particularly the production of films. This meta-cinematic narrative shadows both the superficial and poetic narrative of the film in following Mamo's gradual progress toward both the concert in Iraqi-Kurdistan and his own death, realized through his visions, deteriorating health, and moments where he directly acknowledges this inevitability. Near the end of the film, Mamo becomes overwhelmed by the intolerable nature of his trip and lies down in a grave, asking his sons to throw dirt on him. The various setbacks in the film, difficulty crossing borders, the confiscation of musical instruments, and the detaining of the musical group's female singer, aggregate to illustrate what is intolerable to Mamo in his current environment. Namely, the restrictions posed by the state that prevent any proclamation or expression of Kurdish identity. Just as Boualem sees leaving Bab el-Oued as the only way out of an intolerable situation in *Bab El-Oued City*, Mamo sees death as his only escape.

Turning to a potential reading in light of Mamo's role as the only real bearer of Kurdish nationalism, the message of the film seems clear at face value: Kurdish nationalism is dying out. I believe that this is a misreading, however, and that Ghobadi argues not that Kurdish nationalism is dying, but that it must take another path in the current ideological climate. In 2004, the time of *Half-Moon*'s release, President Mohammad Khatami was in power and known for granting more freedom to artists within Iran (see Zeydabadi-Nejad 2010; Holtmeier 2012). Regardless, *Half-Moon* was refused an exhibition permit. Ghobadi, known for making films about Kurds, was warned by state officials not to make another Kurdish language film, because it might encourage separatism (see Alikhah 2008 for more on this anxiety). Because Iranian censors check films at three points – the script, during filming, and the finished product – it was possible for Ghobadi to make his film, but for the final product to be refused exhibition within Iran (assuming the script was written in Farsi, or the sensors at earlier points of evaluation cared less about the language). As a result, *Half-Moon* marks a point where Ghobadi turns away from the official Iranian film industry. Later, I will show how Ghobadi's attitude changed post-Khatami, but at the time *Half-Moon* was being filmed, arguing for a minor mode of Kurdish artistic production was a feasible alternative to overt Kurdish nationalism.

This argument is most clearly evidenced in *Half-Moon*'s conclusion, when Niwemang and one of Mamo's sons find his lifeless body. Mamo has crawled into the mysterious coffin of his dreams and his corporeal body has passed away, finally granting him reprieve from the restrictions he found intolerable. Niwemang and Mamo's son find another life within the coffin, however, as they reach inside Mamo's jacket and discover manuscripts of the Kurdish songs he has been working on for the past 7 years. Throughout the film, Mamo reiterates this time-line and although it is difficult to determine the exact time that *Half-Moon* takes place, it is likely that placing it seven years earlier correlates with use of chemical weapons on the town of Halabja in Iraq, in 1988. These attacks are a key event in the relationship between Kurds and surrounding nations, as they are evidence that Saddam Hussein committed genocide against non-combatant populations, potentially as retribution for earlier Kurdish moves for independence. Since the attacks on Halabja, however, Mamo has been anticipating the liberation of Kurdish peoples by writing music. And while the freedom concert is an outright display of Kurdish liberation, Mamo's strategy was not to arrive at the concert in Iraq to present himself as the bearer of Kurdish nationalism, but to start laying the rhizomatic groundwork through his sons, Hesho, and the music he has recorded and disseminated. He clearly knew he was traveling towards his own death, but the movement of the characters throughout the film and the various responses to Mamo's musical celebrity are evidence of the rhizomatic infrastructure Mamo was establishing, and from which Kurdish identity emerges – not in opposition to surrounding nation states, but as a way of resisting attacks on Kurdish culture and identity that benefit these nation states by keeping the Kurdish populations docile.

The film's ending emphasizes this point, with Mamo's corpse appearing against a black background accompanied by the sounds of a crowded concert, suggesting that the remaining sons were able to hold the musical event. As viewers, we see no images of the concert, however, because the concert itself was not the goal as the film suggests early on, but rather it is that the music being shared among the Kurdish people. The concert as representation of Kurdish identity cannot be shown – it must be substituted with a blank screen – because, as Yildiz and Taysi argue, the Kurds have become more politically sophisticated from centuries of oppression by surrounding powers, taking the form of resilient rhizomatic group affiliations. That is not to say that classical rebellions following the model of *Battle of Algiers* have not taken place in Kurdish regions, but that Ghobadi's films suggest the efficacy of rhizomatic biopolitical networks are the future, rather than such oppositional politics. Ghobadi ends on a positive note for Kurdish peoples, however: even though a classical Kurdish nationalism must die, the last image in *Half-Moon* shows Mamo's corpse opening his eyes, indicating that his efforts were not in vain, for

Figure 3.2 *Half-Moon* (2006).

they have sown the seeds for an emergent people to come – the production of subjectivity prompted by the intolerable – though in this new resistance subjectivity takes a fragmentary form through contemporary cinematic politics.

No One Knows About Persian Cats and Musical Diversity in Tehran

Ghobadi's latest film, *No One Knows about Persian Cats*, is drastically different from his previous films, proving his break from the Iranian film industry. Unlike his other features, this film was made completely under the radar: without funding or a permit from the Ministry of Culture and Islamic Guidance, using forged papers for necessary equipment and personnel, and released streaming on the internet for Iranian audiences. And while Ghobadi has been labeled a rural filmmaker for setting his previous films in remote regions of Iran, *No One Knows about Persian Cats* explores the heart of Tehran and its urban environments. Like *Half-Moon*, however, the film also contains narrative ruptures in the form of sound situations. These sound situations take the form of various music videos interspersed throughout the film, which interrupt the narrative and cause it to stutter. In this instance, I use the term music video because each sequence lasts the length of a single song, not because they follow a particular popular music video aesthetic. Instead, the music videos in *No One Knows about Persian Cats* often blend in with the surrounding narrative, while including cuts that break away from the otherwise causal connections in the film, usually becoming a montage that highlights a particular demographic of the city. And while the music in each of these sequences is diverse, ranging from blues to heavy metal, the scenes themselves are distinctly Iranian, depicting Iranian peoples and land/cityscapes. In doing so, the film suggests that while the musical genres it depicts are banned by the Iranian state, they exist in an immanent relationship with actual Iranian subjects. Like in *Half-Moon*, these ruptures in cinematic time also represent ruptures in the majoritarian discourse, which cannot account for the actual populations of Iran.

No One Knows about Persian Cats follows two young musicians, Negar and Ashkan, as they try to form a band in order to enter a music contest in London, which would allow them to leave Iran and pursue their dreams of becoming indie-rock musicians. This premise allows Ghobadi to set up a narrative structure similar to that of his two previous films, *Marooned in Iraq* and *Half-Moon*, this time with the protagonists traveling throughout Tehran looking for musicians rather than in the corners of Kurdistan, as Ghobadi depicted his earlier films. This narrative structure evokes the genre of road movies with scenes of the pair traveling and seeing various sites in Tehran, as if the film itself is mapping out the diversity of the city. Each time they visit a band to ask them if they would be willing to play a part in their project, we see the band play a song, functioning as a form of music video playing the music over scenes from the film, but also images unrelated to the events of the narrative. Just as the scenes map the diversity of Tehran, these songs map the diversity in Tehran's music scene and the subjects that inhabit it, as the musicians play everything from traditional Persian music to hip-hop. The diversity in locations, musical genres, and, more subtly, social classes, indicate the film's politics: rather than the hegemonic Islamic entity that Iran's laws and regulations suggest, Tehran is a place of possibility, where despite the official facade, people have the ability to define their own direction. Significantly for Ghobadi's public debate with Kiarostami, this includes the choice to leave Iran, but also the choice to stay and fashion a unique subjectivity within Iran.

While *No One Knows about Persian Cats* is not a musical – it is perhaps difficult to define what genre the film belongs to – Richard Dyer's work on the musical reveals a great deal about the film in showing an important distinction between the more traditional genre of the musical and Ghobadi's film. For Dyer, musicals have a particular social function, to present "Alternatives, hopes, wishes . . . the sense that things could be better, that something other than what is can be imagined and maybe realized" (Dyer 2002: 20). If not presenting utopia outright, musical numbers are the vehicle that deliver the realization or possibility of alternatives, hopes, and wishes through the "extraordinary mix of . . . the historicity of narrative and the lyricism of [musical] numbers" (Dyer 2002: 35). *No One Knows about Persian Cats* operates according to a combination of genres that oscillate between historicity, or the everyday problems the musicians in Tehran must deal with, and a lyricism that introduces a new visual and rhythmic structure to the film.

Unlike Dyer's lyricism, however, there is little indication of utopia in the musical sequences of *No One Knows about Persian Cats*. Instead, these sequences present seemingly indexical images of gritty streets, the homeless and poor, and Islamic law being carried out in Tehran. Compounded by lyrics that describe the inequities of Tehran, the musical sequences are often further removed from utopia than the non-musical narrative of the film. In other words, the musical sequences present an even more realistic account of life in Tehran, even if politically selective in terms of what events are shown. In doing so, these images exist in an immanent relationship with the actual subjects of Tehran, rather than operating as the dominant narrative or the even more transcendent morality tales the Ministry of Culture and Islamic Guidance privilege through funding schemes.

For Dyer there is a more basic force at work within this utopian drive though. The utopian operation in narratives present a potential future, what is-not but could-be, rather than the more common notion of utopia as a perfect world.[4] Rather than a transcendental blueprint for society, *No One Knows about Persian Cats* presents a not-yet-being open to change and innovation by focusing on the collective desire of musicians in the film, and the desire to express a core-component of their subjectivity in the form of differing musical genres. Despite its tragic conclusion, *No One Knows about Persian Cats* exemplifies this narrative drive towards the presentation of not-yet-being through the affective sound situations that take the form of music videos. The ability of these sound situations to present this not-yet-being comes from the affective nature of these sequences as a form of pragmatic utopianism by coupling their documentary-style footage with often energetic, moving music. Rather than dreaming of another world, they are firmly grounded in the historical world of Tehran, Iran in the late 2000s even as they move spectators emotionally through their rhythms and lyrics.

Dyer makes the argument that "We are moved by music, yet it has the least obvious reference to 'reality' – the intensity of our response to it can only be accounted for by the way music, abstract, formal though it is, still embodies feeling" (Dyer 2002: 21). In the case of *No One Knows about Persian Cats*, the film presents a violent contradiction between the musical-affect and the images of its song sequences. Many of the music sequences in *No One Knows about Persian Cats* juxtapose images of an impoverished and repressive environment and lyrics that describe that environment with music full of upbeat vitality. Though textual description cannot do justice to the affective nature of the music, each song includes rhythms and melodies that clash with the visually and lyrically represented elements. While the images and lyrics illustrate contemporary problems in Tehran and Iranian society more generally, it is the feeling of the music that suggests change is possible. By mobilizing feeling toward the situations depicted by the images, the music itself introduces the not-yet-being in these sequences by introducing hope on an embodied register for the viewer. As a result, the musical sequences in *No One Knows about Persian Cats* exercise a productive power – rather than presenting a new, utopian reality, the juxtaposition of vitally felt music and images of class-based struggle motivate thought and action towards these issues.

The most poignant sequence that demonstrates this juxtaposition between the vitality of the music and the visual and lyrical depictions

Figure 3.3 *No One Knows About Persian Cats* (2009).

occurs when Nader visits the famous hip-hop artist Hichkas to enlist him for Negar and Ashkan's band. This sequence parallels the real life debate between Ghobadi and Kiarostami regarding a desire to leave Iran as a result of political difficulties. At this point in the film, Negar and Ashkan are trying to move to London, to leave Iran for the foreseeable future. While critical of the ruling regime, Hichkas delivers a monologue on top of a building under construction that clearly defines his desire to remain within Iran:

> We came up here to shoot a video. To check out the streets from above. To show 'em that this is Tehran! Know what I'm saying? We came up here so we can scream, wake up the city, all these buildings. If we sing underground, the sound won't go past the floor. We used to sleep on the streets. We grew up here. Everything is here! Our work . . . Our lives, our romances, our friendships . . . I swear, there's no other place to be, bro. What we do . . . what's it called? Persian rap. Right? That means it's for right here.

Despite Kiarostami's charge that Ghobadi doesn't care about Iran, his inclusion of Hichkas's strong sentiment here suggests otherwise. Furthermore, this sentiment connected with the following musical sequence suggests a strong desire to transform the current state of affairs in Iran, defining a belief in Iran. The musical sequence begins with aerial shots of buildings in Tehran, reflecting Hichkas's desire to "wake up the city." The sequence jumps between various citizens of Tehran going about their daily life and labors: a man carries trash to the dump, another works a jackhammer on a street construction project, and many are shown looking into the camera, as if about to provide testimonial to the topics of the music. But instead of speaking for themselves, the music speaks for these characters as the lyrics point to socio-economic inequity in Tehran.

Halfway through the song, the lyric says: "A hobo stands next to a Benz. He isn't worth enough to rent it. Me, you, him came from a single drop. Look at the gap between us. It's not gravity that makes the world spin. Money makes the world go round. Today, it's money first, God second for everyone, peasant or boss." Calling out the hypocrisies in Iran's religious leadership, Hichkas mobilizes listeners or viewers towards political issues not only by bringing their attention to these inequities, but also through the affective hip hop beat and the emotion of the lyrics. The music inspires the viewer to move, and perhaps, as Hichkas might intend, mobilizes the subjects in Tehran to act on the inequality of their lives.

Another sequence notable for its radical alterity to Persian musical traditions depicts the practice session of a heavy metal band. This session is notable for several reasons, including its depiction of women and the contraction of hepatitis by band members as a result of the conditions they practice their music in. As with Hichkas' monologue, comments from one of the band members about their music precedes the actual sequence. The member of this band relates: "We used to play heavy metal but we changed, we softened up the lyrics. It used to be much heavier, but now we sing in Persian. It's closer to Iranian culture. People can relate to it more easily." This sentiment is carried out visually in the accompanying musical sequence that depicts various people around Tehran, like the Hichkas sequence but with less emphasis on labor. Titled 'No Fences,' this song's visual sequence shows another non-musical subject-group in its focus on people riding motorcycles and dirt bikes. Scenes of people doing wheelies on motorcycles and going off large dirt ramps on dirt bikes accompany lyrics like "Open your eyes – I'm tired. There's no room in your cage for me." The target of this statement appears to be the Iranian government, as the video cuts to candid footage of the Iranian military shot out of a car window, along the with the lyrics "My words were not criminal, though they were hanged." In the most striking shot in the sequence, a dirt biker removes their helmet to reveal that the rider is a woman, while the lyrics scream "The fences around your mind cannot contain me." In a rare event, and one that illustrates the unofficial status of this film, the woman, without veil or headscarf, looks at the camera and laughs, a direct violation of Sharia law. Just as the musicians play their heavy metal, the sequence depicts other individuals or communities sharing a common interest that is resistant to the restrictions of the current regime. This sequence takes a tragic turn, however, as halfway through the song the drummer falls off his seat and must be taken to the hospital. After explaining what happened, the doctor informs them that the drummer has hepatitis and that they all must be tested. The doctor ends his lecture by saying: "You're crazy, rehearsing in a cowshed!" Due to the type of music they play, however, the cowshed is the only place the band could find to practice. Like the female biker without a veil, these subjects are relegated to the periphery, which can be a dangerous place to inhabit.

The opposition between mainstream subjects and those that inhabit the periphery is a basic concern of *No One Knows about Persian Cats*, and reflects its status as a contemporary political film in its critique of majoritarian discourses. Ghobadi conceived this film after a period of depression attributed to his inability to make films. After Ghobadi defied the order of officials not to film *Half-Moon* predominately in the Kurdish language, they restricted his ability to make films, sending him into depression – Bahman Farmanara, another Iranian filmmaker with transnational ties has echoed this feeling of depression after being refused production and exhibition permits (Holtmeier 2012). In an interview with *Filmmaker Magazine*, Ghobadi has said of *No One Knows about Persian Cats*:

> Censorship, repression, and pressure: these are the things that brought me to [this] film. I had been trying to make another film for three years, but the government gave me a very hard time and would not release permission for it. I was kept at home and I couldn't do anything; it was a struggle day after day. Often I thought about committing suicide. (Macaulay 2010)

A friend convinced him to engage his other passions rather than committing suicide or leaving Tehran, so Ghobadi entered the underground music scene in Tehran. While producing his own music under the radar, Ghobadi met the musicians who appear in *No One Knows about Persian Cats* and decided to make a film not only about them, but with them. By allowing characters to play themselves, Ghobadi creates intercessors who take part in telling their own stories. This storytelling is not, however, "a return to myth but a production of collective utterances capable of raising misery to a strange positivity, the invention of a people" (Deleuze 1989: 222). In other words, not a return to the myth of Tehran established by Islamic officials and repressive laws or even the institution of a counter-myth, but a collection of voices that point towards the future of a newly self-invented people.

This collection of voices is present in Tehran as a group of musicians consciously working to increase their agency and improve conditions of life in the officially-enforced religious environment that their homeland has become. *No One Knows about Persian Cats* details the struggles of these individuals while allowing them to formulate their own positions about their work and their homeland. After refusing to leave Iran with Negar and Ashkan, renowned Iranian rapper Hichkas explains: "Trust me, for me there's nothing like outside here 'cause what I speak for is the heart of this place." And while the musicians in the film may want to speak for their own version of Tehran, their method of doing so is not to present some unattainable utopia through their art, but to spread an intensity vitally felt through their music that mobilizes the desire to work towards a better, more co-operative future. *No One Knows about Persian Cats* illustrates this aesthetic strategy by coupling images of the present to be changed with the music that penetrates the repression in order to reveal change as a real possibility – a possibility that can be talked about, but more importantly, a possibility that can be felt. These musicians, including Ghobadi himself, cannot face the prospect of not making music, being forced to make the music of the dominant discourse, or even of being forced to make their music differently. This impossibility results in the fragmentation of a so-called national subject into the many subjects with their respective musical tastes and desires for the future that describes Tehran in reality.

While *No One Knows about Persian Cats* follows what I argue to be a productive political program throughout the majority of its running time, Ghobadi, like Allouache in the Chapter Two, finishes on a pessimistic note, which reads as a clear argument regarding the political environment of Iran at the time of the film's production. Ghobadi's hope that the people of Iran will continue to reinvent themselves and express their unique interests despite political and existential regulations is tempered by Ashkan's possible death at the end of the film. His injury occurs after police arrive at a party Ashkan is attending during the final moments of the film. Panicked by their presence, Ashkan attempts to flee from a nearby window and falls to the ground. In a strategy striking for such a musical film, the loud screams, yells, and music of the party cuts to silence at the moment Ashkan begins to flee. During this sequence, the only sound is the hollow thump as his body hits the pavement. During a long shot on Ashkan's motionless body from above, an acoustic guitar begins to play, accompanied by Negar's mournful voice soon after. After the long shot, the music continues to play and a montage cuts between the concert that was to be Ashkan and Negar's parting show, Negar listening to music on a rooftop with a pained expression on her face, shots of Negar and Ashkan together that appear to be memories, fireworks, a woman dancing with flames, and Ashkan playing at (presumably) a different concert in the past. During this montage, Negar falls backwards at one point, suggesting that she has thrown herself off the rooftop, but the film does not confirm this act. Instead, the film ends on an overhead shot of Ashkan's bloody face as he is wheeled into a hospital. The film does not end with a definitive narrative conclusion, but several things are clear: the arrival of the police officer, who comes to discipline the errant subjects at the party, prompts Ashkan to jump out of the window, and this act that leads to a sensory-motor disruption of the film by a montage.

This sequence disrupts the expected conclusion of the film, that Negar and Ashkan will successfully reach their goal in traveling to London, and the formal causal connections among events and images thanks to the montage confusing the time and space between them. If, in *Half-Moon*, Mamo faces something intolerable in the restriction of Kurdish expression which eventually ends in his death, here the regulatory function of the police presents a similar encounter with this intolerable form of bio-power. Like *Half-Moon* also, however, the film does not end with death alone. While the indie rock duo will probably not make it to London for their concert, Ashkan's broken and bloodied face entering the hospital suggests the potential for his survival. In fact, Negar and Ashkan, (a real musical duo outside of the film), did make it to London, so that while the film presents the current regulatory measures inside Iran as intolerable, the reality of these musicians' situation is that they will continue to make music, even if they must leave Iran to do so. Considering the ending of *Bab El-Oued City*, however, Negar and Ashkan's departure may be just as evident of the intolerable nature in contemporary Iran for musicians. By not revealing this non-diegetic reality, that Negar and Ashkan make it to London, Ghobadi presents a political message for the population of Tehran, advocating change rather than departure.

Sonic Strategies for Fragmenting Subjects

Ghobadi's films that I have discussed here operate on various levels in order to construct the grounds for a people to come. Rather than defining the identity of the Kurds or the musical youths in Tehran, they construct an assemblage that links the films to affect and possibility – the possibility for characters, and viewers by proxy, to take part in the construction of their own subjectivities. *Half-Moon* argues through non-causal sound-situations that outright displays of Kurdish nationalism, such as the freedom concert, cannot be represented in films – an argument we can extend through Yildiz and Taysi to the media and political conversations about nations as well. *No One Knows about Persian Cats* works on an affective level to mobilize desires to change the present images of Tehran, suggesting a new, politically and culturally motivated people dedicated to the future of Tehran. Each of these films focus on minor subjectivities in Iran, insofar as the subjects promoted by state laws and regulations can be posited as majoritarian subjectivities, in that they respond to the Islamic ideology that permeates Iranian culture, filmmaking, and politics. While Ghobadi may not be overtly political, his films are politically productive, as they lay the groundwork for social change and the emergence of a new social-ecology in Iran.

While each film I have addressed here operates according to a sonic strategy that reveals a different operation of time – *Half-Moon* by injecting a future-time into the present of the narrative and *No One Knows about Persian Cats* by introducing musical sequences – they both include sound situations that interrupt or fragment the narrative. These moments interrupt the majoritarian time of the films, or the causal and linear film-time, and create, as Herzog puts it, "distinct temporal occurrences that are always open to the outside" (Herzog 2009: 16). The introduction of an exterior, I argue in turn, creates a difference that allows for the emergence of new subjects in these films – or subjects that the majoritarian discourse imposed by cinematic censorship cannot represent. In *Half-Moon*, the sound situations break with a nationalist discourse, and generates a Kurdish desire that networks Kurds through music. *No One Knows about Persian Cats* makes recourse to sound situations that resemble music videos, but focus on realist examples rather than fantasy. The lyrics and affective emotion of these songs prompts a turn toward changing the present reality in Tehran, a transformation made possible by the break with causal narrative. Chapter Four, while not focusing on music and sound situations to the same degree, similarly explores the realist and quotidian space created through a break with state-based filmmaking and censorship in China. Through these breaks with a linear, teleological narrative, which risks a return to a majoritarian conclusion, Ghobadi's films create a space inside Iran from which a new people might be conceived.

After examining Ghobadi's later films more closely, I find Kiarostami's criticism of Ghobadi a little ironic. Despite Kiarostami's accusations that Ghobadi is deserting Iran, Ghobadi's films seem to be in no way outward looking, but instead focus on the contemporary problems of Iranian populations. By prompting these populations to work towards the construction of their own futures, Ghobadi's position seems to be clearly situated within Iran. With this in mind, it is unfortunate that Ghobadi has been forced to leave Iran because of being blacklisted from film production. Though he dedicates himself to the creation of future peoples, like the characters in his films, he himself can no longer pursue the construction of hope inside Iran.

Ghobadi's departure from Iran provides a fitting case study for looking at the construction of contemporary political cinema, though. As I have argued at the beginning of this chapter, the dominant discourse in Iranian filmmaking is the Islamic ideology that dictates the construction of film-texts in material and ideological terms. While Ghobadi's films do not nec-essarily stand in opposition to Islamic law – even *No One Knows about Persian Cats* almost entirely follows the restrictions of the Sharia placed on filmmaking in Iran, despite not actually going through the Ministry of Culture and Islamic Guidance – they allow the emergence of a people that is critical of religion being used to reinforce the regulatory power of a ruling class. And while these films can be banned, the people they depict (and construct) cannot, and they will continue to emerge as a force of change within Iran. This variation is already present in the media, as the validity of Ahmadinejad's election was questioned by Iranians referring to themselves as the Green Movement. Rather than directly critiquing the majoritarian Islamic ideology, these contemporary political films establish the grounds for change at a molecular level through the production of a more diverse people than official discourses can account for.

Notes

1. See also Sadr 2006 for a more detailed, historical discussion, as censorship has long played a role in Iran.
2. In 'The Mass Production of the Senses: Classical Cinema as Vernacular Modernism,' Hansen argued that Hollywood exports led to a global/mass cultural understanding of cinema in relation to Hollywood's classical conti-nuity style.
3. Because of *Half-Moon*'s release in 2006, it is unlikely that the Kurdish sat-ellite stations that began broadcasting in 2006 were around when Ghobadi began filming. For more information, see: Alikhah 2008: 100–101.
4. Describing the formal nature of Utopian fulfillment in Bloch, Jameson illus-trates that "the movement of the world in time towards the future's ultimate moment, and the more spatial notion of that adequation of object to subject which must characterise that moment's content . . . [These] correspond to dramatic and lyrical modes of the presentation of not-yet-being" (Dyer 2002: 35). The basic narrative function described by Jameson and Bloch describes a potential people to come, using Deleuze's language, through the presen-tation of "not-yet-being." This also elucidates the function of hope within the Frankfurt school, which allows art the power to impact real people and motivate change, not by presenting a new, better world, but by mobilizing the desire to change what is. In this respect, this focus on futurity and not necessarily utopia reflects an immanent, Deleuzian politics concerning belief in the world as opposed to belief in transcendental ideals or morals.

CHAPTER 4

Jia Zhangke's Aimless Youths: Witnessing Economic Reform in the People's Republic of China

> I hope it is a newly-built world, a newly-built
> culture. It is not to rebel against anything, it is just a new culture.
> Jia Zhangke (2002)[1]

In films such as *Xiao Wu* (1997) and *Ren xiao yao/Unknown Pleasures* (2002), Jia Zhangke films the Birth Control Generation (BCG): youth born soon after the one child policy was introduced to China in 1978–1979. Because of economic reform and the resulting shifts in psychological and social structures, Jia describes this generation as suffering from feelings of emptiness, bleakness, and loneliness, and uses the following analogy: although there may be many roads connected by motorways, "you don't know what the direction is, or which is the way forward" (Jia 2002). He juxtaposes his characters in *Unknown Pleasures* to his characters in *Zhantai/Platform* (2000), noting that, although the latter drift, they still "have a kind of music" (Jia 2002). Though all three films belong to what Michael Berry calls his 'hometown trilogy,' focusing on the Shanxi province, in *Xiao Wu* and *Unknown Pleasures* characters lack the expectations that drive the characters in *Platform*. In the same interview, Jia compares his filmmaking practice to the uncertain lives of his birth control generation characters: "I think making a film is like exploring . . . you know roughly the direction, you know where you are going, but on the road, what experience you will have, what you will see and feel, you don't know that at all" (Jia 2002). Jia Zhangke's concept of filmmaking, which mirrors the aimlessness of his characters, operates within a pre-hodological space, the psychological space before action. This space allows Jia to juxtapose social and economic transformations with the lived experience of young people in China, upsetting the ordering tendencies of state logic.

As the quote that opens this chapter illustrates, he seeks not to create an oppositional political cinema, but one that expresses the experience of the new generation of Chinese after the one child policy whose overwhelming

characteristic, Jia argues, is aimlessness itself. Despite eschewing an oppositional politics, necessary as a result of PRC censorship, he maintains a
critical focus on the effects of globalization and capitalism in China through
to his more recent works such as *A Touch of Sin* (2013) and *Mountains May
Depart* (2015). As a result, his earlier peripatetic approach constitutes not
a thoughtlessness towards these issues, but a specific formal and political
strategy in which he addresses the contemporary moment in China. The
pre-hodological experience he creates reveals the divisive effects of economic reform on individual subjects in the post-socialist era.

Ghobadi and other Iranian filmmakers eventually critical of the state, like
Mohsen Makhmalbaf, started their careers working within the state-managed
filmmaking system and eventually sought ways to make films without the
state. Sixth Generation Chinese films, while sharing a similar relationship
with state-based censorship, followed the opposite trajectory. Certain Sixth
Generation directors such as Jia Zhangke and Wang Xiaoshuai desired to
produce independent films because of the difficulties of starting out in
the PRC state-controlled studio system. While their films may have been
political in content, in the early- to mid-1990s, the PRC's management of
film studios made their attempt to work outside state institutions a blatant
move in its own right. Initial attempts at independent filmmaking did not go
unnoticed by the government, and films such as Wang's *The Days* (1993),
Zhang Yuan's *Beijing Bastards* (1993), and He Jianjun's *Red Beads* (1994)
were banned, prompting a governmental blacklisting of these young directors, newly graduated from the Beijing Film Academy.

As a result, Sixth Generation directors have been perceived as under-
mining state order from the beginning of their careers. Unlike in the
Iranian context, however, incurring the state's ire proved to be a smart
business decision for many of these directors, as it allowed them to tap
into global flows of circulation, distribution, and capital. Using this international success, Jia Zangke re-entered the home market in China with
his first officially accepted film, *The World* (2004). While Jia claims otherwise, his desire to find distribution in China despite overseas fame suggests a political motivation, considering that his films address increasing
economic reform and transformation in China and its impact on Chinese
subjects. All three of the films discussed in this chapter chart the emergence of subjects structured by their relation to global capitalism's spread
of cultural and economic ideologies.

By focusing on subjects caught up in a transitional phase for China,
economic liberalization and urbanization in particular, Jia's films highlight the ability of certain subjects to adapt to broader global economic
transformations and the tragic consequences for those who cannot. Jia's

films, such as *Xiao Wu*, *Unknown Pleasures*, and even the officially accepted *The World*, operate according to a post-socialist realism, which counters state-sponsored ideologies with a focus on existential experiences (Berry 2007, McGrath 2007, and Zhang 2007a). This gap between official discourses on economic reform and the experiences of subjects depicted in Jia's films points to a rupture in the majoritarian narrative of the PRC. Jia first depicts this rupture through characters who witness the evolving economic structures around them, and whose witnessing is aesthetically intensified by a post-socialist realist approach to time, notable for its long takes and slow pace, which Jason McGrath likens broader trends in international art cinema (McGrath 2007: 89). This combination of character psychology grounded in film style provides a uniquely cinematic premise in the form of pre-hodological spaces for an argument regarding the effects of shifting economic structures on the lived experience of subjects in China.

By operating within the space before actions are taken, Jia's characters question, and lead viewers to question, the efficacy of China's rapid economic growth. In focusing on subjects that cannot weather the transition taking place in China and those dispossessed by its effects, Jia's films point to intolerable features of this economic growth through the failures of biopolitical production. In Jia's films, characters are marked by their failure to become globalized capitalists, while witnessing and sometimes actively questioning the success of those who do become part of this international elite. These failures, and their depiction on screen, create another space where the liberalization of China's economy can be questioned. Key to the creation of this space, however, is that it comes not through an overtly oppositional politics that would substitute another political or economic mode for the PRC's ideology. Instead, Jia's films draw upon the difference between perceptions of globalism and actual felt effects, and collapse distinctions between these registers to reveal an immanent terrain where minor and majoritarian positions coexist, both in terms of critical attitudes toward globalization and its supposed agents. In other words, Jia creates dichotomies in his films only to collapse them, refuting a solution. In doing so, Jia's political claim prompts a more active, rather than ideologically driven, approach to the intolerable features of the rapid economic growth and urbanization in China.

The Pickpocket and the Peddler: Dichotomies of Labor in *Xiao Wu*

Xiao Wu follows the pickpocket Xiao Wu amid urbanization in Fenyang as he enters the stage of his life where his friends have begun moving on, getting jobs, and getting married. A number of his friends begin to find purpose in particular things in their lives, but Xiao still embodies the aimlessness Jia discusses in interviews. In *Xiao Wu*, the form of the film reflects the aimlessness of its protagonist through its seemingly directionless nature. Xiao Wu picks pockets, meets old friends, and goes about his daily life, but the character lacks driving motivations or goals just as the film lacks a coherent narrative arc. Describing the aimlessness that this filmic form evokes, Chris Berry and McGrath argue that the stylistic conventions, including long takes and narrative distension, contribute to "a radical vision of postsocialist realist time countering any master narrative of teleological progress" (McGrath 2007: 90). These master narratives appear in the mediated representations on radio and television in *Xiao Wu*. Amidst Xiao Wu's drifting about Fenyang, the government announces new policies to crack down on pickpockets and petty criminals. The news is delivered through radio broadcasts, and the police set up a booth to inform the public, prompting Xiao Wu's friends who have moved on from their lives of petty crime to continually urge Xiao Wu to "calm down for a while," because "they mean it this time." Xiao Wu brushes the advice aside, claiming that he has stopped pickpocketing.

Often the advice from friends involves suggesting that Xiao Wu pick up a new trade, as they proceed to remark on his once-criminal friend Xiao Yong's success, "Take a look at Xiao Yong, he's really on the way up." Eventually, a dichotomy is established between Xiao Wu and Xiao Yong that marks Xiao Wu as unsophisticated or backwards because he relies on the skills he learned in his youth, rather than taking up modern business practices to keep up with the PRC's market-oriented reforms initiated in 1978 (Chu and So 2010: 46). Xiao Yong, on the other hand, is heralded as adept at these new business practices, and he is featured on television and nominated model entrepreneur. As a result, a master narrative – insofar as it is constructed by the state and propagated through state media within the film – results in a dichotomy that distinguishes Xiao Wu's old/ illegitimate business practices from Xiao Yong's new/legitimate business practices, aimlessness versus clear purpose, pre-hodological space versus hodological space. The film compounds this separation through formal features that reflect pre-hodological space and help to articulate Xiao Wu's story.

The film disrupts the veracity of this official dichotomy and invites political critique by confusing what constitutes legitimate or good business practices, and thereby questioning state logic. The dichotomy begins to break down when Xiao Wu responds to his new girlfriend Mei Mei calling him a big spender by saying, "I'm an artisan . . . I work with my hands." Although he may be trying to hide his true occupation as a pick-pocket from his romantic interest, he also crafts a romantic view of his labor. While he claims no extra-moral position, Xiao Wu is different from your average pickpocket. In the beginning of the film, he is tasked with recovering an ID that was inside of a stolen wallet, because "getting a new id isn't easy." He successfully finds the ID, helping it get back to its owner, and toward the end of the film the viewer learns that Xiao Wu has been putting the ID cards of all the wallets he steals in mailboxes where they are turned into the police station and eventually returned to their owners. In this respect, Xiao Wu's actions portray him as more honorable and com-passionate than your average petty thief.

The film reveals Xiao Yong's business, on the other hand, to be the exporting of cigarettes and semi-legal prostitution. Xiao Wu compares his trade to Xiao Yong's by arguing, "his money from illicit cigarette deals and club girls [isn't] so clean, either!" Xiao Wu recognizes that Xiao Yong's entrepreneurship is arguably more deplorable than his own petty theft, but the community of Fenyang hardly recognizes this as Xiao Yong donates 30,000 Yuan to the Hope Project. The confusion of this previously established dichotomy illustrates the way that *Xiao Wu* operates as a work of post-socialist realism through stripping ideological positions of their truth-value. McGrath defines post-socialist realism by arguing, "rather than professing to show an ideological truth that underlies apparent real-ity, it seeks to reveal a raw, underlying reality by stripping away the ideo-logical representations that distort it" (McGrath 2007: 83-84). Xiao Yong is only *officially* a model entrepreneur, or an entrepreneur according to PRC-established ideology. In fact, his donation of 30,000 Yuan shows him to be an adept manipulator of the media, which helps to construct the master narrative itself in the film. Xiao Wu on the other hand is officially a petty criminal, but as viewers follow his experiences firsthand, they find a more complicated character. Drawing Xiao Yong's officially approved role towards the realities of the thief begins to present questions of whether the officially sanctioned position is as pure as state-sanctioned ideology would have it appear.

While a majoritarian discourse emerges from the changing economy depicted in *Xiao Wu*, privileging a new capitalist class, the film also exam-ines the divisions created in populations through the change in market practices. This is accomplished by delving in to the psychological life space of its characters as reflected in the play between hodological and pre-hodological narrative structures. As the film follows Xiao Wu, the viewer does not experience Xiao Yong's psychological life space formally. Instead, the film illustrates Xiao Wu's marginalization through its depiction of the failure of a more traditional life-narrative. Halfway through the film, Xiao meets a woman named Mei Mei who works as a companion at a karaoke bar. Xiao Wu falls in love with Mei Mei, which prompts him to construct a socially approved and ideologically appropriate trajectory as illustrated through the sudden clarity of narrative direction this encounter creates. Prior to this point, Xiao Wu has little direction in his life, a seeming lack of goals and motivations, and it is difficult to determine what action he will take next in the film. This pre-hodological abundance of narrative potential is reined in, however, when Xiao Wu goes through a process of individuation as he shifts his focus towards Mei Mei. For a time, Xiao Wu's narrative drive becomes similar to Xiao Yong's. The first indicator of this narrative shift is Xiao Wu's engagement party and quest to buy an engagement ring. Xiao Wu's goals become clear to himself and viewers of the film as his desire to buy a wedding ring for Mei Mei creates a narrative direction accompanied by causal events – romancing Mei Mei, celebrating with friends, and purchasing an engagement ring. Unlike the first half of the film, the narrative picks up pace as Xiao Wu courts his new love interest and the dichotomy between Xiao Wu and Xiao Yong collapses, resulting in the film losing its earlier critical focus on the deleterious effects of rapid urbanization.

This brief experiment with a clear narrative direction soon crumples, however, creating a sharp distinction between a hodological and pre-hodological narrative. Mei Mei disappears, halting the causal sequence of events established by Xiao Wu's relationship with her. Confused, he wanders up and down the street, eventually deciding to go to Mei Mei's apartment, which she has vacated. The camera takes Xiao Wu's point of view as his eyes wander around the vacated apartment, and he begins to become agitated, communicating his subjectivity. Angry, he returns to his parents' home and offers the wedding ring to his mother, signaling the end of this brief narrative direction constructed in the film. Including this sequence in the middle of the film heightens the viewer's sense of the film's overall aimlessness. The Mei Mei interlude stands as an example of what narrative direction might look like in *Xiao Wu*. Before plunging back into its pre-hodological nature marked by Xiao Wu's wandering, the film returns to its critique of ideology in another way by mimicking earlier, socialist realist films.

Xiao Wu's return to his parents' home reveals his distance from another ideology-driven narrative when he returns the ring intended for Mei Mei. The film lapses into a parody of older socialist realist films, as Xiao Wu's father questions the veracity of the ring: "We've been poor peasants for three generations . . . Is it made of gold or copper?" and, after a brief interlude, begins talking about farming with his other son: "Are the fields ploughed . . . What'll you plant this year?" Xiao Wu sits off to the side, not able to take part of this conversation about legitimate occupations. When Xiao Wu realizes the ring he gave his mother was given to his brother for his engagement, Xiao Wu becomes upset, asking for the ring back. His father replies, "There are family rules to be respected" and "If I'd known, I would have drowned you in a urinal at birth," responding to Xiao Wu's breach of collective, familial protocol and status as a thief. After being chased out of the house by his father with a stick, a single long shot depicts Xiao Wu's departure, which marks the return of the film's meandering nature.

Beginning as a long shot of Xiao Wu walking down a dirt road, the frame remains static as he walks into a medium close-up. The camera then begins to rotate slowly in a 270 degree turn, as a loudspeaker discusses the reunification of Hong Kong. In contrast with the promised reintegration with wealthy, modern Hong Kong, this shot depicts a village with dirt roads and dilapidated stone buildings in probing detail through narrative distension. Focusing on the role that narrative distension has played in Chinese cinema, Harry H. Kuoshu argues that it functions "like the unresolved, often meandering plots of the modernist novel . . . or the voids in the slowly unrolled Chinese scroll painting, both of which call upon and make space for the audience to engage in critical thought" (Kuoshu 2002: 297). Xiao Wu, cast out of the socialist realist narrative, does not know what action to take, which compounds with the aimlessness of the camera to exemplify the pre-hodological aspect of the film. In this same shot, Xiao Wu approaches the camera, pauses, and looks from side to side, seemingly unsure of which direction to take before the shot begins to rotate. At this moment, he exists in the pre-hodological space before action, where he and the viewers in turn are left to witness the juxtaposition of the loudspeaker that plays "anyone who wants a slice of pork, please come to my house," an idealized reference to modernization and the small town where Xiao Wu's family lives.

Eventually, Xiao Wu wanders back into Fenyang where he watches shop owners vacating their buildings to make way for them to be demolished and rebuilt as part of China's reconstruction, a component of the economic reform sweeping China. Xiao Wu's friend comments critically, "The old stuff is coming down, but I see nothing new." Because Mei Mei's departure quashed Xiao Wu's hope of settling down, he returns to his old aimlessness and eventually attempts to pick a pocket while wandering amongst the shops of Fenyang. He is caught in the act, and brought into the police station. In the film's most surreal moment, Xiao Wu is left to watch a television program on Fenyang's new, harsher criminal policies, in which various townsfolk are interviewed about Xiao Wu's own arrest. Each person discusses how appreciative they are that Xiao Wu has been arrested. The conversations shown on the TV are clearly part of an official program dedicated to reinforcing a particular ideological understanding of crime and petty theft in Fenyang, running counter to other responses to Xiao Wu throughout the film that treat him as a person rather than a label: thief. The film ends with Xiao Wu being handcuffed to a telephone pole in public, as crowds gather to look at him with curiosity, the preceding song querying with its lyrics: "May I ask you all, who is the hero?"

With this ending, *Xiao Wu* argues that there is no place for the lived reality of the lower classes within the urbanization and market reform Xiao Wu witnesses through his wandering. In the last moments of the film, where Xiao Wu is handcuffed to a pole in public, the camera turns to the actual bystanders in Fenyang who were walking down the street during the filming of this scene. In these final moments of *Xiao Wu*, Jia introduces the factual through filming real people, as they naturally congregate to see what is happening. The camera turns to film their curiosity, and the lack of condemnation in their demeanor casts doubt upon the truth of Jia's status

Figure 4.1 *Xiao Wu* (1997).

as criminal, despite the earlier staged interviews with citizens of Fenyang, and thereby denaturalize ideology. The focus on a real audience reiterates the question posed by the song: "who is the hero?" *Xiao Wu* ultimately breaks from its fictional narrative to show real people on the streets of Fenyang, and in the final images of this film these spectators seem to bear no moral judgment on Xiao Wu despite his being handcuffed.

The coexistence of the television interviews and these individuals on the street refocuses on the earlier pre-hodological nature of the film. Obviously, this is staged to some extent, as the spectators could be expected to be curious about the camera, and Xiao Wu is being filmed, but it nevertheless presents a break with the dichotomy that labeled Xiao Wu a criminal, which fragments the clear-cut notions of proper subject-positions that the state attempts to mobilize in the film. As China's economy begins globalizing and becoming more capitalist, *Xiao Wu* reveals the effects of market reform on individuals and fragments official attempts to construct a singular understanding of these subjects. This operates through the pre-hodological narrative of the film, as Xiao Wu wanders about the city, and takes on extra significance in the final moments of the film as it suggests wider participation of the Chinese people in this pre-individuated state of uncertainty about official visions of economic reform in China.

Questionable Freedoms: Nothing to Do in *Unknown Pleasures*

Unknown Pleasures follows two protagonists who exemplify the BCG in general for Jia. Scholar Zhang Zhen contends that the documentary method of *Xiao Wu* – shooting on location, using non-professional actors, and even including the public not affiliated with the film – was "critical for the particular kind of story [Jia] wanted to tell about people *in* their social milieu. It is an aesthetic grounded in social space and experience" (Zhang 2007b: 19). This interest in social milieus informs the setting for *Unknown Pleasures* as well, however, the latter film includes "a pair of stylish and attractive lead characters" that makes the film seem "to have a younger and hipper appeal bordering on the commercial," as McGrath notes (McGrath 2007: 104). In other words, the protagonists of *Unknown Pleasures* depict what Robert Moore refers to as China's millennial youth. He points out that this is endemic to "children of the Cultural Revolution generation. Largely because of globalization, their viewpoints and attitudes are profoundly different from those of their parents" (Moore 2005: 357). In this film, Jia seems to be catering to an even more specific demographic of urban youths, who will be viewing this film in film clubs and on

pirated video compact discs (VCDs), two themes addressed explicitly in
Unknown Pleasures. Indicative of globalization's influence, Moore's study
of Chinese youth cultures shows that "Millennial Chinese describe their
individualistic tendencies in terms of freedom" (Moore 2005: 372). Like
Xiao Wu, the interplay between a pre-hodological space and a hodological
space, in terms of formal representation and narrative drive, plays a central role in the film. The film largely follows a set of characters that exist
within a pre-hodological dimension linked to the theme of freedom, albeit
a questionable freedom. The film concludes with two of the protagonists
attempting to forcefully create a hodological space for themselves – an
act that ultimately fails and reveals precisely the questionable nature of
freedom.

Despite the seeming savvy with which Jia targets a particular generation, the film's narrative has little to say about the future or direction
of this generation, repeating the aimlessness and pre-hodological nature
of *Xiao Wu*. The refusal to say anything about the direction of this generation plays out to such a degree that the film becomes an almost banal
exploration of relatively affluent youth culture, when compared to *Xiao
Wu*. The characters wander around the city, shop for and watch videos, and hang out in cafés. At one point, there is an explosion in the city
prompting the characters to act, but this provides only a flirtation with a
more directed narrative, reminiscent of Xiao Wu's brief fling in *Xiao Wu*.
Whereas the psychopolitics of *Xiao Wu* were bound up in the juxtaposition between legitimate and illegitimate business practices or life choices,
the psychopolitical space of the characters in *Unknown Pleasures* illustrates
their relationship with media and its influence over their understanding of
the world. Far from depoliticizing this experience, however, the film draws
the ideologies of the state and of media together in their shared obfusca-
tion of reality.

The setting of the film is a bleak city, Datong, full of demolished buildings and construction sites, reminding the viewer China's rapid urban
development. In his study of *Still Life* (2006), Erik Bordeleau examines
the role such settings play in Jia's films, focusing on the "empty time of
progress and the vital need to stop the present . . . so that each [character]
can conjugate his life in the present" (Bordeleau 2013: 29). This charac-
terization of the setting is useful, in that *Unknown Pleasures* is ultimately
about the failure of its characters to join their lives with a present purpose,
while the city seems to be transforming around them. McGrath adds that
creating "a bombed-out looking backdrop . . . silently repudiates the col-
orful fashions of its youthful protagonists" (McGrath 2007: 104). This
juxtaposition plays out thematically and narratively as well as visually, in

the way that these characters wander in the film unable to find ways to occupy their time. McGrath's reading of this aimlessness explains the genesis of the supposed freedom of the characters in the film:

> The film's Chinese title, meaning "allowed to wander free and easy," is borrowed from a contemporary popular song that appears twice in the film. The song title itself echoes the Daoist philosopher Zhuangzi, who used *xiaoyao*, or "carefree wandering" to describe the ideal state of spiritual freedom. One of the film's protagonists, nineteen-year-old Bin Bin, is enamored of a cartoon version of the Monkey King from the classic Chinese novel *Journey to the West* (Xiyou ji)--an embodiment of a similar ideal combination of empowerment, freedom, and enjoyment. (McGrath 2007: 104)

Ironically, while these characters are allowed to wander among the dilapidated buildings and construction sites of Datong, they lack all three characteristics of the Monkey King: empowerment, freedom, and enjoyment. These attributes are characteristic of individuals who have the power to determine their course in life, and are completely missing from the film's three main protagonists: Bin Bin, Xiao Ji, and Qiao Qiao. Bin Bin and Xiao Ji are unable to secure jobs for themselves, their relationships constantly falter, and at no point do the characters seem to find pleasure in their time spent watching television or wandering around town. At times, the characters even quote the Monkey King, but it only contributes to widening the gap between the fictional Monkey King's achieved freedom, and the aimless wandering of the three protagonists.

Preceding the ultimate attempt by Bin Bin and Xiao Ji to establish a more purposeful hodology in the film, the characters try several times to create direction in their lives, failing each time. Bin Bin attempts to shape his own future by joining the military, which would provide him work that the depressed Datong lacks, but he is refused due to a health condition. Xiao Ji, who pursues Qiao Qiao romantically, is thwarted in his efforts by local thug Qiao San. At one point, Qiao Qiao, fed up with Qiao San, starts pushing him as they are having a conversation inside his bus. Qiao Qiao reiterates this physical action a dozen times, but it seems to have no real effect on Qiao San and does not alter the course of their conversation or relationship in any meaningful way. There are several scenes like this in the film where a particular physical action is repeated for 10–15 iterations, and speaking of another scene where Xiao Ji repeatedly tries to ride his motorbike up a dirt bank, Jia states in an interview that these repetitive moments are a "reminder to the characters that they are actually existing" (Jia 2002). This question, as to whether the characters actually exist, points to an extreme lack of agency, and impotency of the characters' abilities to shape their futures. This impotency indicates a significant characteristic of the film's version of freedom – the characters are free to wander around the city, but not to establish a narrative for themselves that would create momentum, purpose, or a causal sequence of events that might direct their lives.

This lack of agency in the characters of *Unknown Pleasures* illustrates the way that it differs from *Xiao Wu* in its depiction of hodological states. Xiao Wu wanders, but apart from his brief encounter with Mei Mei, he does not seem to have the same desire to construct a narrative for himself as do the characters of *Unknown Pleasures*. Rather than brushing up against state-sponsored media, as Xiao Wu does in *Xiao Wu* with the loudspeaker announcements and official television broadcasts, the characters of *Unknown Pleasures* are shaped by their consumption of media for the purposes of entertainment, and thus have a different relationship with ideology. Namely, their view of the world, shaped by media discourses like the Monkey King, clashes with their existential experiences in Datong. Desire emerges from these media-constructed ideologies and structure the subjectivities of the characters. Whereas one might view the pre-hodological space as a productive place of potential – the characters are free to approach the world in any way they choose, take any course of action they can think of – the concept itself is apolitical, and its significance depends on the context in which it operates. Here, the directionless nature of the characters in *Unknown Pleasures* creates a pre-hodological narrative, but presents it as a questionable freedom, because the characters are not actually able to enter into a relationship with the world in a meaningful way. The film foregrounds this in its conclusion, as the characters, powerless throughout the film, attempt to forcefully create a place for themselves in a world they find intolerable.

Ultimately, *Unknown Pleasures* is pessimistic in its outlook for the generation of youths growing up during this urbanization and transition of economies. At the end of the film, Xiao Ji and Bin Bin decide to take radical action by robbing a bank to establish a narrative for themselves. Tonglin Lu locates the locus of this idea in American pop culture, more specifically, *Pulp Fiction*, which is referenced by the characters earlier in the film (Lu 2006: 136). In these films, the characters see an American ideology associated with clear hodological path established by characters that take action regardless of consequences, and thereby make a place for themselves in the world – just as they might resort to criminal action to make a place from themselves in Datong. Their attempted robbery fails, however, with Xiao Ji fleeing on his motorcycle and Bin Bin being taken to jail by the police. Although Bin Bin perhaps pays the heftier price, Xiao

Ji's retreat is more emblematic of the film in general. While riding back towards Datong on a mostly empty highway in the middle of nowhere, Xiao Ji's bike breaks down. He slowly rolls to a stop, and is left in an even bleaker setting than where he began, with even less mobility. Eventually, he hitches a ride, but the message seems clear: he can't get anywhere on his own. Bin Bin, on the other hand, is asked to stand and sing in the police station. He sings *Ren Xiao Yao*, the popular song about carefree wandering described earlier. The fact that he sings this while imprisoned reinforces the irony of this song as a theme song for the generation of youths followed in the film. Again, the desire for freedom, empowerment, and enjoyment is juxtaposed with the realities of life for the characters. In the film, Xiao Ji and Bin Bin's decision to rob a bank is their final attempt to establish a psychological sense of direction through which they might make sense of their lives and perceive some sort of movement or purpose. Better to be bank robbers than to not exist at all, Jia's commentary suggests. Ultimately, their plan is founded on an imaginary American ideology perpetrated through the spread of popular culture globally, and they fail.

While seemingly less political than *Xiao Wu*, *Unknown Pleasures* communicates the experience of young people who are forgotten by the PRC's rapid transformations, even as they have greater access to global media. This global media offers only hollow and unrealistic ideologies, similar to the problematic construction of the proper businessman in *Xiao Wu*. Although *Unknown Pleasures* is pessimistic, its pessimism becomes a device to mobilize subjective formations of perception and encourage the audience to question the sense of freedom communicated in the film

Figure 4.2 *Unknown Pleasures* (2002).

through pop songs and foreign media. *Unknown Pleasures* focuses on personal, existential experiences, but they are collective and collapse the distinction between this private, existential register and public concerns regarding the economic liberalization of China and forced modernization as seen in Datong. Jia himself refers to this connection when declaring his films different from those of the Fifth Generation, which "had nothing to do with the reality of China at the time" (Jia 2008). Jia's intention is to depict Datong and the Chinese situation in general in 2001 as he finds them, using his realist style to that end. *Unknown Pleasures* is set just prior to Hu Jintao taking leadership of the PRC, when economists were concerned that "China was developing a social structure not unlike Latin America" where wealth was distributed drastically unevenly, even though – or rather, because – economic reforms were well under way, as illustrated by the constant destruction and construction in *Unknown Pleasures* (Fewsmith 2008: 237). While the youth of Datong are subject to a set of personal experiences, these personal experiences are immediately connected to a larger collective experience regarding China's economic situation.

The Problem of Distribution as the Solution to Distribution

Jia's foray into independent filmmaking with *Xiao Wu* led officials to include Jia in a governmental blacklist of a group of directors most commonly associated with the Sixth Generation; simultaneously, the film also garnered international acclaim. The success of many Sixth Generation filmmakers depended upon the distribution of these films as "Banned in China," which was proudly proclaimed on releases in the West. Although it is impossible to say whether or not these films would have had the same critical success abroad had they been welcomed by the PRC, the ban certainly enabled marketing schemes of Western distributors and piqued the interest of Western film critics. The PRC's eventual acceptance of Jia and other Sixth Generation filmmakers raises some important questions. Was it because the filmmakers stopped their political efforts, and anesthetized their films so that they could make a profit with audiences at home, what Sheila Cornelius calls "the taming effect of commercialism" (Cornelius 2002: 108)? Or did the PRC see a growing voice in these directors, one they needed to co-opt lest it become more critical and more popular? With increasing market reforms, the PRC's cultural arm may increasingly resemble Western culture industries, but with this resemblance comes the critical efforts of certain artists to exploit dominant artistic, economic, and political practices.

The initial venture of Sixth Generation Chinese filmmakers into global markets predated the success of Fifth Generation epics such as *Hero* (2002) and *House of Flying Daggers* (2004), albeit in the less popular festival circuits and networks of distribution, and emerged mainly as a response to the filmmaking environment in China at the time. As a relative latecomer to the Sixth Generation filmmaking scene, Jia learned from the experience of comrades such as Wang Xiaoshuai and Zhang Yuan who both entered state-run studios after graduating from the Beijing Film Academy. Both Wang and Zhang encountered frustration in these positions, as their time at the Beijing Film Academy did ensure them work at studios, but did not ensure them an environment where they would have the capacity to direct or create their own films. Not only did all production go through the state-run industries at the time, but to their apparent dismay, there was a hierarchical system that required would-be filmmakers to work their way up before being allowed to create a film. Because Wang and Zhang eschewed the state run system of production and distribution, however, they had to find alternative methods of distributing their films. The biggest alternative market for these directors, and most immediately successful as the awards they received indicate, was the global film festival market.

As I mentioned previously, Sixth Generation films in general, and Jia's films in particular, have been criticized as self-orientalizing by virtue of their globalization – or pandering to international crowds, as more severe critics would argue. Speaking of Jia in particular, Tonglin Lu complicates this straight correlation between accessing global markets and self-orientalizing:

> Instead of praising the new world order, [Sixth Generation films] often question the process that has given birth to their own production and question the value system that has formed the basis of their existence – the capitalist mode of production – by portraying the "localized" lifestyle of an underprivileged urban population. In their documentary or documentary-like portrayals of ordinary Chinese urbanites, they debunk the myth of China as a success story of globalization, a myth disseminated by both the official media in China and the "free press" in the West in order to advance the interests of both the Communist state and multinational corporations. (Lu 2006: 124)

There are two important points to consider in this assessment. First, the films depict realities predicted by economists where in globalized economies wealth is concentrated in smaller pockets and peoples are localized or trapped despite globalization's promise of mobility. Second, the charge of self-orientalizing against these directors may come from the state itself as a nationalist official ideology, when a documentary or documentary-like depiction of people reinforces impressions of China's differences. This occurs when the depiction shows a reality that government officials do not want to circulate globally – a reason censorship is often applied in Iran as well. Whereas critics seem to be locating the presentation of difference as a tactic on the part of Sixth Generation filmmakers, these filmmakers are realistically documenting the consequences of increasing, often disruptive globalization. Furthermore, in Jia's films at least, globalization plays a constant role in the existential experiences of the characters, lending evidence to his insight. In *Xiao Wu*, Xiao Yong presents an example of the globalizing elite as he sells cigarettes abroad; Xiao Wu, on the other hand, is part of the population whose world is further localized by Xiao Yong's business, becoming increasingly narrow and without possibility. In *Unknown Pleasures*, the protagonists appear to be fashionable purveyors of pop culture, but it turns out their upwardly mobile appearance and aspirations are betrayed by their lack of opportunities. All of these characters, Xiao Wu and the protagonists of *Unknown Pleasures*, bear witness to global politics and the (re)distribution of biopower as markets shift to reflect China's globalization.[2]

Rather than a sellout to the global marketplace, as his critics would have it, I argue that Jia presents a critical account of how globalization affects people at home within China. While it is the case that Jia could both sell out to the global market and simultaneously critique the same process of globalization he participates in, since making his film *The World* (2004) he has not only returned to making state sponsored films in China, but has maintained critical success abroad while also accessing markets at home. Although this can also be seen as selling out to the state and denouncing his roots as an independent filmmaker, Jia is very vocal about his intentions in returning to filmmaking with the state's consent. First, Jia has stated that it is very important to him that his banned films are distributed via VCD on the black market, despite the fact that he receives no monetary compensation for the sales of these VCDs (Jia 2008). This can mean only that he is interested primarily in widening the distribution of his films through VCD rather than making a profit from them. In terms of his entering the mainstream, Jia "insists he is motivated by access to audience, not money" (Pickowicz 2006: 4). Jia's focus is not on profit, but his art, or its social and political impact. Second, though his films after *The World* in 2004, have all been made with state consent, they still maintain, I argue, the same critical edge as his earlier, banned films. Pickowicz uses the metaphor of dancing to describe the way that underground filmmakers have to negotiate regulations in the content of their films, which is useful in understanding how they are able to maintain the critical edge of their films (Pickowicz 2006: 6).

As a result, Jia's maneuvering through and around state regulations demonstrates that he isn't selling out the way that one would traditionally define it – for monetary gain – but he is selling out to secure better access to the audiences that might be politically affected by his films.

I will now turn to the first film Jia made with state approval, *The World*, which focuses explicitly on the effects of globalization. *The World* examines a cross section of people working at the Beijing World Park in their social milieu, a theme-park style attraction that offers a tour of the world without leaving Beijing. The park exists as a material example of globalization, but the film also investigates the localization taking place in Beijing as populations congregate there for work – resulting in what Dudley Andrew has called the "mismatch of provincial and urban experience" in this film (Andrew 2010: 84). *The World* exposes the effects of globalization by bearing witness to how it impacts particular areas and peoples. In examining these effects, *The World* also exposes something intolerable about global market politics and mobilizes spectators to recognize that which is intolerable in their own lives. In doing so, *The World* and Jia's subsequent films have the power to reinforce a belief in the world and one's power to change it. By showing that Jia's later films work politically in the same fashion as his earlier films, I also show that his consistency indicates that he has not sold out commercially, and more importantly that he has not succumbed to the chilling effect associated with directors who return to state-approved filmmaking – that is, his message has not been suppressed by the majoritarian market forces of the culture industry.

The World in Private: Global Movement, Personal Trauma

Jia's *The World* marks the director's entry into officially approved filmmaking in China. As a film that discusses the effects of globalization, however, *The World* follows the critical trajectory of Jia's earlier films. Both in content and in form, *The World* addresses globalization with its international funding, transnational actors, and depiction of global locales.[3] Set in the Beijing World Park, where one can "visit the world without leaving Beijing," characters walk between Egypt and London almost seamlessly, implying an underlying global and material connection. Actors come from other countries to work at the Beijing World Park, constituting a global movement accentuated by legal and language barriers. While the film received exhibition and attention in China, having been accepted by PRC officials, the film was even better received internationally by critics and on the festival circuit in addition to exhibition in theaters abroad. Both thematically and industrially, *The World* focuses more consciously on globalization than Jia's earlier films. This presents an interesting question: how does Jia maintain a critique of globalization in this film, while the film itself operates as a product of globalization? I argue that Jia maintains a political edge by focusing on the localization that is part of globalization, and despite the fact that the film seems like a globalized product, the stories focus on local concerns: in particular, the movement of migrant workers to Beijing and the effects of globalization on Beijing's economy. In doing so, Jia questions the efficacy of global capitalism and focuses on the fragmentation that results between urban and rural, wealthy and poor, local and global. Furthermore, *The World* reveals this inequality to be intolerable through the dichotomy established between workers at the Beijing World Park and the peripheral characters they come into contact with, which exposes the difference between perceived benefits of globalization and its felt effects.

Although the film follows many characters, *The World* mainly centers on Tao, a performer at the Beijing World Park, and Taisheng, a security guard, who are in a relationship from the beginning of the film. The story itself meanders – there are several plots that are picked up and then abandoned – but key characters include migrant workers from Shanxi and performers from Russia who have come to work at the Beijing World Park. Two important peripheral characters from these populations are Little Sister, Taisheng's childhood friend who comes to Beijing from a rural area looking for work, and Anna, a Russian performer who quickly becomes trapped in Beijing and is forced to turn to prostitution. While Tao and Taisheng make up the bulk of the narrative, and do not experience much trouble, Little Sister and Anna illustrate a darker side of globalization and the harsh consequences of the seemingly fluid movement of people in the name of profit or to make a living.

The clear demarcation between the experiences of each of these pairs, however, gives a clear example of the inequality at play, as Tao and Taisheng's lives differ considerably from Anna's and Little Sister's. Ultimately, like Jia's other films, *The World* is about the quotidian lives of its protagonists, but the daily lives of Tao and Taisheng is vastly different from those of Anna and Little Sister. Whereas Tao and Taisheng's daily work seems comfortable, Anna's and Little Sister's work and lives in Beijing are eventually revealed to be downward spirals that leave them in positions from which they cannot escape. While the bulk of Tao and Taisheng's experiences revolve around their romance, Anna's and Little Sister's experiences have a far greater deal of urgency about more basic concerns, such as losing access to passports and the ability to travel. While this illustrates the unequal distribution of wealth previously mentioned as a concern of economic analysts, it extends these larger economic concerns into the existential realm by giving examples of localized individuals and the "trapped freedom" Tonglin Lu argues is a part of *Unknown Pleasures*.

Whereas the characters in *Unknown Pleasures* often quote pop culture to illustrate the location and production of their desires, *The World* uses formal breakage of the narrative in the form of cartoon-vignettes that periodically interrupt it. Often, these vignettes show important communications via text messages between the characters that illustrate moments or turns in their relationships, the text messages themselves linked to the same technologies embedded within globalization, which contribute to their alienation from one another. At other times, they draw on the fantasies of the characters, as in the scene used for the cover of the Zeitgeist release of the digital versatile disc (DVD) that has an airline hostess soaring through the skies without the plane that determines or delineates her destination. These vignettes are important, because they mark moments where the film poses a statement to the viewer in the form of a mental image. The vignette with the flying stewardess, for example, delivers a political statement through the juxtaposition of the film's insistence on globalization and its status as a global product that entraps individuals. The image of the flying stewardess takes on a sad irony – her desire for the freedom of magical flight and the ability to choose her direction herself is juxtaposed with the real life stasis of her life and labor. Similarly, as Taisheng takes his visitors from Shanxi on a tour through the Beijing World Park, he beams at the fact that they can move from Cairo to London seemingly instantaneously. While his happiness at showing his friends from the backward Shanxi this global movement communicates his belief that achieving a semblance of freedom is possible, the fact is that in the film, Taisheng (and viewers of the film) rarely leave the park at all. In this way, Jia's comment on globalization oscillates between poles of freedom and entrapment, or more specifically, the characters' perception of freedom and their actual entrapment.

Françoise Lionnet and Shu-Mei Shih's work on minor transnationalism addresses the dichotomy of perceived freedom and actual entrapment in their discussion of two forms of transnationalism: transnationalism from above and transnationalism from below. Their work is particularly useful in relation to the minoritarian politics developed in *The World*, as it illustrates the simultaneity of processes at work within transnational movements of commodities, labor, and people. Transnationalism from above suggests national boundaries might be overcome, cultures might be hybridized, and human rights expanded as a result (Lionnet and Shih

2005: 6). This utopian view of globalization haunts the theme park setting of *The World* and animates the characters' attitudes throughout the film as they go about their daily work as performers. Eventually, we learn that their lives are more complicated than their performances indicate, but the Beijing World Park itself thrives on its concept of overcoming national boundaries and creating an apparent hybridization of cultures. Later, the film confronts this fantasy of hybridization with seemingly insurmountable obstacles in the form of language and geopolitical barriers. For instance, Anna's only friendship among her new colleagues at the Park is with Tao. They clearly consider each other friends as they meet one-on-one for a meal and attempt to communicate with each other through gestures and by revealing intimate information in their respective languages. This information is revealed to the audience through subtitling, but ultimately neither Anna nor Tao understands precisely what the other is saying. Although they often understand basic sentiments, such as when Anna breaks down and begins to cry, they never truly communicate, because this hybridization encouraged by globalized capitalism does not require personal communication in order to function. In fact, it seems that such communication might pose a risk to business, considering that Anna tries to tell Tao, who might have been able to help her leave the city, that she is trapped and considering prostitution to free herself from Beijing.

Similarly, Little Brother comes to Beijing knowing Taisheng's success. While his movement is not properly transnational, his migration from the country to Beijing shares many characteristics of Anna's transnational movement and is certainly the result of China's globalization. It is clear that he enters an entirely other context – from his different dialect to the way he is treated even by those from Shanxi who have successfully assimilated. It turns out that the only work for migrant laborers is dangerous work, such as construction of new skyscrapers. The work is especially dangerous, it is implied, because the workers are migrant laborers, and there is little concern for their safety. Little Brother's discovery of his bleak prospects belies a utopian view of the movement of peoples, and instead points to what might be human rights violations. The film enforces this argument when Little Brother dies in a construction accident. It turns out that he has been working extra shifts in order to make ends meet, including working dangerous night hours. These examples illustrate transnationalism from below, and as a result, while the film oscillates between freedom and entrapment, it also oscillates between utopian and dystopian views of transnationalism and globalization, revealing a class of people produced by these global flows who would otherwise be invisible.

Figure 4.3 *The World* (2004).

Although there seems to be a movement between two poles in this film, establishing a dichotomy between a utopian view of globalization and dystopian entrapment, I use Lionnet and Shih's analysis to point out the falsity of drawing such a distinction in *The World* (Lionnet and Shih 2005: 7). Lionnet and Shih point out that theorizing a continuum with two extremes is the approach of classical politics, as defined earlier in this project in relation to classical political cinemas. This approach posits a dominant force and a resisting force caught up in a dialectical or revolutionary moment. Instead, Lionnet and Shih understand globalization as a single process whereby both of these positions are established simultaneously. In defining transnationalism from below, they situate these dichotomies as the first points where minor/minority subjects challenge traditional understandings of globalization. *The World* recognizes the simultaneity of dominance and resistance by positing the alienating effects of globalization that ultimately lead the film to its conclusion. Two moments in the film, which are sites of trauma for Tao and Taisheng, reveal previously hidden – to the characters, and perhaps viewers as well – effects of globalization. As with the other films examined in this book, these scenes connect global politics to the private lives of individuals and therefore collapse any notion of separation between public and private concerns. This film pushes this facet of political cinema further, however, by also collapsing distinction between national and global socio-economic currents.

In the case of Taisheng, the death of Little Brother reminds him of his own movement from Shanxi to Beijing in search of work. Whereas Taisheng was relatively sheltered from the hardships of this movement having secured a stable, safe job at the Beijing World Park, his childhood friend's experience shows an alternative outcome of this movement, revealing a less salubrious side of migrant labor. In Tao's case, her close relationship with Anna, despite the language barrier, is based upon their similar positions as performers at the Beijing World Park. In this manner, they mirror each other, except that Tao is Chinese and Anna is Russian, and their difference is articulated in the eventual trajectory of their careers. Tao is a lead performer at the Beijing World Park, and she, like Taisheng, seems to enjoy a degree of job security and enjoyment. Anna, on the other hand, is taken advantage of by her handler, who keeps her passport so that she cannot leave the country, and she does not make enough money even to visit her sister in another city. Though Tao and Anna are similar in many respects, ultimately Anna is a victim of human trafficking, a darker aspect of globalization.

In this way, Tao and Taisheng's personal lives are intimately connected with these global politics, which produce conditions that eventually become intolerable for each of them. These events involving their friends depress the mood of the film, which starts out energetic and lighthearted. After Tao finds a text from Qun, a woman Taisheng seems to desire, on Taisheng's phone at their friend's wedding, their relationship dissolves. When Taisheng shows up at an apartment Tao is housesitting, Tao is silent, and after a long take, the film cuts to another long take of their bodies being found, both having succumbed to gas poisoning. While this seems like an unduly pessimistic moment, the film ends with two lines of dialogue. After the screen fades to black, Taisheng asks, "Are we dead?" Tao replies, "No, this is only the beginning." This ending, at odds with the scenes that lead up to it, suggests a forward looking stance, which asks the audience to consider their deaths and other traumas shown in the film as a motivator. It is not insignificant that this was Jia's first film to receive a widespread release in China, and as such, it seems to say: learn from these examples and know that globalization and the resulting new reforms in China affect you intimately, even if it is not immediately apparent. In doing so, the film fragments the idea of a uniform Chinese people and reveals the various manifest and hidden classes that reside within a seemingly prosperous city such as Beijing.

Pre-hodological Narratives, Pre-individuated Subjects, and Contemporary Politics

In an interview with Scott Foundas, Jia describes a label he found on his films that were being illegally distributed on VCD in Beijing. The label reads as a sort of manifesto: "It is our duty to distribute these films to the people" (Jia 2008). This anecdote illustrates the way in which these films reveal something significant about contemporary China. Those who posted this label on these illegally distributed VCDs believe that there is something within that is valuable enough to inspire the audience to take responsibility for their country and their fellow Chinese citizens. Considering the content of Jia's films, this inspiration seems to come from his critique of globalization, economic reforms, and the general increase in consumer-capitalism in China. Despite the critical consciousness these films are purported to inspire, they do not suggest a specific political program that might mitigate such social issues and inequalities in contemporary China. One might question the efficacy of political films that do not suggest a solution. For both Deleuze and Foucault, however, providing a new political program in place of the old carries the same repressive danger in constructing a homogenous psychopolitical space under the banner of ideology.

In a review of Gilbert Simondon's work in 1966, Deleuze begins to develop a political critique of aesthetics in relation to individuation and character choice aligned with a hodological space. Using Simondon, Deleuze argues that narratives have negative ethical and political implications. He argues that individuation is an "act by which an individual cuts him or herself off from the pre-individual reality from which he or she emerged. As a result, the individual is closed in on a singularity, refusing to communicate, and provoking a loss of information" (Deleuze 2004: 89). In other words, individuals suffer from the closing down of possibilities that results from such individuation. Once a subject or character chooses a narrative path, they are no longer open to other possibilities, this initial choice framing subsequent decisions. An example of this individuated subject might be the character that blindly follows or strictly adheres to ideology, because it informs their world-view and decision-making.

Counter to this, pre-hodological narratives depict "an overlapping world of discrete singularities, which overlaps all the more given that the discrete singularities do not yet communicate, or are not yet taken up in an individuality: such is the first moment of being" (Deleuze 2004: 87). In *Xiao Wu*, the pickpocket, the capitalist, and the farmer illustrate different ways of seeing the world, placing the viewer in Simondon's pre-individuated state – admittedly, by drawing critical attention to PRC announcements. This psychological state affords the individual more potential choice and affirms their power to affect the processes by which individuation occurs. Simondon echoes Deleuze's political concern, later arguing for an understanding of individuation that contains "many types of logic" (Simondon 1992: 317). Films such as *Xiao Wu* and *Unknown Pleasures* help viewers to "pluralize logic" and denaturalize ways of being in the world that might otherwise be taken for granted (Simondon 1992: 317).

In *Xiao Wu*, Jia constructs dichotomies between the petty thieves of Fenyang on the one hand, and the more pervasive criminality of global entrepreneurs peddling cigarettes and prostitutes on the other. This relationship between localized individuals and a global elite will similarly be taken up in Chapter Five which addresses immigration in the United States. In *Unknown Pleasures*, characters wander aimlessly, realizing their own futility and purposelessness in the face of their pop-culture icons. When the two protagonists try to take action, breaking free from their lack of sensory-motor schemata and enter into a sensory-motor scenario inspired by their consumption of media, one is arrested and the other is stranded on a sparsely populated highway. In *The World*, populations most susceptible to being taken advantage of by global markets migrate for economic reasons. These migrant peoples face tragedy at every step, and their more successful counterparts witness the plight of their friends first-hand. In turn, their witnessing communicates these social problems to audiences, who may be unaware of these dispossessed migrant laborers – made more relatable to global festival audiences by its communication through the perspective of their middle-class counterparts.

Jia's subsequent films, such as *24 City*, his documentaries, *A Touch of Sin*, and *Mountains May Depart*, dramatize and reveal the effects of globalization and economic reform on specific individuals. In each film, wealth circulates among a small population who grow rich in China. As a mass medium, film has the potential to reach out to a large portion of the population to deliver Jia's subtle critiques of PRC policy and contemporary economic trends. Simultaneously, Jia has maintained his international acclaim, and has continued to push the boundaries of state censors. Earlier I argued that he deftly maneuvered a return to state-sponsored filmmaking in order to reach a wider Chinese audience with his political films. No longer relying on a domestic audience financially, but aware that his films will be seen by a domestic audience regardless, *A Touch of Sin* includes a character that murders corrupt officials after being blocked from legitimate legal recourse. The film's violent realism is a shocking departure from his previous films, though the political statement changes little. Although he submitted the film to the state censor board, and edited it according to their recommendations, the film still did not receive official release in China although it likely reached a domestic audience through back channels of distribution. *A Touch of Sin* evidences the director's savvy in navigating international and domestic markets while maintaining a critical focus on the rapidity with which China has globalized and the inequality that globalization has produced.

Notes

1. This quote, and subsequent quotes with the same citation, are taken from an interview with Jia Zhangke included in the 2002 Artificial Eye release of *Unknown Pleasures*.
2. David Martin-Jones notices a similar trend in *Police Story* (1985) in *Deleuze and World Cinemas*, albeit without the focus on the localized populations. As the film is from 15 years earlier, the specific populations I address here had not quite emerged yet.
3. For more on the funding, see Andrew 2010: 83.

CHAPTER 5

Ramin Bahrani's Fragmented Dreams: Contemporary American Realist Cinema and the Broken Cliché

In this final chapter, I return to the United States where the events that I discussed in the Introduction – the World Trade Organization protests and the Occupy Wall Street movements – began. These signaled the widespread production of political subjectivity in relation to global flows of capital. In other words, both the World Trade Organization and the Occupy protests revealed the intersection of global economic practices with results that these protesters found intolerable, so much so that they took to the streets. This activism revealed the free market's motto of economic prosperity for all as cliché. The United States as the source of these movements should not come as a surprise, considering the significant critical disjunction between portrayals of opportunity in the United States and the reality its citizens face. Although it is a cultural discourse that has existed since the birth of the nation, the term "American Dream" was coined by James Truslow Adams in 1931 and has been used since then to refer to the opportunities in the United States and the expectations of its citizens. This term has become part of American hegemony through its reification in cultural products such as film and television, as well as outside the culture industries in general political discourse, setting expectations for citizens and for immigrants relocating to the United States. In this chapter, I examine films that both capitalize on this ideology within dominant filmic discourses, and others that critique it by addressing global flows through immigration and reveal the American Dream as a bankrupt ideology.

Films from *The Grapes of Wrath* (1940) to *The Pursuit of Happyness* (2006) have used the American Dream as their central motif, perpetuating the idea as an accurate portrayal of reality. The latter film's happy ending and emotional impact depend upon its ability to concretize the American Dream and its ability to elevate an individual beyond difficult economic circumstances if they just work hard enough. In *The American Dream and Contemporary Hollywood Cinema*, J. Emmett Winn illustrates that this general emphasis on "upward mobility" is a larger trend in Hollywood films that reflect this American ideology (Winn 2007). As part of this process, however, *The Pursuit of Happyness* shows spectators that one needs to fit a particular role, take on a proper worldview, and in this way become the correct subject to obtain this success. As a result, I argue that *The Pursuit of Happyness* does not simply suggest that people can succeed if they work hard enough, but that one must succeed by conforming to a particular class. The production of the appropriate neoliberal subject is emphasized through classical patterns of narrative and editing, which construct the causal connections discussed in the introduction of this book that reify the link between hard work and success as a natural or even inevitable progression.

The films of Iranian-American Ramin Bahrani, on the other hand, expose the American Dream as a broken cliché: an unquestioned ideology that precludes a belief in the world and the creative power of change. While Hollywood films have questioned the efficacy of the Dream, such as the films of Elias Kazan discussed later in this chapter, Bahrani's films provide a contemporary critique through their engagement with the global, networked cinematic politics that guide this book. This contemporary American realist cinema critiques glamorous readings of the American Dream by disrupting mainstream cinematic time with a deliberate insistence on blue collar, immigrant labor. A circuitous narrative structure accompanies this focus on precarious labor in Bahrani's early films, which reveal the endless, risk-laden nature of this kind of work in the United States. Considering the economic hardships of the late 2000s in the United States, film critic A. O. Scott has questioned the efficacy of Hollywood as something that can contribute towards productive political positions in a recessionary culture where the American Dream may no longer be a viable goal. Bahrani's films respond to this line of questioning by revealing the American Dream as a chimera. While this may not sound like a useful political position, I argue that Bahrani's critique of the American Dream produces subjects who reinvest themselves with the world once they are able to break away from the regulatory function of the American Dream. These films construct a new, more sustainable subject, marked by their belief in the world. Bahrani's films fundamentally differ from *The Pursuit of Happyness*, then, by avoiding the film's construction of a sensory-motor schemata that unequivocally links hard work to success.

Nation, Immigration, and the American Dream

The ideology of the American Dream, though it manifests in various ways in the films in this chapter, has its roots in the American colonies' Declaration of Independence in 1776. The second sentence of this document reads,

"We hold these truths to be self-evident, that all men are created equal, that they are endowed by their Creator with certain unalienable Rights, that among these are Life, Liberty and the Pursuit of Happiness." Since this declaration, these "unalienable rights" have remained a part of political discourse in the United States, being articulated in different ways to suit various ends. Over time, the pursuit of happiness has taken on more specificity, becoming the American Dream, which is represented by the image of a white-picket fence and 2.5 kids – in other words: home ownership and the nuclear family (GSS 2010, Hanson and Zogby 2010). Despite the manifestation of this historical evolution in *The Pursuit of Happyness*, the original work that gave us the term American Dream contained critical positions that resonate far better with the work of Ramin Bahrani.

William Clark studies the Dream in relation to contemporary immigration in the United States, and identifies three common elements of the American Dream today: obtaining a reasonable income, secure housing, and political freedom (Clark 2003: 6). For Clark, these values point towards the general idea that today the American Dream, at least for immigrants, is the dream of becoming a part of the middle class in the United States. While he acknowledges that "what makes up the middle-class lifestyle has changed over time," he also admits, "Nevertheless, the combination of an income range and ownership encompasses much that we think of as middle class" (Clark 2003: 8). The concept of the middle-class for immigrants, then, tracks fairly closely to the colloquial white-picket fence, which will be reflected in the films discussed in this chapter. This commonplace ideology, however, has its roots in a more political position that is more relevant to today's economic environment in relation to the power of corporations and globalization.

James Truslow Adams coined the phrase American Dream in his manifesto-like epilogue to his work of American history, *The Epic of America* (1931). This work is largely forgotten by those who use the term today, as it contains a critical perspective not found in the modern discourse on the American Dream, which many see as primarily a dream of material success (Hanson and Zogby 2010: 572). Presciently, Adams even critiques modern perspectives of this American ideology. For example, of the worker in relation to rising wages, he argues:

> He is warned that if he does not consume to the limit, instead of indulging in pleasures which do not cost money, he may be deprived not only of his high wages but of any at all. He, like the rest of us, thus appears to be getting into a treadmill in which he earns, not that he may enjoy, but that he may spend, in order that the owners of the factories may grow richer. (Adams 1931: 418)

Later, he reprehends risky investment banking – likely referencing the emerging Great Depression – relevant to our consideration of *The Pursuit of Happyness*, which ties investment banking to the American Dream. Instead of the modern takes on the Dream, there are two driving concerns for Adams's articulation: first, the key difference between America and Europe as a biopolitical question; second, the construction of a public that holds certain values in common, which reads like a move towards Hardt and Negri's concept of Multitude: collaboration between diverse individuals to develop a new political environment.

As a historian who addresses America's independence from Europe in his historical work, it is not surprising that the difference between America and Europe is key for this thinker's conception of American ideology. Adams frames this as a class issue, or biopolitically as a question of opportunity for certain individuals based on race, class, and even age. He gives several anecdotes throughout his epilogue to *The Epic of America* about European immigrants coming to America and being amazed at the potential afforded them. This potential is not just material, however: one of these anecdotes details the story of a laborer who worked for Adams and with whom he would have stimulating intellectual conversations after the day's work was complete. The laborer lamented that back in Europe he would perhaps be given a few kind words after work, but nothing like the real engagement Adams offered. Adams interprets this as an example of how each society handles class:

> the American dream, that dream of a land in which life should be better and richer and fuller for every man, with opportunity for each according to his ability or achievement. It is a difficult dream for the European upper classes to interpret adequately, and too many of us ourselves have grown weary and mistrustful of it. It is not a dream of motor cars and high wages merely, but a dream of a social order in which each man and each woman shall be able to attain to the fullest stature of which they are innately capable, and be recognized by others for what they are, regardless of the fortuitous circumstances of birth or position. (Adams 1931: 415)

For Adams, the focus on societal differences marks America as a unique site of opportunity in the world. Whether or not this is the case, this key part of the discourse is still relevant today, and is useful in understanding why the American Dream is so often a dream of immigration. As an inherent part of this, however, it is also a dream of class mobility, for immigrants and nationals alike. This passage, which seems to be the most often quoted, emerges today as the belief that class mobility is available to anyone if they just work hard enough. Thus, this part of Adams' text coincides most closely with today's American ideology.

Later, however, Adams begins to move in the direction of Multitude as part of his class critique. While shared values among a people alone do not constitute the Multitude (for example, racial nationalists/exclusionary communities likely share values), Adams articulates this concept of shared values among a society of diverse individuals. This begins as a critique of the attempts of corporations and government to lead the people:

> We can look neither to the government nor to the heads of the great corporations to guide us into the paths of a satisfying and humane existence as a great nation unless we, as multitudinous individuals, develop some greatness in our own individual souls. Until countless men and women have decided in their own hearts, through experience and perhaps disillusion, what is a genuinely satisfying life. (Adams 1931: 426–427)

He uses the Library of Congress as a case study for what this should look like:

> As one looks down on the general reading room, which alone contains ten thousand volumes which may be read without even the asking, one sees the seats filled with silent readers, old and young, rich and poor, black and white, the executive and the laborer, the general and the private, the noted scholar and the schoolboy, all reading at their own library provided by their own democracy. It has always seemed to me to be a perfect working out in a concrete example of the American dream – the means provided by the accumulated resources of the people themselves, a public intelligent enough to use them, and men of high distinction, themselves a part of the great democracy, devoting themselves to the good of the whole, uncloistered. (Adams 1931: 426)

What is notable about this example is not just that a diverse population is making use of the resource that is the Library of Congress, but that this resource has been constructed and maintained by this diverse population. This reveals that Adams' original conception of the American Dream was less a meditation on opportunity, material goods, and property as it is generally characterized today. Rather, it is more a meditation on co-operation within the Multitude, including its ability to declare independence from previous systems of value, in this example, that of corporations, by constructing its own system. The original interpretation of the American dream has clearly been forgotten in its current incarnation, but this chapter argues that certain independent filmmakers from the United States return to the earlier version of the dream through their critical attitudes toward its contemporary manifestation.

Defining the American Dream as the achievement of a middle class lifestyle in the United States highlights two populations that are the clear recipients of this dream as a result of their precarious position in American society: certain immigrants moving to the United States and United States citizens below the poverty line. It follows that these populations would feature largely in films that integrate the American Dream into their stories. The *Pursuit of Happyness* approaches the subject of poverty in the United States from the standpoint of a film that uncritically ascribes to and perpetuates the American Dream both as obtainable and as a material objective. This film is an important example in that most of its emotional impact derives from the wish-fulfillment of the American Dream. As a result, the film operates in accord with what T. Kerr has referred to as the "vast amorphous propaganda machine" that perpetuates beliefs in the efficacy of the American Dream (Kerr 1996: 74). It also depicts a process in which an African-American man transitions directly from invisibility and homelessness to a position of stability at a wealthy investment banking firm. Crucial to this film is the idea that its protagonist only needed to work hard enough to transcend the constraints of his class, race, and environment, which is a notion compounded by the causal logic of the film. I then turn to the films of Ramin Bahrani, who focuses on immigrant populations in the United States, fragmenting notions of a homogenous American subject. As works of contemporary American realism, Bahrani's films take us closer to Adams' political aspirations, and suggest a renewed value in Adams' work in contemporary America.

The Pursuit of the Same Happiness

The Pursuit of Happyness follows the story of the real life Chris Gardner, who lived on the streets for a year with his son while participating in an internship at Dean Witter Reynolds, a stock brokerage firm. Gardner previously worked in the medical industry in a variety of roles, but decided to make a career change after talking to a man in a red Ferrari whose material wealth, exemplified by the car, prompted him to ask the man how he made his money. While better depicted in films such as *The Joneses* (2009), this material motivation is important because it illustrates how Gardner's desire for success is not the desire for a unique vision of success, but the same as that of one's neighbor. In the film, Gardner's girlfriend leaves him, taking all of his belongings while he is in jail for unpaid parking tickets. Despite this setback, he succeeds in obtaining and completing a competitive internship with Dean Witter Reynolds, eventually becoming an employee and financially successful. This movement from owning very little to becoming a wealthy individual typifies the perceived potential inherent in the American Dream.

Based on Gardner's story, *The Pursuit of Happyness* follows a similar narrative, but embellishes key points to strengthen the impact of the American Dream as the film's driving ideology. These embellishments, combined with the formal features of the film, contribute to the affective or emotional response the film solicits. The combination of narrative, emotional response, and ideology makes the film a clear example of what Kerr referred to as the propaganda machine that perpetuates the American Dream, which promotes ideology as regulatory biopower. While it would be an overstatement to say that all of Hollywood conforms to this model, the way *The Pursuit of Happyness* does so unproblematically hints at its status as majoritarian and cliché – in other words, the film caters to the desire of viewers to follow this ideology as natural. Furthermore, contrary to Adams's original vision, the film takes the individualism inherent in modern concepts of the American Dream to an extreme through its insistence on conformity and the promotion of an ideal subject much like the promotion of particular subjects in the previous chapters, such as the revolutionary subject in *Battle of Algiers* or the business man Xiao Yong in *Xiao Wu*.

The individualist ethos of *The Pursuit of Happyness* makes it a prime example of Deleuze's concept of the action-image, where causal relationships are clear and provide momentum for the narrative. As I argued in earlier chapters, action-images do not just move the narrative but also tend to restrict the proliferation of identity or the co-presence of different temporalities, histories, and subjectivities. *The Pursuit of Happyness* takes this a step further by placing the struggle in the hands of Gardner alone, as is the custom with Hollywood narratives, rather than in the hands of a numerous but coherent and unified people as in the earlier example of *Battle of Algiers*. As David Martin-Jones argues, such an individualist ethos formally promotes a "linear continuity of spatialised time" (Martin-Jones 2006: 22). The argument Martin-Jones makes regarding the action-image illustrates an important connection between action-images and contemporary conceptions of the American Dream. Action-images are based on clear causal connections and agents who have the ability to directly control their circumstances, while the American Dream includes the belief that an individual can define their future through their hard work, which allows them to create a causal relationship between the present and the future based on their ability to affect their circumstances. This linear relationship between agency and potential success typifies attitudes toward hard work in the United States (Hanson and Zogby 2010: 574; GSS 2010: 573). In this respect, the qualities that Deleuze sees in the action-image are similar to the qualities deemed part of the contemporary American Dream. As a result, it is not surprising that so many popular Hollywood films operate according to this individualist ethos or action-image when it is simultaneously a reflection of popular ideologies.

While the individualist ethos of *The Pursuit of Happyness* sets up a clear narrative teleology for the film – the viewer can be fairly certain that Gardner will triumph in the end – the film also operates according to a particular idea of success. The notion of material accomplishment is created by juxtaposing wealthy businessmen with their poorer counterparts, starting with the encounter between Gardner and the man with a Ferrari. The linear notion of time and causality is established through the narrative in which Gardner struggles and prevails consistently despite numerous setbacks. His continual achievement in face of the setbacks he encounters contributes to the film's affective nature as it plays with the spectators' identification with Gardner, the difficulties he faces, and the eventual joy or relief resulting from his overcoming of these obstacles. For instance, a mentally ill man steals one of his valuable medical imaging devices, and parking tickets accumulate that eventually result in the booting of his car. Throughout these trials, Gardner never questions either his desire for material success or its sustainability. The red Ferrari, the business suit, and the ability to blend in with the white businessmen around the table at Dean Whitter are the consistent goals of the film.

Importantly, the businessmen at Dean Whitter are separated from the more diverse populations in the film that are seen when Gardner is riding the bus or taking his son to daycare. While one could argue that this is problematic in terms of race and gender because the men at Dean Whitter are white, or that it is simply accurate, because successful business people in the 1980s were predominately white men, the film makes it clear that the white businessmen are elevated above the rest of the population in terms of Gardner's desire. Following Hardt and Negri, the film may be making a rather complicated argument about class at this point: that it is a complicated subjective constellation of discourses about material wealth (even brand consciousness), race, gender, and social hierarchies. Even if this is the case, however, the film is clear about its movement, following the trajectory of the American Dream from poor to wealthy as its African-American protagonist ascends from a realm of diversity to that of a particular socio-economic and racial class. As a result, *The Pursuit of Happyness* privileges a particular identity and subject position as appropriate to the American Dream, a departure from Adams' example of diverse individuals working together at the Library of Congress being the greatest achievement of the American Dream.

This notion of subjective conformity plays out from the beginning of the film, as indicated by the misspelling of happiness in the film's title. In the film, Gardner encounters the spelling of happiness with a "y" on the side of the daycare where he takes his son. The daycare is one of the places we see subjects other than the white businessmen and the African-American Gardner. The daycare is run by a family of Chinese-Americans, which the film highlights by having certain members of the family speak only in Chinese, even as Gardner carries on a conversation with them in English. In the face of this potential difference, the film opens after its title sequence and inspirational soundtrack with Gardner addressing a man sweeping up outside the daycare: "Excuse me, when is somebody going to clean this up? And the Y, we talked about this, it's an I, in happiness it's an I. There is no Y in happiness." In this scene, the film reifies its greater teleology: proper spelling, a clear definition of success, and the assumption of the role of the successful subject (one who has more successfully assimilated than these Chinese-Americans in this scene).

The differentiation between subjects carries on throughout the film, such as Gardner's interactions with the mentally ill homeless man who becomes the antagonist of a dichotomy between success and the lack of it. The homeless man is a constant threat to Gardner, not just because the man steals his medical imaging machine, but also a reminder of what Gardner might become should he fail at his internship. As a concrete representation of failure in the film, the homeless man further delineates the direction of Gardner's goal by playing upon stereotyped representations of the homeless as mentally ill (and completely other). In creating a linear movement where Gardner extricates himself from poverty, the film illustrates the reductive nature of the individualist American Dream despite its simultaneous alignment of success with whiteness. His goal not only includes becoming materially wealthy, but also avoiding the threat of the precarious other, marked out biopolitically in the film either racially or through illness.

In operating according to the sensory-motor schema in both form and ideology, *The Pursuit of Happyness* presents a notion of the American Dream quite different from its original incarnation in 1931. Most prominently, what was once a dream about the potential of co-operation and the opportunities for diverse individuals has become the dream of transcending diversity to assume a privileged role in this film. In this operation, *The Pursuit of Happyness* illustrates the way in which such an ideology might result in the consolidation of an idealized subjectivity. Kerr would no doubt agree, as the purpose of a propaganda machine can only be the spread of ideas, attitudes, and subjectivities benefiting a particular class of people, despite the author's larger desire in his work to re-envision the American Dream as a productive force (Kerr 1996).

The consolidation of subjectivity is important to understanding the difference between past and present versions of the American Dream in its appeal to the under-privileged and immigrants. A consolidated subjectivity achieves something akin to what Max Horkheimer and Theodor Adorno see as mass alienation in response to the culture industry. The authors explain that the culture industry operates as a distraction through laughter and desire, and as a result alienates people from their own suffering (Adorno 2002: 110). Whereas immigrants and the under-privileged might focus on a sustainable life style, they instead put their faith in hard work and its causal relationship with economic prosperity, which in reality does not necessarily guarantee the dreams they aspire to. In fact, the remarkable nature of Chris Gardner's story suggests that more often than not, hard work does not lead to success like his. In this respect, the film operates biopolitically in promoting a particular way of life, which takes on a regulatory dimension considering the collective ways of living or community-building this film eschews. While it would be difficult to call this an example of political cinema, it is a film that contributes to problematic ideologies that contemporary political cinemas critique.

The Broken Cliché in Contemporary American Realist Cinema

In turning to films that critique the ideological function associated with the American Dream, I look to contemporary American realist cinema, which presents it as a broken cliché. Contemporary American realist cinema returns to questions posed by Adorno and Horkheimer in relation to the culture industry, which I take up in the Introduction to this book. As I argued in the Introduction, the culture industry is a useful way to understand Deleuze's concept of cliché within his cinematic politics. Deleuze turns to this problem of cliché when he asks what happens when the methods of Hitchcock, Eisenstein, and Gance are taken up by mediocre directors. He responds: "When grandeur is no longer that of the composition, but a pure and simple inflation of the represented, there is no cerebral stimulation or birth of thought. It is rather a generalized shortcoming in author and viewers" (Deleuze 1989: 164). Deleuze extends his critique by arguing that "mass-art . . . has degenerated into state propaganda and manipulation, into a kind of fascism which brought together Hitler and Hollywood, Hollywood and Hitler" (Deleuze 1989: 164). Deleuze's argument borrows from Adorno in drawing a connection between Hitler and

RAMIN BAHRANI'S FRAGMENTED DREAMS   147

Hollywood in how they control the production of subjects. In this comparison, Deleuze makes a strikingly pro-filmic argument when he names
viewers as part of the ideological equation: it isn't just about directors
making boring films, it is about boring films making boring people, or
subjects locked into a particular ideology. It is this strict repetition that
is intolerable or, as Anna Backman Rogers puts it: "It is this exposure of
meaninglessness at the heart of supposedly meaningful human activity
that is 'intolerable and unbearable'" (Rogers 2011: 4). Through their realist approach and emphasis on labor, Ramin Bahrani's early films critique
the American Dream as an intolerable cliché.

It is important to note a distinction I make in referring to Bahrani's
films as 'contemporary' American realist cinema. Deleuze discusses
American realism in relation to the American Dream at length in *Cinema 1*
as being a key example of the action-image. He describes the "model which
produced the universal triumph of American cinema" as: "Affects and
impulses now only appear as embodied in behavior, in the form of emotions
or passions which order and disorder it. This is Realism . . . On this level, it
does not exclude fiction or even the dream. It can include the fantastic, the
extraordinary, the heroic and above all melodrama" (Deleuze 1986: 141).
What is necessary, rather, is that linear time and causality are embodied
within actors who react, even if only emotionally, to the challenges the film
presents. Elias Kazan, through founding the Actors Studio with its emphasis on method acting, presents the limit of this embodied realism, wherein
"the American Dream and the action-image grow tougher together. The
American Dream is affirmed more to be a dream, nothing more than a
dream, contradicted by the facts; but it draws from this a sudden burst
of increased power since it now encompasses actions such as betrayal and
calumny" (Deleuze 1986: 157). In other words, Kazan's cinema is not so
much a critique of the American Dream, but a more powerful realization of
it because Kazan's films rely less on historical conditions, which Deleuze
associates with Eisenstein's films, and instead on embodied behaviors, emotions, and affect. As Richard Rushton argues, this is particularly stressed
in the post-War period with the onset of the crisis of the action-image:
"For Kazan, according to Deleuze, this ethical battle is nothing less than
the battle for the American dream, a dream which becomes more and more
difficult to uphold over the war, but which Kazan's films . . . work cease-
lessly to reaffirm" (Bettinson and Rushton 2010: 118). Rushton develops
his reading of Kazan further in *Cinema After Deleuze*, where he argues
that Kazan's characters must find themselves in relation to an established
and hegemonic ideology, "characters are at the mercy of that American
vision [and must] try to find their place within it" (Rushton 2012: 39).

This sense of a classical American realism differs from the contemporary American realism of Bahrani in that the latter refuses to posit the American dream as a naturalized ideology, and instead frames it as cliché.

The political concern for Deleuze, in relation to cliché and the culture industry, is how to promote what he calls a belief in the world, which encourages individuals to think in terms of possibility rather than repetition. In a similar vein, Ronald Bogue postulates the political response to intolerable realities: "The only viable response to the intolerable is to think differently, to disconnect the world's networks of certainties and pieties and formulate new problems that engender as yet unmapped relations and connections" (Bogue 2010: 122). In other words, it is necessary to have a belief in the immanent or existential possibilities inherent in one's immediate experience. Because the question of belief in the world involves breaking away from the reliance on cliché, Bogue suggests that film must construct a line of flight by no longer relying on the usual ways of thinking and the usual subjects of representation.

Offering a potential method of moving away from a reliance on cliché, D. N. Rodowick argues that the answer to Deleuze's challenge of belief is not through simply formulating new problems by revealing the clichés at work, however, but working through "an anticipatory time—of contingency, the purely conditional, the nondetermined or not yet" (Rodowick 2010: 109). When the action, story, plot, or linearity of a film breaks down, Rodowick explains, the character of the seer emerges in cinema, and "the seer . . . alienated both within herself and from the world . . . sees farther, better, and deeper than she can react or think" (Rodowick 2010: 110). As a result, the figure of the seer does not take the automatic or clichéd narrative path, but instead engages in thought – that is, the production of new connections between subjects and their environments. For Julian Reid the ultimate political potential of Deleuze's cinematic thought lies in the possibility of "our becoming seers" alongside these characters on screen, because the seer has the potential to witness what is intolerable and unbearable in life (Reid 2011: 231). In other words, there is something about certain films, for Reid, post-War films in particular, which have a pro-filmic effect on spectators that allows them to see clichés as intolerable.

A. O. Scott identifies a similar function of cinema in what he dubs "Neo-Neo-Realism" (Scott 2009). Scott's Neo-Neo-Realist canon includes films by Ramin Bahrani, Ryan Fleck, David Gordon Green, So Yong Kim, Jim McKay, and Kelly Reichardt. Scott's article in the *New York Times* drew critical attention for the claims it made regarding the glossy nature of Hollywood in light of the real hardships of the post-9/11 world (Brody

2009 and Rowin 2009). Especially inflammatory was his question 'What kind of movies do we need now?' Scott follows this by arguing:

> It's a question that seems to arise almost automatically in times of crisis. It was repeatedly posed in the swirl of post-9/11 anxiety and confusion, and the consensus answer, at least among studio executives and the entertainment journalists who transcribe their insights, was that, in the wake of such unimaginable horror, we needed fantasy, comedy, heroism. (Scott 2009)

Scott's argument reflects the general concerns of the Frankfurt School, and perhaps unsurprisingly so, if contemporary political cinema returns to such a theoretical framework. Addressing reasons why *Wendy and Lucy* (2008) would never be considered for an Oscar, while *Slumdog Millionaire* (2008) won Best Picture, Scott points out that despite both films focusing on economic hardship, "in its story and in its exuberant, sentimental spirit, [*Slumdog Millionaire* is about] the magical power of popular culture to conquer misery, to make dreams come true. And the major function of Oscar night is to affirm that gauzy, enchanting notion" (Scott 2009). In other words, the Oscars ceremony perpetuates/affirms majoritarian values. Scott's statement could fit *The Pursuit of Happyness* just as easily as *Slumdog Millionaire*. Scott counters this function of Hollywood media, answering his own question regarding what movies we need, by suggesting, "it would be worth considering that what we need from movies, in the face of a dismaying and confusing real world, is realism" (Scott 2009). Where Scott identifies realism, he includes the avoidance of particular Hollywood clichés that perpetuate ideologies such as the American Dream. If Scott identifies a type of political cinema appropriate to recessionary America, Deleuze's cinematic framework adds philosophical gravitas to this contemporary political discussion with his focus on sensory-motor connections and their disruption.

Bahrani acknowledges this intersection between contemporary American attitudes and a sensory-motor schemata that privileges certain ideologies. Responding to a question regarding the seeming lack of clear endings in his films, Bahrani explains, "moral endings aren't true to life since life has no intrinsic morality. If you look at Persian poetry, it has an acceptance of life as it is. That's disturbing to most American viewers and you don't find it much in American movies. I find the opposite disturbing" (Porton 2008). Instead of ending his films with clichéd narrative closure, Bahrani leaves his films relatively open ended, a style he borrows from Kiarostami and other Iranian directors. While there is something evocative of Iranian cinema in Bahrani's use of narrative form, such a case could be made for most of the Neo-Neo-Realist films Scott names, and this discussion of endings is only one example of Bahrani's treatment of cinematic time wherein the sensory-motor schemata breaks down. While the characters of contemporary American realist films are often motivated to move towards a particular goal, that goal is never actually realized, unlike in *The Pursuit of Happyness*, where Gardner finally secures his fortune. In doing so, contemporary American realist cinema creates the anticipatory time Rodowick refers to, the non-determined or not yet, and shifts focus from the goals of his characters to their basic realities and experiences.

The focus on the everyday lives of Americans, without the injection of Hollywood glamor and grand narratives, promotes the creation of subjects with a belief in the world that allows them to critique the intolerability of the American Dream as an empty cliché. Elsewhere, Bahrani has said that what Scott calls Hollywood wish-fulfillment tales "create massive confusion" (Scott 2009). To combat this confusion, Bahrani's films revel in the tangible interactions, gestures, and feelings of characters from moment to moment. These films do not construct a belief in the world just because they seem true to life, however, but because their characters have an immanent relation with the worlds they inhabit. In other words, they are not able to transcend their milieu, as Gardner does, but instead must react and exist within it. The immanent relationship these characters have with their worlds forces them toward the position of the seer, returning to Reid's argument, and helps to politicize spectators.

The seers of contemporary American realist films are different from those Deleuze first identifies in the post-War period. Not only do they come from quite different circumstances, the seers in Bahrani's films are not purely products of the time-image as Deleuze originally argued. David Martin-Jones has similarly appropriated the concept of the seer to understand the role a child plays in the Argentinian film *Kamchatka* (2002), arguing that this change in context requires a new understanding that goes beyond Deleuze's movement- and time-image categories (Martin-Jones 2011: 70). Whereas Martin-Jones focuses on the child seer's ability to present history cinematically, the seers I refer to are more invested in disconnecting networks of certainties, as Bogue argues, through their powers of vision. Reid clarifies this idea in his juxtaposition of the classical concept of the seer with this contemporary usage:

> Classically, within theater, the seer was conceived and portrayed in his or her exceptionality . . . a highly particular power to whom a people turned at moments of crisis, giving them direction with which to recover their bearings, in order to resume the journey on which they would eventually secure their truths. What modern cinema does, however, is to democratize the seer by depicting him or her in everyday life while also laying stress on the quotidian and fugitive experience of "seeing" within postwar societies. (Reid 2011: 228)

Reid's distinction between types of seers helps to differentiate between a classical politics and a contemporary one. The classical seer served a didactic function: it taught a people what to do or how to be. The contemporary seer does not teach or act, but witnesses as a see-er, one who sees. Similarly, the characters in contemporary American realist films often witness rather than act as agents, and in doing so recognize something in contemporary society that subjects operating according to sensory-motor schemas do not.

Such characters exist in an immanent relationship with their environments, creating a more intimate linkage with their surroundings – the settings, the mise-en-scène, and other characters – than is possible in either the action-image with its focus on causal connections or the purely optical-image with its complete lack of causal connections. This difference is important to the political potential of seeing in the context of constructing a belief in the world. These seers construct a belief in an immanent causality rather than a transcendental one, and this has the potential to inspire a belief in people's ability to act and choose realistically rather than according to ideology. Bahrani's films in particular illustrate how seer-like figures encounter the American Dream as a broken cliché, and in doing so begin a transition, as biopolitical production, from active agents to seers that reveal the falsities of clichés.

Man Push Cart: Sisyphean Time and the American Dream

An Iranian-American educated at Columbia University, Ramin Bahrani travelled to Iran to complete his thesis project *Strangers* (2000). This point has often been used by critics to suggest something Iranian about the style of his films (Kauffman 2008 and 2009; Porton 2008; Sandhu 2009). Despite this stylistic influence, his first three feature films – *Man Push Cart* (2005), *Chop Shop* (2007), and *Goodbye Solo* (2008) – focus on resolutely American issues, including particular locales in the United States, immigration in the United States, and the American Dream. Bahrani focuses on diverse communities of individuals or relationships between subjects with drastically different backgrounds, whether in race, class, or nationality. In particular, Bahrani has a preoccupation with the day-to-day experiences and labor of these individuals: *Man Push Cart* follows the push cart vendors of New York City, *Chop Shop* explores the Iron Triangle and the mechanics who work there, and *Goodbye Solo* probes the life of a taxi driver in North Carolina. Focusing on quotidian lives and environments helps Bahrani reveal the sociopolitical layers immanent to the subjects he depicts. In doing so, Bahrani's posits a different relationship with the American Dream by framing it as untenable, and in turn reveals the role of particular communities with diverse demographics, neighborhoods and their locations/environments, and forms of labor in relation to the production of political subjectivity.

Ramin Bahrani's *Man Push Cart* details the life of a Pakistani immigrant as he goes about his daily life as a pushcart vendor one year after his wife's death. Bahrani cites Albert Camus' adaptation the Myth of Sisyphus as a "key inspiration to the creation of *Man Push Cart*," which is reflected in repeated scenes of main character Ahmad laboriously moving his cart into place (Bahrani 2005). In addition to the visual depiction of Ahmad's labor, this inspiration also plays out in the narrative of the film as Ahmad works toward the dream of owning his own pushcart – a dream that is dashed when his newly purchased cart is stolen. While a romantic encounter with a woman named Noemi takes up a nominal amount of *Man Push Cart*'s narrative, the film's primary focus is on immigration and class difference in New York City. Ahmad, once a rock star in Pakistan, encounters a score of other Pakistani immigrants working in New York, but they exist in vastly different socio-economic circumstances. Some are other pushcart vendors like Ahmad, but others are successful businessmen, like Mohammad, whom Ahmad encounters early on in the film.

The distinction between these characters illustrates Zygmunt Bauman's concept of localization within globalization, discussed in the Introduction to this book. Bauman argues that "Globalization divides as much as it unites; it divides as it unites – the causes of division being identical with those which promote the uniformity of the globe" (Bauman 1998: 2). He later explains that this is a "predicament neither pleasurable nor endurable in the world in which the 'globals' set the tone and compose the rules of the life-game" (Bauman 1998: 2). In other words, the effects of localization are intolerable to the individuals that experience them, even as they are naturalized or taken for granted by others. While Bauman refers to larger global processes and the movement of capital, Ahmad's relationship with Mohammad provides an instantiation of this division within a population as it moves globally through the establishment and maintenance of class hierarchies. As the film focuses on Ahmad's personal experience, it collapses the distinction between private and political concerns regarding the formation of subjects within global movements of capital.

Ahmad and Mohammad realize that before coming to New York, they once ran in the same social circles in Pakistan. Mohammad recollects an instance where he attended a party, and Ahmad was the famous musician playing at the party. In Pakistan, Ahmad enjoyed a degree of fame and financial success, as evidenced by the fact that Mohammad and his friends own Ahmad's compact discs. He gave up this career, however, to move to the United States for the sake of his wife, although the details of his decision are not made specific in the film. While the film does not fully reveal Ahmad's motivations, it is clear that this move required him to give up his career and earn a living however he could. In his new country, Ahmad finds work as a pushcart vendor, and a brief flashback shows Ahmad and his wife working happily at their pushcart with their new child. After a few years his wife dies, another instance where the director omits an explanation. Ahmad is left to work the pushcart alone, and Bauman's construct of localization as intolerable is illustrated in Ahmad's lack of socio-economic mobility.

Although Mohammad and his wealthy Pakistani friends promise to help restart Ahmad's music career, these friends treat Ahmad like a day laborer. They ask him to paint their houses and man the ticket booths to their clubs. Ahmad initially welcomes the work, an alternative to his other side job of selling pornographic DVDs to other workers in New York City. As Bauman suggests, however, "Being local in a globalized world is a sign of social deprivation and degradation" (Bauman 1998: 2). Eventually, Ahmad grows weary of the hierarchical relationship that divides him from the successful Pakistani immigrants, and ceases to work for them. Instead, he returns to his pushcart, which Ahmad appears to perceive as more respectable in that Ahmad works to own his pushcart and is his own boss. The director reminds us, however, that this work is a Sisyphean effort in the sense that he works off the cost of the pushcart slowly each day without any discernable progress, which visually plays out as the film repeats shots of Ahmad moving his cart through the streets of New York. These scenes operate as a critique of the American Dream by denying the breakthrough success seen in *The Pursuit of Happyness*, despite Ahmad's hard work.

The sequences of Ahmad pulling his cart into place hold the film together, occurring approximately every ten minutes during the ninety-minute film. They consist of artistically framed pre-dawn shots of Ahmad moving his cart through traffic on his way to set up shop for the day. Often these sequences follow into the morning light as Ahmad preps his bagels and cups for tea. Individual shots emphasize the labor itself through the use of extreme close-ups: a hand lighting a burner, cups being placed atop the coffee machine, two hands folding down the sides of a coffee filter, and donuts being placed inside a display window. In one of these sequences from the beginning of the film, Ahmad himself is shown only in fragments. The close-ups and glimpses at parts of Ahmad – his hands, the back of his head, one of his eyes through a display case – illustrate the

Figure 5.1 *Man Push Cart* (2005).

cramped nature of the pushcart, but also diffuse Ahmad within his work. Through this editing and cinematography, the images produced resonate with Fordist principles of manufacturing, and though the context is quite different, they also resonate with Marxist critiques of the alienated factory worker. In this way, the film suggests we cannot understand Ahmad as a subject in his social and psychological milieus separate from his labor. As is true of contemporary American realist cinema in general, these moments focus on quotidian experiences at length.

By repeating the action of Ahmad pulling his cart into place throughout the film, *Man Push Cart* presents this work as a Sisyphean effort, a monotonous physical task that is repeated indefinitely, and through the camera's deliberate focus on Ahmad pulling the cart, the film shifts attention from narrative progression to the labor itself. The poetic realism of the film's focus on these minute details subtly returns to the film's larger political argument regarding nation and immigration. Ahmad eventually mentions that he is saving up for a new apartment, so that he can live with his son who is currently being taken care of by his in-laws – an attempt to create the stability, shelter, and security promised by the American Dream for what remains of his family. Furthermore, the details, gestures, and labor this film depicts in detail are invisible to the people who buy products from Ahmad, as they take place well before the sun rises and the 9–5 occupants of New York City emerge to purchase their coffees and breakfasts. As one customer tells Ahmad late in the film, arriving before Ahmad has fully set up shop, "I'm usually not up this early." Through its long tracking shots of

Ahmad pushing the cart and close ups of his hands prepping food and cups of tea, the film dwells on an existential register, but the politically evocative quality of *Man Push Cart* can be found in the way it reveals Ahmad's personal desires behind this daily work. As Steven Shaviro argues, global neoliberalism "does not provide an alibi for exploiting workers, so much as it positively works to make the status of the worker, and the process of labor-as-exploitation, literally *unthinkable*" (Shaviro 2011: 79). Bahrani reverses this argument, however, in making labor tangible to viewers. It is not just that Ahmad and the pushcart vendors go through this Sisyphean effort daily, but that this effort reveals the previously unknowable other as full of history, life, dreams, and desires.

While sharing the similarity of a protagonist attempting to provide security for his son, unlike *The Pursuit of Happyness*, *Man Push Cart* ends on a tragic note. Ahmad's cart, which he has just paid off and now owns, is stolen while he buys a toy flute for his son. Lengthier shots than even those of his morning labor track Ahmad as he searches amidst the crowds of New York for his cart. While the action seems frenetic, the deliberate focus of the camera on the failure of the search slows it through the use of long takes. The film asks the spectator to witness Ahmad's loss and desperation for more than five minutes while he looks for his cart. Finally, Ahmad goes to Mohammad to ask for a loan. Without his cart, he cannot work, and he needs five-thousand dollars. Mohammad, however, keeps their hierarchical relationship intact, refusing a loan and berating him for his work on Mohammad's home. Though he keeps up the pretense that Ahmad is a "brother," ultimately the film reinforces Bauman's argument that the wealthy compose the rules of the life-game. Without the ability to work, Ahmad loiters on the street until a friend comes by with car trouble. He asks Ahmad to work his pushcart for him while he takes care of his car, and Ahmad agrees. The film ends mirroring the opening scenes and many quotidian moments throughout the film, with Ahmad setting up shop for the day.

The Sisyphean time presented by the film frames the entirety of its narrative within its circular structure, in addition to the slow and repetitive shots of labor visually depicted on screen. While the theft of his pushcart might seem to mirror the theft of the bike in *Bicycle Thieves* (1948), there is a sense in this older film that Antonio might transcend his economic circumstances if he retrieves his bike, but Bahrani's film argues something different about contemporary America: that for this class the labor is endless; it is not just that Ahmad has somehow missed his opportunity. As soon as Ahmad gets a chance at breaking the Sisyphean cycle and achieving his version of the American Dream by owning his own cart, this opportunity is revealed as unattainable, and he returns to the end-less labor that Bahrani shows us in detail repeatedly throughout the film. In relation to the global flows of people and money in the film, Ahmad returns to his localized existence, where the life of the pushcart vendor defines his daily experience and there seems little chance of upward mobility. While the film works on an ethical register, by arguing that this pushcart vendor is a fully-developed person in his own right rather than a nameless figure, it also works in a more political arena in this conclusion. The film becomes political by enforcing Bauman's critique and revealing the American Dream as an intolerable and broken cliché. The film argues, contrary to the majoritarian discourse surrounding the Dream, that no matter how hard this population works, there is a natural division that imprisons portions of this population in a Sisyphean stasis: even with endless labor there is little hope that they will move beyond their current circumstances.

Ahmad's lack of mobility – a hallmark of Bahrani's cinematic oeuvre that could be extended to his other films – works to both counter the ide-ology of the American Dream and to set up Ahmad as a seer-like figure. On the level of the narrative, *Man Push Cart* makes a clear statement regard-ing the efficacy of the American Dream. Just as Ahmad is about to realize his American Dream – not the glossy dream of fancy cars in *The Pursuit of Happyness*, but at least the more majoritarian American Dream Clark identifies in *Immigrants and the American Dream* – he loses everything he has worked for when someone steals his cart. The fact that bad luck strips Ahmad of his dream in an instant resonates with the current state of affairs in the United States, where a single trip to the hospital can drain one's life savings and plunge one into debt, because of the lack of public health care and a social safety net. Financial security is core to the American Dream Clark identifies in immigrant populations (Clark 2003: 24, 26), but as *Man Push Cart* illustrates, while attempting to achieve this stability, even when making progress, individuals are still susceptible to situations that can force them back to step one. Moreover, achieving the level of financial stability required for a secure, middle class lifestyle is doubly difficult to attain from the position of Ahmad. Due to their precarious existence, the material progress of immigrants in the United States is subject to a type of stuttering that plays out cinematically in *Man Push Cart*.

The depletion of Ahmad's savings and his return to the beginning of his quest for the American Dream not only shakes up Ahmad's life-plan in the narrative of *Man Push Cart*, but also plays out through the repet-itive scenes that make up Ahmad's Sisyphean task. Unlike Gardner, who constantly overcomes the obstacles he faces, Ahmad is constantly unable to act or react effectively to the situations he faces. This is particularly noticeable in the differences between Ahmad and his more successful friend Mohammad. Ahmad constantly downplays the fact that he was a rock star in Pakistan, whereas Mohammad tries to emphasize it to his advantage, at times speaking for Ahmad. After effacing his history as a rock star by responding to Mohammad's claims, "He's kidding," at a party, another successful Pakistani tells him to "Own it." Acting and achieving are the modes of these characters, but in contrast to the outspoken self-aggrandizement of the other characters, Ahmad mostly mumbles his lines throughout the film, which echoes his ineffectual response to the challenges he faces. Towards the end of the film, this stuttering is emphasized when Ahmad actually stumbles in one of the scenes where he is pulling his cart into place. As a result of this constant faltering in speech and action, Ahmad is unable to do much more than observe what goes on around him. This facet of his character is so extreme that he lets Mohammad ask Noemi on dates right in front of him despite their burgeoning romance. *Man Push Cart* makes the claim that these qualities of Ahmad's subjectivity alternately reinforce or are reinforced by his marginal status as an immigrant who is not able to achieve the Dream, and if this is the case it suggests a particular feature of the class of subjects within the United States who are economically insecure. If seer-like characters also engender the potential of our becoming-seers as Reid puts it, Ahmad's status and the cinematic presentation of this status has the potential to reveal to the spectator a new way of seeing the economic precariousness pervasive in the United States, should they not already be experiencing it firsthand.

This cinematic stuttering in all its iterations ruptures the sensory-motor schema that defines majoritarian cinematic time. This strategy presents a rupture in the clear narrative progression of the film and opens it up to potential readings that allow for new political speech in relation to the film's precarious subjects. Simon O'Sullivan argues that the rupture in straightforward narratives,

> gives such art a utopian function inasmuch as part of its being is somehow located elsewhere. Importantly, and following Deleuze, and Deleuze and Guattari, we can understand this as a specifically immanent utopia – intrinsically connected to the present, made out of the same materials, the same matter (after all what else is there?) but calling 'for a future form, for a new earth and people that do not yet exist.' (O'Sullivan 2009: 248)

Through its entangling of subjects and socio-economic circumstances, *Man Push Cart* certainly engenders an immanent political community, but this does not otherwise necessitate the utopian nature of thinking. Instead, through stressing daily experience and labor, *Man Push Cart* moves towards the emergence of the Multitude by developing a collective enunciation that speaks to a diverse population. The co-operation and mutual support of the diverse populations comprising the street-food scene of New York with its multiple languages and different histories work with the film's formal organization to construct a Multitude alongside the rupture of cliché cinematic modes.

The impractical and unattainable American Dream in *Man Push Cart* points directly to the class divide that Ahmad finds intolerable in the film. After Ahmad's cart is stolen, he turns to Mohammad in desperation, because of his earlier profession of good will and brotherhood between the two. Mohammad rejects Ahmad's request for money to keep his business going, however, and aggressively demands that Ahmad leave his apartment. Ahmad finally lashes out, knocking Mohammad on the ground. The violence is minor and does not resolve the situation, but rather marks the point in the film where Ahmad fully realizes the intolerability of his economic insecurity, the fruitlessness of his hard work, and falsity of his American Dream. Realizing the infeasibility of the Dream in relation to the class difference engendered in Ahmad and Mohammad's global movements allows Ahmad (and by implication, the viewers) to turn to a more active approach to the world that does not rely on this majoritarian ideology. While the film ends on a relatively mournful note, with Ahmad once more repetitively working at a pushcart, there is a sense that this is a repetition with a difference: when asked by a customer if he'll be filling in for his friend for a while, he responds, "Yeah, only for a little while," suggesting new horizons unstymied by the Dream that structured the previous repetition in the film. This reading is encouraged in light of Bahrani's next film, *Chop Shop*, where Ahmad appears again in a new role, having left the pushcart scene.

Chop Shop and Realist Immanence

Chop Shop charts the experience of a young boy named Ale as he takes a job at Willets Point, or the Iron Triangle, in New York and pursues his dream of buying a food truck so that he and his sister can work together. The Iron Triangle earned its name from the many junkyards and automobile repair shops that have moved into the area, establishing it as a unique destination for automobile repairs. As depicted in the film, individuals in need of car repairs can travel to Willets Point for a one-stop shopping experience, as there are many repair garages sitting side-by-side with various auto parts. Willets Point is off the grid, so much so that it has been refused infrastructural improvements to streets and sewers in the past, and customers can haggle with the owners of the repair shops, no doubt making it a much more affordable option than auto shops elsewhere in the city. As a result of its existence more or less outside the protection of the law, Willets Point also attracts questionable business practices. *Chop Shop* addresses prostitution, the stripping of stolen cars, and child labor. The setting and what appears to be a separation from normal conditions for citizens of the United States marks the Willets Point of *Chop Shop* as an area with a very different economic discourse. In spite of its gray-market position, this discourse is not altogether un-American, however: the complete disavowal of government, law, and thriving of free market relations also makes Willets Point a bastion of uncompromised neoliberalism. Despite his surroundings, Ale stands out like a beacon of optimism or the last vestige of the American Dream in this place. In this respect, the narrative of *Chop Shop* closely follows that of *Man Push Cart*, with Ale saving the money he earns and stashing it in a secret savings tin. However, also like *Man Push Cart*, Ale's dreams are dashed just as it seems he is about to achieve the goal of owning his own food truck. The final shattering of Ale's dream is the last step in a process that has broken down Ale's childlike naiveté throughout the film. In doing so, the film actively works to replace transcendent aspirations and dreams with an immanent realism that Ale cannot avoid as a localized subject.

The film begins with an homage to Kiarostami's *Taste of Cherry*, as Ale waits with a group of day-laborers trying to get picked up for some work. The difference between *Taste of Cherry* and *Chop Shop* is important in this instance, however, in that Ale is the subject of the film, a laborer himself, rather than the wealthy protagonist of Kiarostami's film. Ale is not picked for work despite his vocal desire for a job, so he stows away in the back of the foreman's truck anyway. The foreman eventually catches Ale and kicks him out, giving him some money for breakfast. In the next scene, we find Ale and his friend selling candy on the subway, as Ale gives his speech: "Excuse me ladies and gentlemen sorry for the interruption, my name is Alejandro, we are not going to lie to you, we are not here selling candy for no school basketball team, in fact I don't even go to school and if you want me to go back to school I have candy for you." Similar to the repetition in *Man Push Cart*, this sequence begins to repeat shortly after it concludes. These scenes illustrate Ale's ingenuity in navigating the capitalist environment, even though he lives outside mainstream channels of labor and pay. They also illustrate his desire to work hard, a point that is reiterated when his friend connects him with a shop owner in the Iron Triangle.

Throughout the film, Rob, Ale's boss in the Iron Triangle, respects Ale's work ethic, emphasizing this film's approach to the contemporary American Dream. In addition to working for Rob, Ale finds various other ways to make money in the film such as working for Ahmad, the same character from *Man Push Cart*, who now owns a shop in the area. Because Rob provides Ale with a small apartment in his shop, he invites his sister Isamar to come live with him. That he is able to provide a home for his sister and, he thinks, a relatively secure situation resonates with Clark's middle class dream. After moving in, Isamar also begins working in the Iron Triangle at a food truck. Ale and Isamar's life seems good, and there are scenes where Ale and Isamar go shopping and buy expensive sneakers, a sign of relative financial success. Up until this point, the film has documented the unique community of the Iron Triangle and Ale's pursuit of the American Dream, but the narrative begins to break down when Ale discovers that his sister has been working as a prostitute at a truck stop nearby. It turns out that their relative security, the ability to buy nice clothes and grape soda, is built upon Isamar's prostitution. Ale's idealism is further compromised when, upon finally purchasing the food truck he has been saving for, Ahmad explains that it will never pass a health code inspection. This penultimate event in the film simultaneously breaks down Ale's ability to blindly follow the American Dream and the notion that the Iron Triangle is a neoliberal paradise.

Figure 5.2 *Chop Shop* (2007).

When Ale shows his new food truck to Ahmad, the following conversation takes place:

> Ahmad: Ale are you stupid or something?
> Ale: What?
> Ahmad: Look inside this place man, all of this stuff has got to pass health code.
> Ale: They don't do a health code around here. They don't even care about it.
> Ahmad: Ale man, look at this grill, okay, it has rust on it. Of course it does.
> Ale: So what?
> Ahmad: It says it right here, did you even read this? [referring to bill of sale]

Earlier in the film Isamar points out that Ale has never gone to school. It is likely that he does not know how to read, a product of the supposed freedom from government intervention Ale raises when he says "they don't do health code around here." As Ahmad points out, however, regardless of whether or not the truck must pass a health code, the truck is still in no shape to operate a business out of. He explains, "You're going to spend $10,000 to fix that [buying new kitchen equipment] . . . I used to have one of these," in a nod to *Man Push Cart*. At this point in the film, the previously industrious Ale now makes a number of abortive gestures to solve his problems, and the narrative begins to stutter. He attacks his friend who introduced him to the man that sold him the food truck, but his friend has no idea what is happening and the fight dissolves soon after it starts. He plays around in the defunct food truck, shifting the gears that clearly do not work. He fails to respond to the several solutions that Ahmad offers, even after Ahmad reiterates, "let me know what you want to do." When Rob confronts him about the poorly managed purchase, he dumbly responds, "Can I have my pay?" The request is oddly not connected to any causal situation, almost as if Ale did not even hear Rob's questions about the van, and it is quickly rejected.

Whereas his previous connection to the American Dream structured his relationship with work by forming a clear trajectory from his present labors to a successful future, Ale's empty actions in this sequence illustrate the destabilization of the causal connection that informs the ideology of this film. Previously a smooth talker, Ale's response to questions concerning the worthlessness of his cart is a vacant gaze and illustrates a shift in his subjectivity. After once more wandering around his defunct truck, he heads to the nearby stadium where he steals a woman's purse. He succeeds at this action resulting from his spiral into desperation, but everyone he approaches refuses to buy the pilfered phone he finds in the purse – eventually, he tosses the useless object back in with his stash of unsold bootleg DVDs. When Isamar asks Ale why he's trying to sell the phone, he says, "I'm working. You should be working too." This veiled reference to her prostitution reveals Ale's disenchantment with his previous idealism. He obliquely acknowledges that Isamar has been prostituting herself, and also seems to finally see what is going on around him. In other words, he enters the position of the seer who "sees farther, better, and deeper than she can react or think," as Rodowick puts it (Rodowick 2010: 110). Stripped of his ability to act in line with the majoritarian ideology in the pursuit of goals that has previously structured his life, Ale witnesses some of the reality around him. In *Chop Shop* the reality that Ale perceives helps to mitigate the confusion both Scott and Bahrani suggest pervades contemporary Hollywood productions and American society.

After Ale discards the unsold phone, the film cuts to a short sequence where he and Ahmad start dismantling the food truck, the final signal that he has given up on his dream and the point at which the film's production of subjectivity is most visible. Ale's work is slow and ponderous, and the scene itself is laden with the factors that led to their dismantling of the food truck, which include not just the scenes that preceded this one, but intangible factors such as Ale's constant idealism. In this scene, "objects and settings [*milieux*] take on an autonomous, material reality which gives them an importance in themselves" (Deleuze 1989: 4). Even though the scene seems relatively ordinary, the connotations of Ale's labor create what Patricia Pisters has referred to as a "camera consciousness [that is] no longer defined by the movements it is able to follow or make, but by the mental connections it is able to enter into" (Pisters 2003: 15). This is particularly true in connection with what Adrian Martin has called Social Mise-en-Scène, which imbues the shop and the broken-down food truck set amid the heaps of auto parts as components in the construction of Ale's class-based subjectivity and his relationship with the American Dream (Martin 2009).

The sequence that depicts the dismantling of the food truck is shot in just three long takes. First, a crane shot shows Ale and Ahmad from above as they work on the food truck. The second shot shows Ale in a medium close-up as he stares vacantly into space. During these shots, the cheers and roar of a distant crowd can be heard, emanating from nearby Shea Stadium, providing a soft backdrop to the clicks and clanks of their dismantling of the truck. The third shot follows Ale as he climbs a set of stairs to pack away the steering column from the truck. Towards the end of this shot, the camera drops lower while it tracks Ale's movement to the left, anticipating his bending over to place the steering column on the ground. The camera tilts to follow Ale as he stands up, which suddenly reveals the bright lights of Shea Stadium in the distance and the source of the soundtrack in this scene, and Ale then turns his gaze in that direction. While the defunct truck and the shops strewn with parts provide a Social

Figure 5.3 *Chop Shop* (2007).

Mise-en-Scène that evidences Ale's class-based subjectivity, the sounds within this sequence and the eventual revelation of Shea Stadium's location more precisely describe Ale's newly distanced relationship with the glamor the stadium represents.

The subsequent scene follows Ale as he returns to his workshop apartment. Ale's dispirited gaze reveals the weight of Isamar's absence, as he correctly assumes that she is out working as a prostitute. This fact, now intolerable to Ale, prompts him to set out to look for her. Slow laborious shots follow Ale as he walks to the truck stop in search of his sister. When he realizes she is in a car across the lot, a single long take follows Ale as he opens the car she is in and starts hitting the man she is with. Ale's action marks a turning point in the film: previously aware of Isamar's prostitution, he did nothing, but this time intolerability drives him to act. The scuffle that ensues is short and without conclusion, Ale and Isamar end up running away, but it would be hard to call this a reinvestment of the sensory-motor schema. After the scuffle, nothing fundamental seems to have changed about their situation. Instead, this scene illustrates a shift in Ale's understanding of the world and his own place within it. Previously, he grappled with an intangible dream of owning property and achieving a form of economic prosperity, but it was not a belief in his immediate environment but a belief in the ability of the American Dream to transcend it that overshadowed his experience. Now he is able to see the real injustices around him and, seemingly, seeks to change them, illustrating the transformation or production of subjectivity.

This is no new Hollywood tale, however: Ale does not end prostitution in the Iron Triangle by force of his justice alone – this is why his action in this case is relatively unsuccessful with indeterminate consequences – but he at least acts in favor of the reality he wants to create. In other words, Ale now has the power of choice that he lacked as he followed what he believed to be a personal dream. Rather than confronting his sister earlier in the film, he used the money she made to contribute to buying the food truck, meaning he really made no choice at all, or because he had yet to become politicized, he was not able to accurately assess the possibilities in the situation. While Hollywood glamour might render a number of political questions invisible in its privileging of narrative progression in the way of *The Pursuit of Happyness*, in the particular case of *Chop Shop*, giving up on the American Dream allows Ale to confront, or at least to see as injustice, prostitution in his community.

Ale's revelation and transition from blindly following an ideology to becoming a person of choice or autonomy moves towards "a future form, for a new earth and people that do not yet exist," as O'Sullivan acknowledges, which is a form that is immanent to the present (made from the same material, rather than a complete substitution or transcendence) (Deleuze and Guattari 1994: 108). Nevertheless, Bahrani's work casts doubts on the utopianism of such a move. Utopianism suggests idealism; contemporary political cinema is based on the biopolitical production of subjectivity, however, which has no predetermined relationship with the future, and rejects utopianism because there is no blueprint for the future. What is important to Deleuze and Scott both, is that characters and spectators engage in a becoming-political where they are able to turn toward their immediate environments and their ability to interact with and change them. For Scott, realism has the potential to make people realize that gaudy Hollywood tales do not mitigate real life suffering. In the early 1940s, Adorno made a similar argument regarding Hollywood cinema and its goal of creating consumers. Currently, some independent filmmakers in the United States are moving toward a counter argument to the culture industry by altering cinematic codes and expectations. Despite O'Sullivan's contention, there is no ideal circumstance that would replace the ideologies perpetuated by Hollywood cinema, but in these contemporary American realist films there does exist the possibility of engaging in the biopolitical production of subjectivity on screen that engages the subjectivity of spectators.

The Collapse of the Dream, an Immanent Politics

The American Dream operates according to a form of causality whereby in the United States, hard work elevates the individual to a particular socio-economic position. As an art that is organized around causality in narrative, patterns of editing, and the actions of its characters, political cinema has a decisive role to play in rejecting the causal connections that perpetuate the myth of upward mobility. The sensory-motor schemata of classical cinema is particularly well-suited to wish fulfillment tales, where the actions of an individual character allow them to triumph over adversity. *The Pursuit of Happyness* is a representative example of this type of story, as it perpetuates the American Dream as an achievable ideal and follows a character driven by his belief in this causality. The extent to which spectators respond positively to the structure of *The Pursuit of Happyness* suggests that the American Dream is a majoritarian ideology in the United States, structuring the way people think and the political decisions that they make. The reciprocal emotional exchange between subjects who ascribe to these ideologies and the films that derive from them create a feedback loop where these majoritarian ideas and subjects feed upon and reinforce one another. These filmic discourses also construct a situation where it becomes impossible to choose otherwise, as the correct narrative or subject position is already laid out. This position restricts the potential for political discussion, however, as it relies on the conformity of subjects and desires. The contemporary political cinema I turn to, however, begin to break down reliance on the American Dream and introduce the fragmentation of this national ideology, which allows an immanent politics.

The early films of Bahrani reject causality and disrupt the American Dream via repetition, interruption, and a deliberate focus on the gestures of labor. By interrupting the narrative linearity that moves towards the transcendence of a character's circumstances, his films reveal a network of diverse individuals that resonates with Adams' vision in *The Epic of America*. *Man Push Cart* mainly follows a community of Pakistani immigrants but also includes immigrants from Latin America and Spain, as well as African-American and white nationals. *Chop Shop*, again taking place in New York, follows a pair of Latin American youths as they intermingle with the similarly diverse group of people working in the Iron Triangle. Bahrani's next film, *Goodbye Solo* (2008), adds the Senegalese main character Solo to the mix of subjects. Solo is a particularly multicultural character – he comes from a former colony of France, and speaks Wolof and French as well as Spanish, acquired through his relationship with a Latin-American woman. Like *Goodbye Solo*, Behrani's other films display a similar diversity through their use of multiple languages and presentation of a variety of positions in relation to economic status, race, and gender. While these films follow precarious populations that may be most susceptible to the American Dream, they simultaneously illustrate its fantasy – that hard work does not invariably lead to the success promised in the Dream. The sober endings of these films, with each protagonist returning to work in their communities, illustrates a more realistic and sustainable vision of the American Dream that resembles more closely what James Truslow Adams originally described.

Bahrani's later works follows the same political direction, but they are distinct from the perspective of the film industry. *At Any Price* (2012) and *99 Homes* (2014) are both driven by star power and relatively mainstream distribution deals. They differ politically, however, in their analytic approach to the American Dream. *At Any Price* examines the evolution of modern agricultural practices and the impact of global farming corporations on family-owned farms. Protagonist Henry Whipple, played by Dennis Quaid, comes to realize that the American Dream is no longer sustainable in the era of big business. Similarly, *99 Homes* examines the US housing market bubble and crash of the late 2000s. Dennis Nash, played by Andrew Garfield, becomes caught up in an outfit profiting from the housing crash by evicting residents. After extricating himself from poverty, he briefly aspires to the glamorous lifestyle of the profiteers he works for before realizing the breach of ethics he commits on their behalf. While it would be difficult to call either of these films morality tales, because they still include the relatively open endings and an existential emphasis, they offer less of a focus on labor itself than Bahrani's earlier films. Instead, they analyze specific structures and symptoms of global capital and economic crisis more explicitly.

The original articulation of the American Dream described a diverse group of individuals working together to create a resource that they might share together, something evoked by the push cart scene in New York or the mechanic communities of the Iron Triangle. While such communities might not be an example of economic prosperity, they at least depict a sustainable association of individuals who make a living. I am not arguing that these communities present a utopian future, but their depiction in these films at least allows for the proliferation of different voices, rather than a unified espousal of a particular ideology or identity. As a result, these films provide an alternative to majoritarian cinemas, both politically and stylistically. Rather than chasing a transcendental idealism, these films inspire audiences to work towards new, collaborative solutions immanent to the world these characters exist in, and suggest the potential for these communities to work together. Their conclusions are not as fantastic as in *The Pursuit of Happyness*, but rather suggest smaller examples of where one can begin a productive process of experimentation that leads to a new political reality. The films avoid Hollywood glamour, because it involves a turning away from the world in a movement that suggests not real world change, but a dream of another world. In this move, contemporary American realist cinema offers films that suggest an immanent solution, critiquing majoritarian cinematic and social discourses through their depiction of labor, diverse subjects, and the falsity of overburdened ideology.

I end this book by turning to the United States for two reasons. First, as part of the larger cinematic project in this book, it illustrates how contemporary political films are not global cinemas responding to the hegemony of Hollywood or United States cinema, but films that operate like Deleuze and Guattari's minor texts in disrupting dominant modes of storytelling and thereby disrupting dominant stories around the world. As I argued in the case of Bahman Ghobadi: the dominant discourse within Iran's media industries is not Hollywood. This necessitates a more flexible understanding of ideology and its structuring of repressive biopolitics. In other words, a turn away from Foucault's institutions as the source of repressive biopolitics – for example, Hollywood understood as its more archaic classical studio system, which no longer actually exists. Such a perspective would track more closely to Deleuze's 'Societies of Control' – for example, vast networks of screen media, delivered via theaters, the internet, cell phones, screens in public, etc. situated variably around the world. In this regard, I want to remove Hollywood as the repressive center of any cinematic politics, though it undoubtedly has sway with regard to politics in the United States as shown in the case of *The Pursuit of Happyness*. As I conclude in the Introduction to this book, however, I also hesitate from suggesting that there is no connection between these films from around the world that are nonetheless responding to their own political contexts.

Which leads me to the second reason I end with Bahrani's films: they return to the economic and structural questions I begin with in the Introduction regarding the World Trade Organization protests, the rise of neoliberal markets, and the global redistribution of populations. While the World Trade Organization protests in Seattle were inspired by injustices around the world, the United States is not exempt from the effects of the large scale economic shift, including the production of precarious populations and migrants seeking work. Of course, writing from 2017, this topic has become everyday political conversation with now President Trump's desire to build a wall between Mexico and the United States in order to restrict the flow of people. Such a reactionary response, not focused on processes or root causes, provides the most concrete evidence that the issues discussed in the films within this book are the most prevalent political issues of the contemporary world. This is far from a United States or North American issue, however, as Ai Wei Wei's *Human Flow*

(2017) illustrates by documenting similar crises of migration around the world. Bahrani's films do not give us the scope of *Human Flow*, but they do provide individual accounts, which is the remit of all of the films in this book, that prompt the precariousness leading to the *Human Flow* – the individual pricks, points at which our societies and environments have been wounded, cut open so that people flow like blood.

If the contemporary political cinema I have defined here has one role then, it is to magnify these minor stories, these existential accounts, which taken together are not minor at all. But 'minor' in a philosophical sense, for Deleuze and Guattari, has never meant small, only subject to being silenced by certain societal norms in terms of what people say and how they say it, film content and form. What the films in this book show us, alongside a film like Ai's, is that we are reaching a tipping point, a crisis, signaled by the reinforcing of boundaries around the world. How we got here is the story of contemporary political cinema.

Bibliography

Adams, James Truslow (1931), *The Epic of America*, Boston: Little, Brown, & Co.

Adorno, Theodor W. and Max Horkheimer [1944] (2002), *Dialectic of Enlightenment: Philosophical Fragments*, Stanford: Stanford University Press.

Alikhah, Fardin (2008), "The Politics of Satellite TV in Iran," in Mehdi Semati (ed.), *Media, Culture and Society in Iran: Living with Globalization and the Islamic State*, London: Routledge.

Andrew, Dudley (2010), "Time Zones and Jetlag: the Flows and Phases of World Cinema," in Nataša Ďurovičová and Kathleen Newman (eds), *World Cinemas, Transnational Perspectives*, New York: Routledge, pp. 59–89.

Appadurai, Arjun (2006), *Fear of Small Numbers*, Durham, NC: Duke University Press.

Armes, Roy (2006), *African Filmmaking: North and South of the Sahara*, Bloomington: Indiana University Press.

Austin, John Langshaw (1975), *How to Do Things with Words*, Oxford: Clarendon Press.

Baudry, Jean-Louis (1985), "Ideological Effects of the Basic Cinematographic Apparatus," in Bill Nichols (ed.), *Movies and Methods: Volume II*, Berkeley: University of California Press, pp. 531–542.

Bauman, Zygmunt (1998), *Globalization: the Human Consequences*, Cambridge: Polity Press.

Berry, Chris (2007), "Getting Real: Chinese Documentary, Chinese Postsocialism," in Zhang Zhen (ed.), *The Urban Generation: Chinese Cinema and Society at the Turn of the Twenty-first Century*, Durham, NC: Duke University Press, pp. 115–136.

Bettinson, Gary and Richard Rushton (2010), *What is Film Theory?*, Maidenhead: Open University Press.

Bogue, Ronald (2010), "To Choose to Choose—to Believe in This World," in David Norman Rodowick (ed.), *Afterimages of Gilles Deleuze's Film Philosophy*, Minneapolis: University of Minnesota Press, pp. 115–134.

Bordeleau, Erik (2013), "Jia Zhangke's Still Life: Destruction as Intercession," *Scapegoat*, 3, pp. 26–29.

Boundas, Constantin V. (2006), *Deleuze and Philosophy*, Edinburgh: Edinburgh University Press.

Brody, Richard (2009), "About 'Neo-Neo Realism'," *The New Yorker*, March 20, 2009. <https://www.newyorker.com/culture/richard-brody/about-neo-neo-realism> (last accessed May 24, 2018).

Brown, William (Forthcoming), "Listening to the Future: The Film-Philosophy of Abderrahmane Sissako," in Ewa Mazierska and Lars Kristensen (eds), *Third Cinema, World Cinema and Marxism*.

Brown, William and Matthew Holtmeier (2013), "Machinima: Cinema in a Minor or Multitudinous Key?" in Jenna Ng (ed.), *Understanding Machinima: Essays on Filmmaking in Virtual Worlds*, New York: Bloomsbury, pp. 3–21.

Butler, Alison (2002), *Women's Cinema: The Contested Screen*, London: Wallflower.

Butler, Judith and Athena Athanasiou (2013), *Dispossession: The Performative in the Political*, Cambridge: Polity Press.

Castells, Manuel [1996] (2010), *The Rise of the Network Society*, Oxford: Wiley-Blackwell.

Chaliand, Gérard (1993), *A People Without a Country: The Kurds and Kurdistan*, New York: Olive Branch Press.

Chomsky, Noam (1999), *Profit over People: Neoliberalism and Global Order*, New York: Seven Stories.

Chomsky, Noam (2012), *Occupy: Reflections on Class War, Rebellion, and Solidarity*, Westfield: Zucotti Park Press.

Chu, Yin-wah and Alvin Y. So (2010), "State Neoliberalism: The Chinese Road to Capitalism," in Yin-wah Chu (ed.), *Chinese Capitalisms: Historical Emergence and Political Implications*, New York: Palgrave Macmillan.

Clark, William A. V. (2003), *Immigrants and the American Dream: Remaking the Middle Class*, New York: Guilford.

Cornelius, Sheila (2002), *New Chinese Cinema: Challenging Representations*, London: Wallflower.

Dabashi, Hamid (2001), *Close Up: Iranian Cinema, Past, Present, and Future*, New York: Verso.

Deleuze, Gilles [1983] (1986), *Cinema 1: The Movement-image*, Minneapolis: University of Minnesota Press.

Deleuze, Gilles [1985] (1989), *Cinema 2: The Time-Image*, Minneapolis: University of Minnesota Press.

Deleuze, Gilles (2004), *Desert Islands and Other Texts 1953–1974*, Los Angeles: Semiotext(e).

Deleuze, Gilles (1992), "Postscript on the Societies of Control," *October*, 59, pp. 3–7.

Deleuze, Gilles, and Félix Guattari [1980] (1998), *A Thousand Plateaus: Capitalism and Schizophrenia*, Minneapolis: University of Minnesota Press.

Deleuze, Gilles, and Félix Guattari [1975] (1986), *Kafka: Towards a Minor Literature*, Minneapolis: University of Minnesota Press.

Deleuze, Gilles and Félix Guattari [1991] (1994), *What is Philosophy?* London: Verso.

Ďurovičová, Nataša and Kathleen Newman (2010), *World Cinemas, Transnational Perspectives*, New York: Routledge.

Dyer, Richard [1992] (2002), *Only Entertainment*, New York: Routledge.

Eleftheriotis, Dimitris (2010), *Cinematic Journeys: Film and Movement*, Edinburgh: Edinburgh University Press.

Espinosa, Julio Garcia (1979), "For an Imperfect Cinema," *Jump Cut: A Review of Contemporary Media*, 20, pp. 24–26.

Fewsmith, Joseph (2008), *China since Tiananmen: From Deng Xiaoping to Hu Jintao*, New York: Cambridge University Press.

Foucault, Michel (2004), *"Society Must Be Defended": Lectures at the College De France 1975–76*, London: Penguin.

Frangville, Vanessa (2016), "Pema Tseden's *The Search*: the Making of a Minor Cinema," *Journal of Chinese Cinemas*, 10:2, pp. 106–119.

Gabara, Rachel (2010), "Abderrahmane Sissako: Second and Third Cinema in the First Person," in Rosalind Galt and Karl Schoonover (eds), *Global Art Cinema: New Theories and Histories*, Oxford: Oxford University Press, pp. 320–333.

Ghobadi, Bahman (2002), "Interview with Director Bahman Ghobadi," *Marooned in Iraq* (DVD): distributed by Wellspring.

GSS (2010), "Getting ahead by Hard Work versus Lucky Breaks," *Public Opinion Quarterly*, 74:3, p. 573.

Hanson, Sandra and John Zogby (2010), "The Polls—Trends: Attitudes About the American Dream," *Public Opinion Quarterly*, Volume 74, Issue 3, 2010, pp. 570–584.

Hardt, Michael and Antonio Negri (2000), *Empire*, London: Harvard University Press.

Hardt, Michael and Antonio Negri (2006), *Multitude: War and Democracy in the Age of Empire*, London: Penguin Books.

Hardt, Michael and Antonio Negri (2011), "The Fight for 'Real Democracy' at the heart of Occupy Wall Street," *Foreign Affairs*, October 11, 2011.

Harvey, David (2007), *A Brief History of Neoliberalism*, New York: Oxford University Press.

Held, David (1999), *Global Transformations: Politics, Economics and Culture*, Stanford: Stanford University Press.

Herzog, Amy (2009), *Dreams of Difference, Songs of the Same: The Musical Moment in Film*, Minneapolis: University of Minnesota Press.

Higson, Andrew (2000), "The Limiting Imagination of National Cinema," in Mette Hjort and Scott MacKenzie (eds), *Cinema and Nation*, London: Routledge, pp. 15–25.

Hjort, Mette (2005), *Small Nation, Global Cinema: The New Danish Cinema*, Minneapolis: University of Minnesota Press.

Holtmeier, Matthew (2012), "An Exiled Filmmaker under House Arrest: Bahman Farmanara's Smell of Camphor, Fragrance of Jasmine," *Middle East Journal of Culture and Communication*, 5, pp. 135–148.

Holtmeier, Matthew (2010), "Post-Pandoran Depression or Na'vi Sympathy: *Avatar*, Affect, and Audience Reception," *Journal for the Study of Religion, Nature, and Culture*, 4:4, pp. 414–424.

Huntington, Samuel P. (1993), The Clash of Civilizations? *Foreign Affairs*, summer, pp. 22–49.

Huntington, Samuel P. (1996), *The Clash of Civilizations and the Remaking of World Order*, New York: Simon and Schuster Paperbacks.

Jia, Zhangke (2008), "Moving Pictures," *Good*, April 1, <http://www.good.is/post/moving_pictures/> (last accessed May 31, 2010).

Kauffman, Stanley (2008), "Stanley Kauffman on Chop Shop and Paranoid Park," *New Republic*, 238:4, pp. 32–33.

Kauffman, Stanley (2009), "Stanley Kauffman on Goodbye Solo and the Song of Sparrows," *New Republic*, 240:7, pp. 26–27.

Kerr, Thomas D. (1996), *Chasing after the American Dream*, Commack: Kroshka.

Klein, Naomi (2007), *The Shock Doctrine: The Rise of Disaster Capitalism*, New York: Metropolitan/Henry Holt.

Kuoshu, Harry (2002), *Celluloid China: Cinematic Encounters with Culture and Society*, Carbondale: Southern Illinois University Press.

Le Sueur, James D. (2010), *Algeria Since 1989: Between Terror and Democracy*, London: Zed Books.

Lionnet, Françoise, and Shumei Shih (2005), *Minor Transnationalism*, Durham, NC: Duke University Press.

Lu, Tonglin (2006), "Trapped Freedom and Localized Globalism," in Paul Pickowicz and Yingjin Zhang (eds), *From Underground to Independent: Alternative Film Culture in Contemporary China*, Lanham: Rowman & Littlefield, pp. 123–142.

Macaulay, Scott (2010), "Bahman Ghobadi on Improvisation, 'Persian Cats,' and Kiarostami," *Filmmaker Magazine*, April 15, 2010.

Maimon, Vered (2012), "Beyond Representation: Abbas Kiarostami's and Pedro Costa's Minor Cinema," *Third Text*, 26:3, pp. 331–344.

Marks, Laura U. (2000), *The Skin of the Film: Intercultural Cinema, Embodiment, and the Senses*, Durham, NC: Duke University Press.

Marshall, Bill (2001), *Quebec National Cinema*, Montreal: McGill-Queen's University Press.

Martin, Adrian (2009), "At Table: The Social Mise en Scène of How Green Was My Valley," *Undercurrent*, 5.

Martin-Jones, David (2006), *Deleuze, Cinema and National Identity: Narrative Time in National Contexts*, Edinburgh: Edinburgh University Press.

Martin-Jones, David (2011), *Deleuze and World Cinemas*, London: Continuum.

Martin-Jones, David (2004), "*Orphans*, a Work of Minor Cinema from Post-devolutionary Scotland," *Journal of British Cinema and Television*, 1:2, pp. 226–241.

Martin-Jones, David and María Soledad Montañez (2013), "Uruguay Disappears: Small Cinemas, Control Z Films, and the Aesthetics and Politics of Auto-Erasure," *Cinema Journal*, 53:1, pp. 26–51.

McGrath, Jason (2007), "The Independent Cinema of Jia Zhangke: From Postsocialist Realism to a Transnational Aesthetic," in Zhang Zhen (ed.), *The Urban Generation: Chinese Cinema and Society at the Turn of the Twenty-first Century*, Durham, NC: Duke University Press, pp. 81–114.

Mitchell, William John Thomas, Bernard E. Harcourt, and Michael Taussig (2013), *Occupy: Three Inquiries in Disobedience*, Chicago: The University of Chicago Press.

Miles, William F. S. (2007), *Political Islam in West Africa: State-society Relations Transformed*, Boulder: Lynne Rienner Publishers.

Moore, Robert L. (2005), "Generation Ku: Individualism and China's Millennial Youth," *Ethnology*, 44:4, pp. 357–376.

Mottahedeh, Negar (2008), *Displaced Allegories: Post-Revolutionary Iranian Cinema*, Durham, NC: Duke University Press.

Mouffe, Chantal (2013), *Agnostics: Thinking the World Politically*, London: Verso.

Mulvey, Laura (1975), "Visual Pleasure and Narrative Cinema," *Screen*, 16, pp. 6–18.

Naficy, Hamid (2001), *An Accented Cinema: Exilic and Diasporic Filmmaking*, Princeton: Princeton University Press.

Naficy, Hamid (1994), "Veiled Visions/Powerful Presences: Women in Postrevolutionary Iranian Cinema," in Mahnaz Afkhami, and Erika Friedl (eds), *In the Eye of the Storm: Women in Postrevolutionary Iran*, Syracuse: Syracuse University Press, pp. 131–150.

Natali, Denise (2005), *The Kurds and the State: Evolving National Identity in Iraq, Turkey, and Iran*, Syracuse: Syracuse University Press.

Okeowo, Alexis (2015), "The Film That Dares to Humanize Jihadists," *The New Yorker*, March 5, 2015.

Oudart, Jean-Pierre (1990), "Cinema and Suture," in Nick Browne (ed.), *Cahiers du Cinema: The Politics of Representation*, Cambridge, MA: Harvard University Press, pp. 45–57.

O'Sullivan, Simon (2009), "From Stuttering and Stammering to the Diagram: Deleuze, Bacon and Contemporary Art Practice," *Deleuze Studies*, 3:2, pp. 247–258.

Patton, Paul (2008), "Becoming-Democratic," in Ian Buchanan and Nicholas Thoburn (eds), *Deleuze and Politics*, Edinburgh: Edinburgh University Press, pp. 178–195.

Pickowicz, Paul (2006), "Social and Political Dynamics of Underground Filmmaking in China," in Paul Pickowicz and Yingjin Zhang (eds), *From Underground to Independent: Alternative Film Culture in Contemporary China*, Lanham: Rowman & Littlefield, pp. 1–22.

Pisters, Patricia (2006), "Arresting the Flux of Images and Sounds: Free Indirect Discourse and the Dialectics of Political Cinema," Ian Buchanan and Adrian Parr (eds), *Deleuze and the Contemporary World*, Edinburgh: Edinburgh University Press.

Pisters, Patricia (2016), "The Filmmaker as Metallurgist: Political Cinema and World Memory," *Film-Philosophy*, 20, pp. 149–167.

Pisters, Patricia (2003), *The Matrix of Visual Culture: Working with Deleuze in Film Theory*, Stanford: Stanford University Press.

Pisters, Patricia (2012), *The Neuro-Image: A Deleuzian Film-Philosophy of Digital Screen Culture*, Stanford: Stanford University Press.

Porton, Richard (2008), "An Interview with Ramin Bahrani," *Cineaste*, 33:3, pp. 44–48.

Prochaska, David (2003), "That was Then, This is Now: *The Battle of Algiers* and After," *Radical History Review*, 85, pp. 133–149.

Purcell, Mark (2013), *The Down-Deep Delight of Democracy*, Oxford: Wiley-Blackwell.

Reid, Julian (2011), "A People of Seers: The Political Aesthetics of Postwar Cinema Revisited," *Cultural Politics*, 7:2, pp. 219–238.

Restivo, Angelo (2000), "Into the Breach: *Between* The Movement-Image *and* The Time-image," in Gregory Flaxman (ed.), *The Brain Is the Screen: Deleuze and the Philosophy of Cinema*, Minneapolis: University of Minnesota Press, pp. 171–192.

Rodowick, David Norman (1997), *Gilles Deleuze's Time Machine*, Durham, NC: Duke University Press.

Rodowick, David Norman [1988] (1994), *The Crisis of Political Modernism: Criticism and Ideology in Contemporary Film Theory*, Berkeley: University of California Press.

Rodowick, David Norman (2010), "The World, Time," in D. N. Rodowick (ed.), *Afterimages of Gilles Deleuze's Film Philosophy*, Minneapolis: University of Minnesota, pp. 97–114.

Rogers, Anna Backman (2011), "Making Nothing Happen: The Transition from Reactive Nihilism to Affirmation in Jim Jarmusch's *Broken Flowers*," *Alphaville: Journal of Film and Screen Media*, 2, pp. 1–12.

Rowin, Michael Joshua (2009), "Review of *Goodbye Solo*," *Cineaste*, 34:3, pp. 47–49.

Rushton, Richard (2012), *Cinema After Deleuze*, London: Continuum International Publishing Group.

Sadr, Hamid Reza (2006), *Iranian Cinema: A Political History*, New York: I. B. Tauris.

Sandhu, Sukhdev (2009), "A New Way Must be Seen," *Vertigo*, 4:3, p. 44.

Sassen, Saskia (2014), *Expulsions: Brutality and Complexity in the Global Economy*, Cambridge, MA: The Belknap Press of Harvard University Press.

Sassen, Saskia (2001), "Spatialities and Temporalities of the Global: Elements for a Theorization," in Arjun Appadurai (ed.), *Globalization*, Durham, NC: Duke University Press, pp. 260–278.

Scarlet, Peter (2007), "Interview with Filmmaker Bahman Ghobadi," *LinkTV*.

Schmitt, Carl [1927] (2007), *The Concept of the Political*, Chicago: University of Chicago Press.

Scott, Anthony Oliver (2009), "Neo Neo Realism," *The New York* Times, March 22, 2009, p. MM38.

Semati, Mehdi (2008), *Media, Culture and Society in Iran: Living with Globalization and the Islamic State*, New York: Routledge.

Shapiro, Michael J. (2009), *Cinematic Geopolitics*, New York: Routledge.

Shaviro, Steven (2011), "The 'Bitter Necessity' of Debt: Neoliberal Finance and the Society of Control," *Concentric: Literary and Cultural Studies*, 37:1, pp. 73–82.

Shaviro, Steven (2003), *Connected, or What it Means to Live in the Network Society*, Minneapolis: University of Minnesota Press.

Shepard, Todd (2011), "Hors-la-loi/Outside the Law," *Fiction and Film for French Historians*, 1:4, http://h-france.net/fffh/the-buzz/hors-la-loioutside-the-law/.

Silverman, Kaja (1983), *The Subject of Semiotics*, New York: Oxford University Press.

Simondon, Gilbert (1992), "The Genesis of the Individual," in Jonathan Crary and Sanford Kwinter (eds), *Incorporations*, Cambridge, MA: Zone Books.

Staff and agencies (2005), "Iran declares ban on western music," *The Guardian*, December 20, 2005 <https://www.theguardian.com/world/2005/dec/20/iran> (last accessed May 24, 2018).

Stam, Robert and Louise Spence (1983), "Colonialism, Racism and Representation: An Introduction," *Screen*, 24:2, pp. 2–20.

Stam, Robert and Louise Spence (1985), "Colonialism, Racism and Representation: An Introduction," in Bill Nichols (ed.), *Movies and Methods: Volume 2*, Berkeley: University of California Press, pp. 632–648.

Stewart, Michelle (2007), "Abderrahmane Sissako: Les Lieux Provisoires of Transnational Cinema," in Tina Chen and David Churchill (eds), *Film, History, and Cultural Citizenship*, Routledge, pp. 335–344.

Szymanski, Adam (2011), "It's All About Love: Félix Guattari's Minor Cinema," *Multilingualism in Popular Arts*, 3:1.

Taub, Amanda (2017), "Myanmar Follows Global Pattern in How Ethnic Cleansing Begins," *The New York Times*, September 19, 2017, p. A4.

Wayne, Mike (2001), *Political Film: The Dialectics of Third Cinema*, London: Pluto Press.

White, Patricia (2008), "Lesbian Minor Cinema," *Screen*, 49:4, pp. 410–425.

Winn, J. Emmett (2007), *The American Dream and Contemporary Hollywood Cinema*, New York: The Continuum International Publishing Group.

Woll, Josephine (2004), "The Russian Connection: Soviet Cinema and the Cinema of Francophone Africa," in Françoise Pfaff, *Focus on African Films*, Bloomington: Indiana University Press, pp. 223–240.

Yau, Ka-Fai (2001), "Cinema 3: Towards a 'Minor Hong Kong Cinema,'" *Cultural Studies*, 15:3/4, pp. 543–563.

Yildiz, Kerim and Tanyel Taysi (2007), *The Kurds in Iran: The Past, Present, and Future*, London: Pluto Press.

Zeydabadi-Nejad, Saeed (2010), *The Politics of Iranian Cinema: Film and Society in the Islamic Republic*, New York: Routledge.

Zhang, Zhen (2007a), *The Urban Generation: Chinese Cinema and Society at the Turn of the Twenty-first Century*, Durham, NC: Duke University Press.
Zhang, Zhen (2007b), "Bearing Witness: Chinese Urban Cinema in the Era of 'Transformation'," in Zhen Zhang (ed.), *The Urban Generation: Chinese Cinema and Society at the Turn of the Twenty-first Century*, Durham, NC: Duke University Press, pp. 1–48.

Index